Programming Quantum Computers
Essential Algorithms and Code Samples

*Eric R. Johnston, Nic Harrigan,
and Mercedes Gimeno-Segovia*

Beijing · Boston · Farnham · Sebastopol · Tokyo

Programming Quantum Computers

by Eric R. Johnston, Nic Harrigan, and Mercedes Gimeno-Segovia

Published by O'Reilly Media, Inc., 1005 Gravenstein Highway North, Sebastopol, CA 95472.

O'Reilly books may be purchased for educational, business, or sales promotional use. Online editions are also available for most titles (*http://oreilly.com*). For more information, contact our corporate/institutional sales department: 800-998-9938 or *corporate@oreilly.com*.

Acquisitions Editor: Mike Loukides	**Indexer:** WordCo Indexing Services, Inc.
Development Editor: Michele Cronin	**Interior Designer:** David Futato
Production Editor: Christopher Faucher	**Cover Designer:** Karen Montgomery
Copyeditor: Kim Cofer	**Illustrator:** Rebecca Demarest
Proofreader: Rachel Head	

July 2019:   First Edition

Revision History for the First Edition

2019-07-03:   First Release

See *http://oreilly.com/catalog/errata.csp?isbn=9781492039686* for release details.

978-1-492-03968-6

[LSI]

Table of Contents

Part IV. Outlook

Preface

Quantum computers are no longer theoretical devices.

The authors of this book believe that the best uses for a new technology are not necessarily discovered by its inventors, but by domain experts experimenting with it as a new tool for their work. With that in mind, this book is a hands-on programmer's guide to using quantum computing technology. In the chapters ahead, you'll become familiar with symbols and operations such as those in Figure P-1, and learn how to apply them to problems you care about.

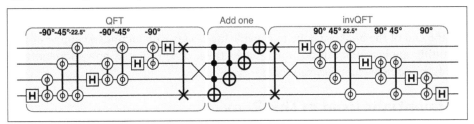

Figure P-1. Quantum programs can look a bit like sheet music

How This Book Is Structured

A tried-and-tested approach for getting hands-on with new programming paradigms is to learn a set of conceptual primitives. For example, anyone learning Graphics Processing Unit (GPU) programming should first focus on mastering the concept of parallelism, rather than on syntax or hardware specifics.

The heart of this book focuses on building an intuition for a set of quantum primitives—ideas forming a toolbox of building blocks for problem-solving with a QPU. To prepare you for these primitives, we first introduce the basic concepts of qubits (the *rules of the game*, if you like). Then, after outlining a set of Quantum Processing Unit (QPU) primitives, we show how they can be used as building blocks within useful QPU applications.

Consequently, this book is divided into three parts. The reader is encouraged to become familiar with Part I and gain some hands-on experience before proceeding to the more advanced parts:

Part I: Programming a QPU
Here we introduce the core concepts required to program a QPU, such as qubits, essential instructions, utilizing superposition, and even quantum teleportation. Examples are provided, which can be easily run using simulators or a physical QPU.

Part II: QPU Primitives
The second part of the book provides detail on some essential algorithms and techniques at a higher level. These include *amplitude amplification*, the *Quantum Fourier Transform*, and *phase estimation*. These can be considered "library functions" that programmers call to build applications. Understanding how they work is essential to becoming a skilled QPU programmer. An active community of researchers is working on developing new QPU primitives, so expect this library to grow in the future.

Part III: QPU Applications
The world of QPU applications—which combine the primitives from Part II to perform useful real-world tasks—is evolving as rapidly as QPUs themselves. Here we introduce examples of existing applications.

By the end of the book we hope to provide the reader with an understanding of what quantum applications can do, what makes them powerful, and how to identify the kinds of problems that they can solve.

Conventions Used in This Book

The following typographical conventions are used in this book:

Italic
Indicates new terms, URLs, email addresses, filenames, and file extensions.

`Constant width`
Used for program listings, as well as within paragraphs to refer to program elements such as variable or function names, databases, data types, environment variables, statements, and keywords.

`Constant width bold`
Shows commands or other text that should be typed literally by the user.

`Constant width italic`
Shows text that should be replaced with user-supplied values or by values determined by context.

This element signifies a tip or suggestion.

This element signifies a general note.

This element indicates a warning or caution.

Using Code Examples

Supplemental material (code examples, exercises, etc.) is available for download at *https://oreilly-qc.github.io*.

This book is here to help you get your job done. In general, if example code is offered with this book, you may use it in your programs and documentation. You do not need to contact us for permission unless you're reproducing a significant portion of the code. For example, writing a program that uses several chunks of code from this book does not require permission. Selling or distributing a CD-ROM of examples from O'Reilly books does require permission. Answering a question by citing this book and quoting example code does not require permission. Incorporating a significant amount of example code from this book into your product's documentation does require permission.

We appreciate, but do not require, attribution. An attribution usually includes the title, author, publisher, and ISBN. For example: "*Programming Quantum Computers* by Eric R. Johnston, Nic Harrigan, and Mercedes Gimeno-Segovia (O'Reilly). Copyright 2019 Eric R. Johnston, Nic Harrigan, and Mercedes Gimeno-Segovia, 978-1-492-03968-6."

If you feel your use of code examples falls outside fair use or the permission given above, feel free to contact us at *permissions@oreilly.com*.

O'Reilly Online Learning

 For almost 40 years, *O'Reilly Media* has provided technology and business training, knowledge, and insight to help companies succeed.

Our unique network of experts and innovators share their knowledge and expertise through books, articles, conferences, and our online learning platform. O'Reilly's online learning platform gives you on-demand access to live training courses, in-depth learning paths, interactive coding environments, and a vast collection of text and video from O'Reilly and 200+ other publishers. For more information, please visit *http://oreilly.com*.

How to Contact Us

Please address comments and questions concerning this book to the publisher:

O'Reilly Media, Inc.
1005 Gravenstein Highway North
Sebastopol, CA 95472
800-998-9938 (in the United States or Canada)
707-829-0515 (international or local)
707-829-0104 (fax)

We have a web page for this book, where we list errata, examples, and any additional information. You can access this page at *http://bit.ly/programming-quantum-computers*.

To comment or ask technical questions about this book, send email to *bookquestions@oreilly.com*.

For more information about our books, courses, conferences, and news, see our website at *http://www.oreilly.com*.

Find us on Facebook: *http://facebook.com/oreilly*

Follow us on Twitter: *http://twitter.com/oreillymedia*

Watch us on YouTube: *http://www.youtube.com/oreillymedia*

Acknowledgments

This book could not have been possible without a supporting team of talented people passionate about quantum computing. The authors would like to thank Michele, Mike, Kim, Rebecca, Chris, and the technical team at O'Reilly for sharing and amplifying our enthusiasm for the topic. Although the authors are responsible for all errors and omissions, this book benefited immensely from the invaluable feedback and inspiration of a number of technical reviewers, including Konrad Kieling, Christian Sommeregger, Mingsheng Ying, Rich Johnston, James Weaver, Mike Shapiro, Wyatt Berlinic, and Isaac Kim.

EJ would like to thank Sue, his muse. Quantum computation started to make sense to him on the week that they met. EJ also sends thanks to friends at the University of Bristol and at SolidAngle, for encouraging him to color outside the lines.

Nic would like to thank Derek Harrigan for first teaching him to talk binary, the other Harrigans for their love and support, and Shannon Burns for her pending Harrigan application.

Mercedes would like to thank José María Gimeno Blay for igniting her interest on computers early, and Mehdi Ahmadi for being a constant source of support and inspiration.

But clichéd as it may be, most of all the authors would like to thank you, the reader, for having the sense of adventure to pick up this book and learn about something so different and new.

CHAPTER 1

Introduction

Whether you're an expert in software engineering, computer graphics, data science, or just a curious computerphile, this book is designed to show how the power of quantum computing might be relevant to you, by actually allowing you to start using it.

To facilitate this, the following chapters do *not* contain thorough explanations of quantum physics (the laws underlying quantum computing) or even quantum information theory (how those laws determine our abilities to process information). Instead, they present working examples providing insight into the capabilities of this exciting new technology. Most importantly, the code we present for these examples can be tweaked and adapted. This allows you to learn from them in the most effective way possible: by getting hands-on. Along the way, core concepts are explained as they are used, and only insofar as they build an intuition for writing quantum programs.

Our humble hope is that interested readers might be able to wield these insights to apply and augment applications of quantum computing in fields that physicists may not even have heard of. Admittedly, hoping to help spark a quantum revolution isn't *that* humble, but it's definitely exciting to be a pioneer.

Required Background

The physics underlying quantum computing is full of dense mathematics. But then so is the physics behind the transistor, and yet learning C++ need not involve a single physics equation. In this book we take a similarly *programmer-centric* approach, circumventing any significant mathematical background. That said, here is a short list of knowledge that may be helpful in digesting the concepts we introduce:

- Familiarity with programming control structures (`if`, `while`, etc.). JavaScript is used in this book to provide lightweight access to samples that can be run online. If you're new to JavaScript but have some prior programming experience, the level of background you need could likely be picked up in less than an hour. For a more thorough introduction to JavaScript, see *Learning JavaScript* by Todd Brown (O'Reilly).
- Some relevant programmer-level mathematics, necessitating:
  - An understanding of using mathematical functions
  - Familiarity with trigonometric functions
  - Comfort manipulating binary numbers and converting between binary and decimal representations
  - A comprehension of the basic meaning of complex numbers
- A very elementary understanding of how to assess the computational complexity of an algorithm (i.e., *big-o* notation).

One part of the book that reaches beyond these requirements is Chapter 13, where we survey a number of applications of quantum computing to machine learning. Due to space constraints our survey gives only very cursory introductions to each machine-learning application before showing how a quantum computer can provide an advantage. Although we intend the content to be understandable to a general reader, those wishing to really experiment with these applications will benefit from a bit more of a machine-learning background.

This book is about programming (not building, nor researching) quantum computers, which is why we can do without advanced mathematics and quantum theory. However, for those interested in exploring the more academic literature on the topic, Chapter 14 provides some good initial references and links the concepts we introduce to mathematical notations commonly used by the quantum computing research community.

What Is a QPU?

Despite its ubiquity, the term "quantum computer" can be a bit misleading. It conjures images of an entirely new and alien kind of machine—one that supplants all existing computing software with a futuristic alternative.

At the time of writing this is a common, albeit huge, misconception. The promise of quantum computers stems not from them being a *conventional computer killer*, but rather from their ability to dramatically extend the kinds of problems that are tractable within computing. There are important computational problems that are easily calculable on a quantum computer, but that would quite literally be impossible on any conceivable standard computing device that we could ever hope to build.[1]

But crucially, these kinds of speedups have only been seen for certain problems (many of which we later elucidate on), and although it is anticipated that more will be discovered, it's highly unlikely that it would ever make sense to run *all* computations on a quantum computer. For most of the tasks taking up your laptop's clock cycles, a quantum computer performs no better.

In other words—from the programmer's point of view—a quantum computer is really a *co*-processor. In the past, computers have used a wide variety of co-processors, each suited to their own specialties, such as floating-point arithmetic, signal processing, and real-time graphics. With this in mind, we will use the term *QPU* (Quantum Processing Unit) to refer to the device on which our code samples run. We feel this reinforces the important context within which quantum computing should be placed.

As with other co-processors such as the GPU (Graphics Processing Unit), programming for a QPU involves the programmer writing code that will primarily run on the CPU (Central Processing Unit) of a normal computer. The CPU issues the QPU co-processor commands only to initiate tasks suited to its capabilities.

A Hands-on Approach

Hands-on samples form the backbone of this book. But at the time of writing, a full-blown, general-purpose QPU does not exist—so how can you hope to ever run our code? Fortunately (and excitingly), even at the time of writing a few prototype QPUs *are* currently available, and can be accessed on the cloud. Furthermore, for smaller problems it's possible to *simulate* the behavior of a QPU on conventional computing hardware. Although simulating larger QPU programs becomes impossible, for smaller code snippets it's a convenient way to learn how to control an actual QPU. The code samples in this book are compatible with both of these scenarios, and will remain both usable and pedagogical even as more sophisticated QPUs become available.

There are many QPU simulators, libraries, and systems available. You can find a list of links to several well-supported systems at *http://oreilly-qc.github.io*. On that page, we provide the code samples from this book, whenever possible, in a variety of

---

1 One of our favorite ways to drive this point home is the following back-of-the-envelope calculation. Suppose conventional transistors could be made atom-sized, and we aimed to build a warehouse-sized conventional computer able to match even a modest quantum computer's ability to factor prime integers. We would need to pack transistors so densely that we would create a gravitational singularity. Gravitational singularities make computing (and existing) very hard.

languages. However, to prevent code samples from overwhelming the text, we provide samples only in JavaScript for QCEngine. QCEngine is a free online quantum computation simulator, allowing users to run samples in a browser, with no software installation at all. This simulator was developed by the authors, initially for their own use and now as a companion for this book. QCEngine is especially useful for us, both because it can be run without the need to download any software and because it incorporates the *circle notation* that we use as a visualization tool throughout the book.

A QCEngine Primer

Since we'll rely heavily on QCEngine, it's worth spending a little time to see how to navigate the simulator, which you can find at *http://oreilly-qc.github.io*.

Running code

The QCEngine web interface, shown in Figure 1-1, allows you to easily produce the various visualizations that we'll rely on. You can create these visualizations by simply entering code into the QCEngine code editor.

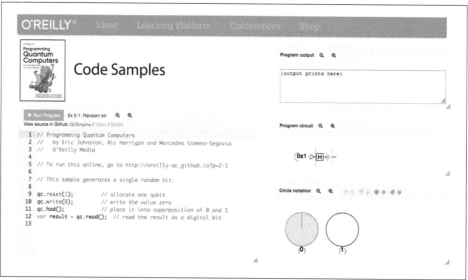

Figure 1-1. The QCEngine UI

To run one of the code samples from the book, select it from the drop-down list at the top of the editor and click the Run Program button. Some new interactive UI elements will appear for visualizing the results of running your code (see Figure 1-2).

Quantum circuit visualizer

This element presents a visual representation of the circuit representing your code. We introduce the symbols used in these circuits in Chapters 2 and 3. This view can also be used to interactively step through the program (see Figure 1-2).

Circle-notation visualizer

This displays the so-called *circle-notation* visualization of the QPU (or simulator) register. We explain how to read and use this notation in Chapter 2.

QCEngine output console

This is where any text appears that may have been printed from within your code (i.e., for debugging) using the `qc.print()` command. Anything printed with the standard JavaScript `console.log()` function will still go to your web browser's JavaScript console.

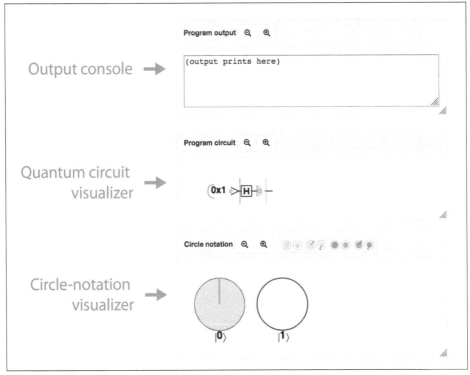

Figure 1-2. QCEngine UI elements for visualizing QPU results

Debugging code

Debugging QPU programs can be tough. Quite often the easiest way to understand what a program is doing is to slowly step through it, inspecting the visualizations at each step. Hovering your mouse over the circuit visualizer, you should see a vertical orange line appear at a fixed position and a gray vertical line wherever in the circuit your cursor happens to be. The orange line shows which position in the circuit (and therefore the program) the circle-notation visualizer currently represents. By default this is the end of the program, but by clicking other parts of the circuit, you can have the circle-notation visualizer show the configuration of the QPU at that point in the program. For example, Figure 1-3 shows how the circle-notation visualizer changes as we switch between two different steps in the default QCEngine program.

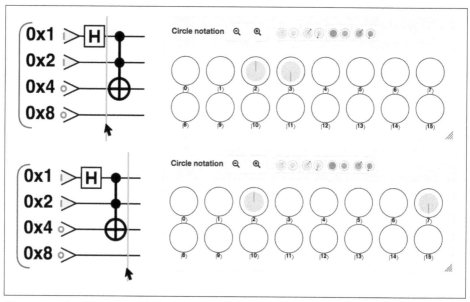

Figure 1-3. Stepping through a QCEngine program using the circuit and circle-notation visualizers

Having access to a QPU simulator, you're probably keen to start tinkering. Don't let us stop you! In Chapter 2 we'll walk through code for increasingly complex QPU programs.

Native QPU Instructions

QCEngine is one of several tools allowing us to run and inspect QPU code, but what does QPU code actually look like? Conventional high-level languages are commonly used to control lower-level QPU instructions (as we've already seen with the JavaScript-based QCEngine). In this book we'll regularly cross between these levels. Describing the programming of a QPU with distinctly quantum machine-level operations helps us get to grips with the fundamental novel logic of a QPU, while seeing how to manipulate these operations from higher-level conventional languages like JavaScript, Python, or C++ gives us a more pragmatic paradigm for actually writing code. The definition of new, bespoke, *quantum* programming languages is an active area of development. We won't highlight these in this book, but references for the interested reader are offered in Chapter 14.

To whet your appetite, we list some of the fundamental QPU instructions in Table 1-1, each of which will be explained in more detail within the chapters ahead.

Table 1-1. Essential QPU instruction set

Symbol	Name	Usage	Description
	NOT (also X)	`qc.not(t)`	Logical bitwise NOT
	CNOT	`qc.cnot(t,c)`	Controlled NOT: `if (c) then NOT(t)`
	CCNOT (Toffoli)	`qc.cnot(t,c1|c2)`	`if (c1 AND c2) then NOT(t)`
	HAD (Hadamard)	`qc.had(t)`	Hadamard gate
	PHASE	`qc.phase(angle,c)`	Relative phase rotation
	Z	`qc.phase(180,c)`	Relative phase rotation by 180 °
	S	`qc.phase(90,c)`	Relative phase rotation by 90 °
	T	`qc.phase(45,c)`	Relative phase rotation by 45 °
	CPHASE	`qc.cphase(angle,c1|c2)`	Conditional phase rotation

Symbol	Name	Usage	Description
	CZ	`qc.cphase(180,c1|c2)`	Conditional phase rotation by 180 °
	READ	`val = qc.read(t)`	Read qubits, returning digital data
	WRITE	`qc.write(t,val)`	Write conventional data to qubits
	ROOTNOT	`qc.rootnot(t)`	Root-of-NOT operation
	SWAP (EXCHANGE)	`qc.exchange(t1|t2)`	Exchange two qubits
	CSWAP	`qc.exchange(t1|t2, c)`	Conditional exchange: `if (c) then SWAP(t1,t2)`

With each of these operations, the specific instructions and timing will depend on the QPU brand and architecture. However, this is an essential set of basic operations expected to be available on all machines, and these operations form the basis of our QPU programming, just as instructions like MOV and ADD do for CPU programmers.

Simulator Limitations

Although simulators offer a fantastic opportunity to prototype small QPU programs, when compared to real QPUs they are hopelessly underpowered. One measure of the power of a QPU is the number of *qubits* it has available to operate on[2] (the quantum equivalent of bits, on which we'll have much more to say shortly).

At the time of this book's publication, the world record for the largest simulation of a QPU stands at 51 qubits. In practice, the simulators and hardware available to most

---

2 Despite its popularity in the media as a benchmark for quantum computing, counting the number of qubits that a piece of hardware can handle is really an oversimplification, and much subtler considerations (*https://ibm.co/2FhLcIE*) are necessary to assess a QPU's true power.

readers of this book will typically be able to handle 26 or so qubits before grinding to a halt.

The examples in this book have been written with these limitations in mind. They make a great starting point, but each qubit added to them will double the memory required to run the simulation, cutting its speed in half.

Hardware Limitations

Conversely, the largest actual QPU hardware available at the time of writing has around 70 *physical* qubits, while the largest QPU available to the public, through the Qiskit (*https://qiskit.org/*) open source software development kit, contains 16 physical qubits.[3] By physical, as opposed to logical, we mean that these 70 qubits have no error correction, making them noisy and unstable. Qubits are much more fragile than their conventional counterparts; the slightest interaction with their surroundings can derail the computation.

Dealing with *logical* qubits allows a programmer to be agnostic about the QPU hardware and implement any textbook algorithm without having to worry about specific hardware constraints. In this book, we focus solely on programming with logical qubits, and while the examples we provide are small enough to be run on smaller QPUs (such as the ones available at the time of publication), abstracting away physical hardware details means that the skills and intuitions you develop will remain invaluable as future hardware develops.

QPU Versus GPU: Some Common Characteristics

The idea of programming an entirely new kind of processor can be intimidating, even if it does already have its own Stack Exchange community (*http://bit.ly/2XICxsY*). Here's a list of pertinent facts about what it's like to program a QPU:

- It is very rare that a program will run *entirely* on a QPU. Usually, a program running on a CPU will issue QPU instructions, and later retrieve the results.
- Some tasks are very well suited to the QPU, and others are not.
- The QPU runs on a separate clock from the CPU, and usually has its own dedicated hardware interfaces to external devices (such as optical outputs).
- A typical QPU has its own special RAM, which the CPU cannot efficiently access.
- A simple QPU will be one chip accessed by a laptop, or even perhaps eventually an area within another chip. A more advanced QPU is a large and expensive add-on, and always requires special cooling.

---

3 This figure may become out of date while this book is in press!

- Early QPUs, even simple ones, are the size of refrigerators and require special high-amperage power outlets.

- When a computation is done, a projection of the result is returned to the CPU, and most of the QPU's internal working data is discarded.

- QPU debugging can be very tricky, requiring special tools and techniques. Stepping through a program can be difficult, and often the best approach is to make changes to the program and observe their effect on the output.

- Optimizations that speed up one QPU may slow down another.

Sounds pretty challenging. But here's the thing—you can replace *QPU* with *GPU* in each and every one of those statements and they're still entirely valid.

Although QPUs are an almost alien technology of incredible power, when it comes to the problems we might face in learning to program them, a generation of software engineers have seen it all before. It's true, of course, that there are some nuances to QPU programming that are genuinely novel (this book wouldn't be necessary otherwise!), but the uncanny number of similarities should be reassuring. We can do this!

PART I

Programming for a QPU

What exactly is a qubit? How can we visualize one? How is it useful? These are short questions with complicated answers. In the first part of the book we'll answer these questions in a practical way. We begin in Chapter 2 by first describing and making use of a single qubit. The additional complexity of multi-qubit systems are then covered in Chapter 3. Along the way we'll encounter a number of single and multi-qubit operations, and Chapter 4 puts these straight to use, describing how to perform quantum teleportation. Bear in mind that the code samples that punctuate our discussion can be run on the QCEngine simulator (introduced in Chapter 1), using the provided links.

CHAPTER 2

One Qubit

Conventional bits have one binary parameter to play with—we can initialize a bit in either state 0 or state 1. This makes the mathematics of binary logic simple enough, but we *could* visually represent the possible 0/1 values of a bit by two separate empty/filled circles (see Table 2-1).

Table 2-1. Possible values of a conventional bit—a graphical representation

Possible values of a bit	Graphical representation
0	● ○ 0 1
1	○ ● 0 1

Now on to qubits. In some sense, qubits are very similar to bits: whenever you read the value of a qubit, you'll always get either 0 or 1. So, *after the readout* of a qubit, we can always describe it as shown in Table 2-1. But characterizing qubits *before* readout isn't so black and white, and requires a more sophisticated description. Before readout, qubits can exist in a *superposition* of states.

We'll try to tackle just what superposition means shortly. But to first give you an idea of why it might be powerful, note that there are an infinite number of possible superpositions in which a single qubit can exist prior to being read. Table 2-2 lists just some of the different superpositions we could prepare a qubit to be in. Although we'll always end up reading out 0 or 1 at the end, if we're clever it's the availability of these extra states that will allow us to perform some very powerful computing.

Table 2-2. Some possible values of a qubit

Possible values of a qubit	Graphical representation
$\lvert 0 \rangle$	$\lvert 0 \rangle$ $\lvert 1 \rangle$
$\lvert 1 \rangle$	$\lvert 0 \rangle$ $\lvert 1 \rangle$
$0.707\lvert 0 \rangle + 0.707\lvert 1 \rangle$	$\lvert 0 \rangle$ $\lvert 1 \rangle$
$0.95\lvert 0 \rangle + 0.35\lvert 1 \rangle$	$\lvert 0 \rangle$ $\lvert 1 \rangle$
$0.707\lvert 0 \rangle - 0.707\lvert 1 \rangle$	$\lvert 0 \rangle$ $\lvert 1 \rangle$

In the mathematics within Table 2-2 we've changed our labels from 0 and 1 to $\lvert 0 \rangle$ and $\lvert 1 \rangle$. This is called *bra-ket notation*, and it's commonly used in quantum computing. As a casual rule of thumb, numbers enclosed in bra-ket notation denote values that a qubit *might* be found to have when read out. When referring to a value that a qubit *has* been read out to have, we just use the number to represent the resulting digital value.

The first two rows in Table 2-2 show the quantum equivalents of the states of a conventional bit, with no superposition at all. A qubit prepared in state $\lvert 0 \rangle$ is equivalent to a conventional bit being 0—it will always give a value of 0 on readout—and similarly for $|1\rangle$. If our qubits were only ever in states $|0\rangle$ or $|1\rangle$, we'd just have some very expensive conventional bits.

But how can we start to get to grips with the more exotic possibilities of superposition shown in the other rows? To get some intuition for the bewildering variations in Table 2-2, it can be helpful to very briefly consider what a qubit actually is.[1]

A Quick Look at a Physical Qubit

One object that readily demonstrates quantum superposition is a single photon. To illustrate this, let's take a step back and suppose we tried to use the *location* of a photon to represent a conventional digital *bit*. In the device shown in Figure 2-1, a switchable mirror (that can be set as either reflective or transparent) allows us to control whether a photon ends up in one of two paths—corresponding to an encoding of either 0 or 1.

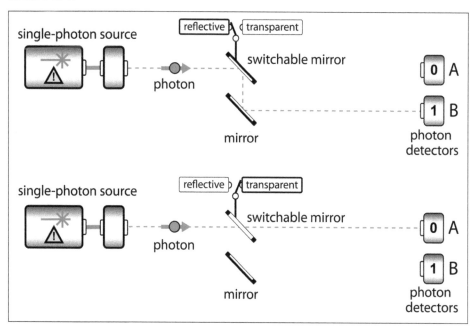

Figure 2-1. Using a photon as a conventional bit

---

1 In this book we'll try very hard *not* to think too much about what qubits really are. Although this may seem a little anticlimactic, it's worth remembering that conventional programming guides almost never revel in the fascinating physical nature of bits and bytes. In fact, it's precisely the ability to abstract away the physical nature of information that makes the writing of complex programs tractable.

Devices like this actually exist in digital communication technology, but nevertheless a single photon clearly makes a very fiddly bit (for starters, it won't stay in any one place for very long). To use this setup to demonstrate some qubit properties, suppose we replace the switch we use to *set* the photon as 0 or 1 with a *half*-silvered mirror.

A half-silvered mirror, as shown in Figure 2-2 (also known as a *beamsplitter*), is a semireflective surface that would, with a 50% chance, either deflect light into the path we associate with 1, or allow it to pass straight through to the path we associate with 0. There are no other options.

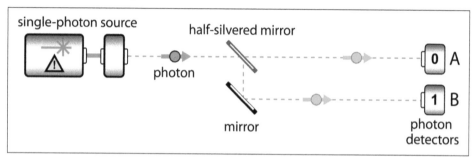

Figure 2-2. A simple implementation of one photonic qubit

When a single indivisible photon hits this surface, it suffers a sort of identity crisis. In an effect that has no conventional equivalent, it ends up existing in a state where it can be influenced by effects in both the 0 path and the 1 path. We say that the photon is in a *superposition* of traveling in each possible path. In other words, we no longer have a conventional bit, but a *qubit* that can be in a superposition of values 0 and 1.

It's very easy to misunderstand the nature of superposition (as many popular quantum computing articles do). It's *not* correct to say that the photon is in both the 0 *and* 1 paths at the same time. There is only one photon, so if we put detectors in each path, as shown in Figure 2-2, only one will go off. When this happens, it will reduce the photon's superposition into a digital bit and give a definitive 0 *or* 1 result. Yet, as we'll explore shortly, there are computationally useful ways a QPU can interact with a qubit in superposition before we need to read it out through such a detection.

The kind of superposition shown in Figure 2-2 will be central to leveraging the quantum power of a QPU. As such, we'll need to describe and control quantum superpositions a little more quantitatively. When our photon is in a superposition of paths, we say it has an *amplitude* associated with each path. There are two important aspects to these amplitudes—two *knobs* we can twiddle to alter the particular configuration of a qubit's superposition:

- The *magnitude* associated with each path of the photon's superposition is an analog value that measures how much the photon has *spread* into each path. A path's magnitude is related to the probability that the photon will be detected in that path. Specifically, the *square* of the magnitude determines the chance we observe a photon in a given path. In Figure 2-2 we could twiddle the magnitudes of the amplitudes associated with each path by altering how reflective the half-silvered mirror is.

- The *relative phase* between the different paths in the photon's superposition captures the amount by which the photon is *delayed* on one path relative to the other. This is also an analog value that can be controlled by the difference between how far the photon travels in the paths corresponding to 0 and 1. Note that we could change the relative phase without affecting the chance of the photon being detected in each path.[2]

It's worth re-emphasizing that the term *amplitude* is a way of referring to *both* the magnitude and the relative phase associated with some value from a qubit's superposition.

For the mathematically inclined, the amplitudes associated with different paths in a superposition are generally described by *complex numbers*. The *magnitude* associated with an amplitude is precisely the modulus of this complex number (the square root of the number multipled by its complex conjugate), while its *relative phase* is the angle if the complex number is expressed in polar form. For the mathematically uninclined, we will shortly introduce a visual notation so that you need not worry about such complex issues (pun intended).

The magnitude and relative phase are values available for us to exploit when computing, and we can think of them as being *encoded* in our qubit. But if we're ever to read out any information from it, the photon must eventually strike some kind of detector. At this point both these analog values vanish—the quantumness of the qubit is gone. Herein lies the crux of quantum computing: finding a way to exploit these ethereal quantities such that some useful remnant persists after the destructive act of readout.

The setup in Figure 2-2 is equivalent to the code sample we will shortly introduce in Example 2-1, in the case where photons are used as qubits.

---

2 Although we introduce the idea of relative phase in terms of relative distances traveled by light, it is a general concept that applies to all flavors of qubits: photons, electrons, superconductors, etc.

Okay, enough with the photons! This is a programmer's guide, not a physics textbook. Let's abstract away the physics and see how we can describe and visualize qubits in a manner as detached from photons and quantum physics as binary logic is from electrons and semiconductor physics.

Introducing Circle Notation

We now have an idea of what superposition is, but one that's quite tied up with the specific behavior of photons. Let's find an abstract way to describe superposition that allows us to focus only on abstract information.

The full-blown mathematics of quantum physics provides such an abstraction, but as can be seen in the lefthand column of Table 2-2, this mathematics is far more unintuitive and inconvenient than the simple binary logic of conventional bits.

Fortunately, the equivalent pictorial *circle notation* in the righthand column of Table 2-2 offers a more intuitive approach. Since our goal is building a fluent and pragmatic understanding of what goes on inside a QPU without needing to entrench ourselves in opaque mathematics, from now on we'll think of qubits entirely in terms of this circle notation.

From experimenting with photons we've seen that there are two aspects of a qubit's general state that we need to keep track of in a QPU: the magnitude of its superposition amplitudes and the relative phase between them. Circle notation displays these parameters as follows:

- The *magnitude* of the amplitude associated with each value a qubit can assume (so far, $|0\rangle$ and $|1\rangle$) is related to the radius of the filled-in area shown for each of the $|0\rangle$ or $|1\rangle$ circles.

- The *relative phase* between the amplitudes of these values is indicated by the *rotation* of the $|1\rangle$ circle relative to the $|0\rangle$ circle (a darker line is drawn in the circles to make this rotation apparent).

We'll be relying on circle notation throughout the book, so it's worth taking a little more care to see precisely how circle sizes and rotations capture these concepts.

Circle Size

We previously noted that the *square* of the magnitude associated with |0> or |1> determines the probability of obtaining that value on readout. Since a circle's filled *radius* represents the *magnitude*, this means that the shaded *area* in each circle (or, more colloquially, its size) is directly proportional to the *probability* of obtaining that circle's value (0 or 1) if we read out the qubit. The examples in Figure 2-3 show the circle notation for different qubit states and the chance of reading out a 1 in each case.

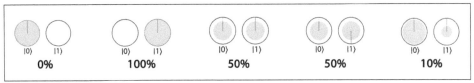

Figure 2-3. Probability of reading the value 1 for different superpositions represented in circle notation

 Reading a qubit destroys information. In all of the cases illustrated in Figure 2-3, reading the qubit will produce either a 0 or a 1, and when that happens, the qubit will change its state to match the observed value. So even if a qubit was initially in a more sophisticated state, once you read out a 1 you'll always get a 1 if you immediately try to read it again.

Notice that as the area shaded in the $|0\rangle$ circle gets larger, there's more chance you'll read out a 0, and of course that means that the chance of getting a 1 outcome decreases (being whatever is left over). In the last example in Figure 2-3, there is a 90% chance of reading out the qubit as 0, and therefore a corresponding 10% chance of reading out a 1.[3] We'll often talk of the filled-area of a circle in our circle notation as representing the magnitude associated with that value in a superposition. Although it might seem like an annoying technicality, it's important to have in the back of your mind that the magnitude associated with that value really corresponds to the circle's *radius*—although often it won't hurt to equate the two for visual convenience.

It's also easy to forget, although important to remember, that in circle notation the size of a circle associated with a given outcome does *not* represent the full superposition *amplitude*. The important additional information that we're missing is the relative phase of our superposition.

Circle Rotation

Some QPU instructions will also allow us to alter the relative rotations of a qubit's $|0\rangle$ and $|1\rangle$ circles. This represents the *relative phase* of the qubit. The relative phase of a qubit's state can take any value from 0° to 360°; a few examples are shown in Figure 2-4.

---

3 The sum of the register's magnitudes must *always* sum up to 1. This requirement is called *normalization*, for more on this see "Caveat 2: The requirement for normalized vectors" on page 183.

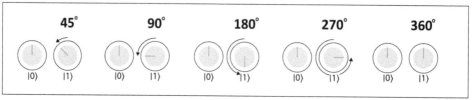

Figure 2-4. Example relative phases in a single qubit

 Our convention for rotating the circles in circle notation within this book is that a positive angle rotates the relevant circle *counterclockwise*, as illustrated in Figure 2-4.

In all the preceding examples we have only rotated the $|1\rangle$ circle. Why not the $|0\rangle$ circle as well? As the name suggests, it's only the *relative* phase in a qubit's superposition that ever makes any difference. Consequently only the *relative* rotation between our circles is of interest.[4] If a QPU operation were to apply a rotation to both circles, then we could always equivalently reconsider the effect such that only the $|1\rangle$ circle was rotated, making the relative rotation more readily apparent. An example is shown in Figure 2-5.

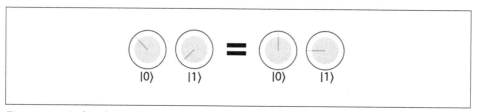

Figure 2-5. Only relative rotations matter in circle notation—these two states are equivalent because the relative phase of the two circles is the same in each case

Note that the relative phase can be varied independently of the magnitude of a superposition. This independence also works the other way. Comparing the third and fourth examples in Figure 2-3, we can see that the relative phase between outcomes for a single qubit has no direct effect on the chances of what we'll read out.

The fact that the relative phase of a single qubit has no effect on the magnitudes in a superposition means that it has no *direct* influence on observable readout results. This may make the relative phase property seem inconsequential, but the truth could not be more different! In quantum computations involving *multiple* qubits, we can

---

4 That only relative phases are of importance stems from the underlying quantum mechanical laws governing qubits.

crucially take advantage of this rotation to cleverly and indirectly affect the chances that we will eventually read out different values. In fact, well-engineered relative phases can provide an astonishing computational advantage. We'll now introduce operations that will allow us to do this—in particular, those that act only on a single qubit —and we'll visualize their effects using circle notation.

In contrast to the distinctly digital nature of conventional bits, magnitudes and relative phases are *continuous* degrees of freedom. This leads to a widely held misconception that quantum computing is comparable to the ill-fated *analog* computing. Remarkably, despite allowing us to manipulate continuous degrees of freedom, the errors experienced by a QPU can be corrected *digitally*. This is why QPUs are more robust than analog computing devices.

The First Few QPU Operations

Like their CPU counterparts, single-qubit QPU operations transform input information into a desired output. Only now, of course, our inputs and outputs are qubits rather than bits. Many QPU instructions[5] have an associated inverse, which can be useful to know about. In this case a QPU operation is said to be *reversible*, which ultimately means that no information is lost or discarded when it is applied. Some QPU operations, however, are *irreversible* and have no inverse (somehow they result in the loss of information). We'll eventually come to see that whether or not an operation is reversible can have important ramifications for how we make use of it.

Some of these QPU instructions may seem strange and of questionable utility, but after only introducing a handful we'll quickly begin putting them to use.

QPU Instruction: NOT

NOT is the quantum equivalent of the eponymous conventional operation. Zero becomes one, and vice versa. However, unlike its traditional cousin, a QPU NOT operation can also operate on a qubit in superposition.

In circle notation this results, very simply, in the swapping of the $|0\rangle$ and $|1\rangle$ circles, as in Figure 2-6.

---

5 Throughout the book we will use the terms *QPU instruction* and *QPU operation* interchangeably.

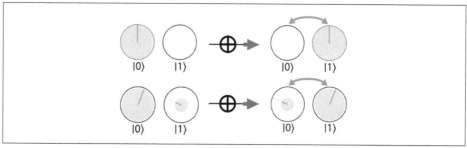

Figure 2-6. The NOT operation in circle notation

Reversibility: Just as in digital logic, the NOT operation is its own inverse; applying it twice returns a qubit to its original value.

QPU Instruction: HAD

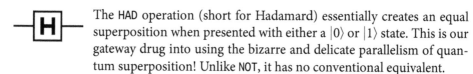

The HAD operation (short for Hadamard) essentially creates an equal superposition when presented with either a $|0\rangle$ or $|1\rangle$ state. This is our gateway drug into using the bizarre and delicate parallelism of quantum superposition! Unlike NOT, it has no conventional equivalent.

In circle notation, HAD results in the output qubit having the same amount of area filled-in for both $|0\rangle$ and $|1\rangle$, as in Figure 2-7.

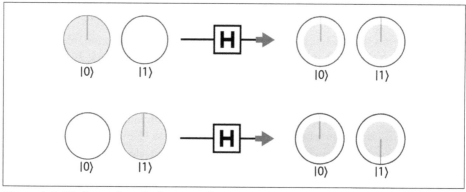

Figure 2-7. Hadamard applied to some basic states

This allows HAD to produce *uniform superpositions* of outcomes in a qubit; i.e., a superposition where each outcome is equally likely. Notice also that HAD's action on qubits initially in the states $|0\rangle$ and $|1\rangle$ is slightly different: the output of acting HAD on $|1\rangle$ yields a nonzero rotation (relative phase) of one of the circles, whereas the output from acting it on $|0\rangle$ doesn't.

You might wonder what happens if we apply HAD to qubits that are *already in a superposition*. The best way to find out is to experiment! Doing so you'll soon notice that the following occurs:

- HAD acts on both the $|0\rangle$ and $|1\rangle$ states separately according to the rules illustrated in Figure 2-7.
- The $|0\rangle$ and $|1\rangle$ values this generates are combined, weighted by the amplitudes of the original superpositions.[6]

Reversibility: Similar to NOT, the HAD operation is its own inverse; applying it twice returns a qubit to its original value.

QPU Instruction: READ

The READ operation is the formal expression of the previously introduced *readout* process. READ is unique in being the only part of a QPU's instruction set that potentially returns a *random* result.

QPU Instruction: WRITE

The WRITE operation allows us to initialize a QPU register before we operate on it. This is a deterministic process.

Applying READ to a single qubit will return a value of either 0 or 1 with probabilities determined by (the square of) the associated magnitudes in the qubit's state (ignoring the relative phase). Following a READ operation, a qubit is left in the state $|0\rangle$ if the 0 outcome is obtained and state $|1\rangle$ if the 1 outcome is obtained. In other words, any superposition is irreversibly destroyed.

In circle notation an outcome occurs with a probability determined by the filled area in each associated circle. We then shift the filled-in area between circles to reflect this result: the circle associated with the occurring outcome becomes entirely filled in, while the remaining circle becomes empty. This is illustrated in Figure 2-8 for READ operations being performed on two different example superpositions.

---

6 For details on the mathematics behind HAD and other common operations, see Chapter 14.

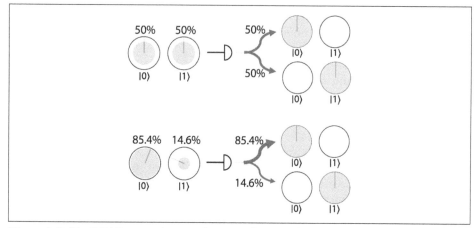

Figure 2-8. The READ operation produces random results

In the second example of Figure 2-8, the READ operation removes all meaningful relative phase information. As a result, we reorient the state so that the circle points upward.

Using a READ and a NOT, we can also construct a simple WRITE operation that allows us to prepare a qubit in a desired state of either $|0\rangle$ or $|1\rangle$. First we READ the qubit, and then, if the value does not match the value we plan to WRITE, we perform a NOT operation. Note that this WRITE operation does *not* allow us to prepare a qubit in an arbitrary superposition (with arbitrary magnitude and relative phase), but only in either state $|0\rangle$ or state $|1\rangle$.[7]

Reversibility: The READ and WRITE operations are not reversible. They destroy superpositions and lose information. Once that is done, the analog values of the qubit (both magnitude and phase) are gone forever.

Hands-on: A Perfectly Random Bit

Before moving on to introduce a few more single-qubit operations, let's pause to see how—armed with the HAD, READ, and WRITE operations—we can create a program to perform a task that is impossible on any conventional computer. We'll generate a *truly* random bit.

---

7 We will see that being able to prepare an arbitrary superposition is tricky but useful, especially in quantum machine-learning applications, and we introduce an approach for this in Chapter 13.

Throughout the history of computation, a vast amount of time and effort has gone into developing Pseudo-Random Number Generator (PRNG) systems, which find usage in applications ranging from cryptography to weather forecasting. PRNGs are *pseudo* in the sense that if you know the contents of the computer's memory and the PRNG algorithm, you can—in principle—predict the next number to be generated.

According to the known laws of physics, the readout behavior of a qubit in superposition is fundamentally and perfectly unpredictable. This allows a QPU to create the world's greatest random number generator by simply preparing a qubit in state $|0\rangle$, applying the HAD instruction, and then reading out the qubit. We can illustrate this combination of QPU operations using a *quantum circuit* diagram, where a line moving left to right illustrates the sequence of different operations that are performed on our (single) qubit, as shown in Figure 2-9.

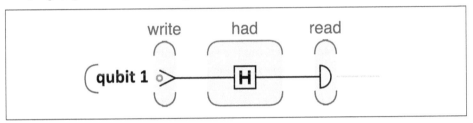

Figure 2-9. Generating a perfectly random bit with a QPU

It might not look like much, but there we have it, our first QPU program: a Quantum Random Number Generator (QRNG)! You can simulate this using the code snippet in Example 2-1. If you repeatedly run these four lines of code on the QCEngine simulator, you'll receive a binary random string. Of course, CPU-powered simulators like QCEngine are approximating our QRNG with a PRNG, but running the equivalent code on a real QPU will produce a perfectly random binary string.

Sample Code

Run this sample online at *http://oreilly-qc.github.io?p=2-1*.

Example 2-1. One random bit

```
qc.reset(1);            // allocate one qubit
qc.write(0);            // write the value zero
qc.had();               // place it into superposition of 0 and 1
var result = qc.read(); // read the result as a digital bit
```

All of the code samples in this book can be found online at *http:// oreilly-qc.github.io*, and can be run either on QPU simulators or on actual QPU hardware. Running these samples is an essential part of learning to program a QPU. For more information, see Chapter 1.

Since this might be your first quantum program (congratulations!), let's break it down just to be sure each step makes sense:

- `qc.reset(1)` sets up our simulation of the QPU, requesting one qubit. All the programs we write for QCEngine will initialize a set of qubits with a line like this.

- `qc.write(0)` simply initializes our single qubit in the $|0\rangle$ state—the equivalent of a conventional bit being set to the value 0.

- `qc.had()` applies HAD to our qubit, placing it into a superposition of $|0\rangle$ and $|1\rangle$, just as in Figure 2-7.

- `var result = qc.read()` reads out the value of our qubit at the end of the computation as a random digital bit, assigning the value to the `result` variable.

It might look like all we've really done here is find a very expensive way of flipping a coin, but this underestimates the power of HAD. If you could somehow *look inside* HAD you would find neither a pseudo nor a hardware random number generator. Unlike these, HAD is guaranteed unpredictable by the laws of quantum physics. Nobody in the known universe can do any better than a hopeless random guess as to whether a qubit's value following a HAD will be read to be 0 or 1—even if they know exactly the instructions we are using to generate our random numbers.

In fact, although we'll properly introduce dealing with multiple qubits in the next chapter, we can easily run our single random qubit program in parallel eight times to produce a random *byte*. Figure 2-10 shows what this looks like.

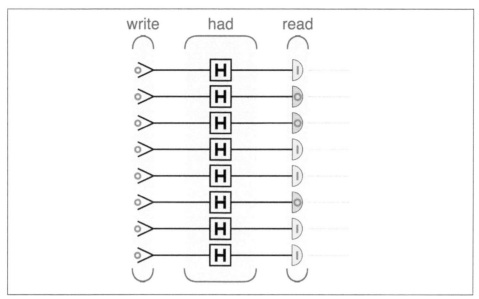

Figure 2-10. Generating one random byte

This code in Example 2-2 for creating a random byte is almost identical to Example 2-1.

Sample Code

Run this sample online at *http://oreilly-qc.github.io?p=2-2*.

Example 2-2. One random byte

```
qc.reset(8);
qc.write(0);
qc.had();
var result = qc.read();
qc.print(result);
```

Note that we make use of the fact that QCEngine operations like WRITE and HAD default to acting on all initialized qubits, unless we explicitly pass specific qubits for them to act on.

Although Example 2-2 uses multiple qubits, there are no actual multi-qubit operations that take more than one of the qubits as input. The same program could be serialized to run on only a single qubit.

QPU Instruction: PHASE(θ)

The PHASE(θ) operation also has no conventional equivalent. This instruction allows us to directly manipulate the *relative phase* of a qubit, changing it by some specified angle. Consequently, as well as a qubit to operate on, the PHASE(θ) operation takes an additional (numerical) input parameter—the angle to rotate by. For example, PHASE(45) denotes a PHASE operation that performs a 45° rotation.

In circle notation, the effect of PHASE(θ) is to simply rotate the circle associated with $|1\rangle$ by the angle we specify. This is shown in Figure 2-11 for the case of PHASE(45).

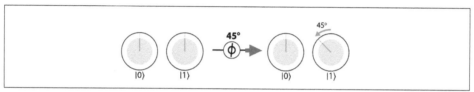

Figure 2-11. Action of a PHASE(45) operation

Note that the PHASE operation only rotates the circle associated with the $|1\rangle$ state, so it would have no effect on a qubit in the $|0\rangle$ state.

Reversibility: PHASE operations are reversible, although they are not generally their own inverse. The PHASE operation may be reversed by applying a PHASE with the *negative* of the original angle. In circle notation, this corresponds to *undoing* the rotation, by rotating in the opposite direction.

Using HAD and PHASE, we can produce some single-qubit quantum states that are so commonly used that they've been named: $|+\rangle$, $|-\rangle$, $|+Y\rangle$, and $|-Y\rangle$, as shown in Figure 2-12. If you feel like flexing your QPU muscles, see whether you can determine how to produce these states using HAD and PHASE operations (each superposition shown has an equal *magnitude* in each of the $|0\rangle$ and $|1\rangle$ states).

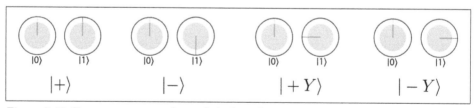

Figure 2-12. Four very commonly used single-qubit states

These four states will be used in Example 2-4, and although one way to produce them is using HAD and PHASE, we can also understand them as being the result of so-called single-qubit *rotation* operations.

QPU Instructions: ROTX(θ) and ROTY(θ)

We've seen that PHASE rotates the relative phase of a qubit, and that in circle notation this corresponds to rotating the circle associated with the $|1\rangle$ value. There are two other common operations related to PHASE called ROTX(θ) and ROTY(θ), which also perform slightly different kinds of rotations on our qubit.

Figure 2-13 shows the application of ROTX(45) and ROTY(45) on the $|0\rangle$ and $|1\rangle$ states in circle notation.

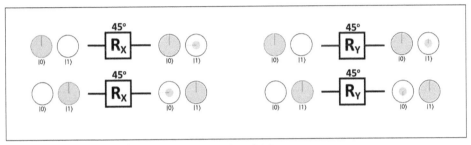

Figure 2-13. ROTX and ROTY actions on 0 and 1 input states

These operations don't *look* like very intuitive rotations, at least not as obviously as PHASE did. However, their rotation names stem from their action in another common visual representation of a single qubit's state, known as the *Bloch sphere*. In the Bloch sphere representation, a qubit is visualized by a point somewhere on the surface of a three-dimensional sphere. In this book we use circle notation instead of the Bloch sphere visualization, as the Bloch sphere doesn't extend well to multiple qubits. But to satisfy any etymological curiosity, if we represent a qubit on the Bloch sphere, then ROTY and ROTX operations correspond to rotating the qubit's point about the sphere's y- and x-axes, respectively. This meaning is lost in our circle notation, since we use two 2D circles rather than a single three-dimensional sphere. In fact, the PHASE operation actually corresponds to a rotation about the z-axis when visualizing qubits in the Bloch sphere, so you may also hear it referred to as ROTZ.

COPY: The Missing Operation

There is one operation available to conventional computers that *cannot* be implemented on a QPU. Although we can make many copies of a *known* state by repeatedly preparing it (if the state is either $|0\rangle$ or $|1\rangle$, we can do this simply with WRITE operations), there is no way of copying some state partway through a quantum computation without determining what it is. This constraint arises due to the fundamental laws of physics governing our qubits.

This is definitely an inconvenience, but as we will learn in the following chapters, other possibilities available to QPUs can help make up for the lack of a COPY instruction.

Combining QPU Operations

We now have NOT, HAD, PHASE, READ, and WRITE at our disposal. It's worth mentioning that, as is the case in conventional logic, these operations can be combined to realize each other, and even allow us to create entirely new operations. For example, suppose a QPU provides the HAD and PHASE instructions, but NOT is missing. A PHASE(180) operation can be combined with two HADs to produce the exact equivalent of a NOT operation, as shown in Figure 2-14. Conversely, a PHASE(180) instruction can also be realized from HAD and NOT operations.

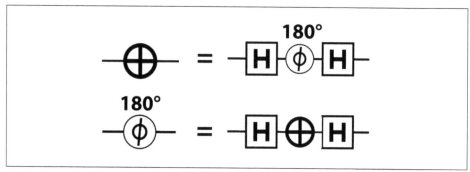

Figure 2-14. Building equivalent operations

QPU Instruction: ROOT-of-NOT

Combining instructions also lets us produce interesting new operations that do not exist at all in the world of conventional logic. The ROOT-of-NOT operation (RNOT) is one such example. It's quite literally the square root of the NOT operation, in the sense that, when applied twice, it performs a single NOT, as shown in Figure 2-15.

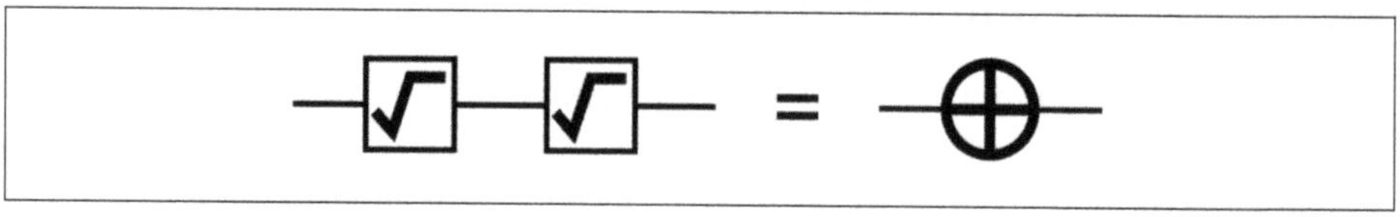

Figure 2-15. An impossible operation for conventional bits

There's more than one way to construct this operation, but Figure 2-16 shows one simple implementation.

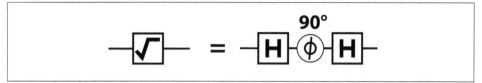

Figure 2-16. Recipe for ROOT-of-NOT

We can check that applying this set of operations twice does indeed yield the same result as a NOT by running a simulation, as shown in Example 2-3.

Sample Code

Run this sample online at *http://oreilly-qc.github.io?p=2-3*.

Example 2-3. Showing the action of RNOT

```
qc.reset(1);
qc.write(0);

// Root-of-not
qc.had();
qc.phase(90);
qc.had();

// Root-of-not
qc.had();
qc.phase(90);
qc.had();
```

In circle notation, we can visualize each step involved in implementing an RNOT operation (a PHASE(90) between two HADs). The resulting operation is shown in Figure 2-17.

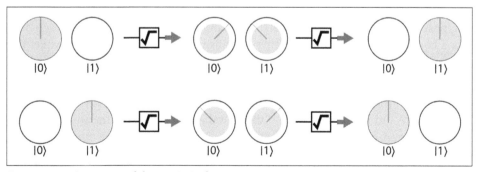

Figure 2-17. Function of the ROOT-of-NOT operation

Following the evolution of our qubit in circle notation helps us see how RNOT is able to get us halfway to a NOT operation. Recall from Figure 2-14 that if we HAD a qubit, then rotate its relative phase by 180°, another HAD will result in a NOT operation. RNOT performs half of this rotation (a PHASE(90)), so that two applications will result in the HAD-PHASE(180)-HAD sequence that is equivalent to a NOT. It might be a bit mind-bending at first, but see if you can piece together how the RNOT operation cleverly performs this feat when applied twice (it might help to remember that HAD is its own inverse, so a sequence of two HADs is equivalent to doing nothing at all).

Reversibility: While RNOT operations are never their own inverse, the inverse of the operation in Figure 2-16 may be constructed by using a negative phase value, as shown in Figure 2-18.

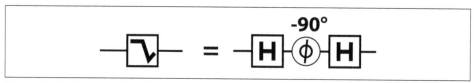

Figure 2-18. Inverse of RNOT

Although it might seem like an esoteric curiosity, the RNOT operation teaches us the important lesson that by carefully placing information in the relative phase of a qubit, we can perform entirely new kinds of computation.

Hands-on: Quantum Spy Hunter

For a more practical demonstration of the power in manipulating the relative phases of qubits, we finish this chapter with a more complex program. The code presented in Example 2-4 uses the simple single-qubit QPU operations introduced previously to perform a simplified version of Quantum Key Distribution (QKD). QKD is a protocol at the core of the field of quantum cryptography that allows the provably secure transmission of information.

Suppose that two QPU programmers, Alice and Bob, are sending data to each other via a communication channel capable of transmitting qubits. Once in a while, they send the specially constructed "spy hunter" qubit described in Example 2-4, which they use to test whether their communication channel has been compromised.

Any spy who tries to read one of these qubits has a 25% chance of getting caught. So even if Alice and Bob only use 50 of them in the whole transfer, the spy's chances of getting away are far less than one in a million.

Alice and Bob can detect whether their key has been compromised by exchanging some conventional digital information, which does not need to be private or encrypted. After exchanging their messages, they test a few of their qubits by reading them out and checking that they agree in a certain expected way. If any disagree, then they know someone was listening in. This process is illustrated in Figure 2-19.

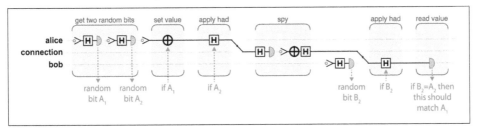

Figure 2-19. The quantum spy hunter program

Here's the code. We recommend trying out Example 2-4 on your own, and tweaking and testing like you would with any other code snippet.

Sample Code

Run this sample online at *http://oreilly-qc.github.io?p=2-4*.

Example 2-4. Quantum random spy hunter

```
qc.reset(3);
qc.discard();
var a = qint.new(1, 'alice');
var fiber = qint.new(1, 'fiber');
var b = qint.new(1, 'bob');

function random_bit(q) {
    q.write(0);
    q.had();
    return q.read();
}

// Generate two random bits
var send_had = random_bit(a);
var send_val = random_bit(a);

// Prepare Alice's qubit
a.write(0);
if (send_val)  // Use a random bit to set the value
    a.not();
if (send_had)  // Use a random bit to apply HAD or not
    a.had();

// Send the qubit!
fiber.exchange(a);

// Activate the spy
var spy_is_present = true;
```

```
if (spy_is_present) {
    var spy_had = 0;
    if (spy_had)
        fiber.had();
    var stolen_data = fiber.read();
    fiber.write(stolen_data);
    if (spy_had)
        fiber.had();
}

// Receive the qubit!
var recv_had = random_bit(b);
fiber.exchange(b);
if (recv_had)
    b.had();
var recv_val = b.read();

// Now Alice emails Bob to tell
// him her choice of operations and value.
// If the choice matches and the
// value does not, there's a spy!
if (send_had == recv_had)
    if (send_val != recv_val)
        qc.print('Caught a spy!\n');
```

In Example 2-4, Alice and Bob each have access to a simple QPU containing a single qubit, and can send their qubits along a quantum communication channel. There might be a spy listening to that link; in the sample code you can control whether or not a spy is present by toggling the spy_is_present variable.

> The fact that quantum cryptography can be performed with such relatively small QPUs is one of the reasons why it has begun to see commercial application long before more powerful general-purpose QPUs are available.

Let's walk through the code one step at a time to see how Alice and Bob's simple resources allow them to perform this feat. We'll refer to comments from the code snippet as markers:

// Generate two random bits
Alice uses her one-qubit QPU as a simple QRNG, exactly as we did in Example 2-2, generating two secret random bits known only to her. We denote these send_val and send_had.

// Prepare Alice's qubit

Using her two random bits, Alice prepares the "spy hunter" qubit. She sets it to value, and then uses send_had to decide whether to apply a HAD. In effect, she is preparing her qubit randomly in one of the states $|0\rangle$, $|1\rangle$, $|+\rangle$, or $|-\rangle$, and not (yet) telling anyone *which* of the states it is. If she does decide to apply a HAD, then if Bob wants to extract whether she intended a 0 or 1, he will have to apply the inverse of HAD (another HAD) before performing a READ.

// Send the qubit!

Alice sends her qubit to Bob. For clarity in this example, we are using another qubit to represent the communication channel.

// Activate the spy

If Alice were transmitting *conventional* digital data, the spy would simply make a copy of the bit, accomplishing their mission. With qubits, that's not possible. Recall that there is no COPY operation, so the only thing the spy can do is READ the qubit Alice sent, and then try to carefully send one just like it to Bob to avoid detection. Remember, however, that reading a qubit irrevocably destroys information, so the spy will only be left with the conventional bit of the readout. The spy doesn't know whether or not Alice performed a HAD. As a result, he won't know whether to apply a second (*inverting*) HAD before performing his READ. If he simply performs a READ he won't know whether he's receiving a random value from a qubit in superposition or a value actually encoded by Alice. This means that not only will he not be able to reliably extract Alice's bit, but he also won't know what the right state is to send on to Bob to avoid detection.

// Receive the qubit!

Like Alice, Bob randomly generates a recv_had bit, and he uses that to decide whether to apply a HAD before applying a READ to Alice's qubit, resulting in his value bit. This means that sometimes Bob will (by chance) correctly decode a binary value from Alice and other times he won't.

// If the had setting matches between sender and receiver but the val does not, there's a spy!

Now that the qubit has been received, Alice and Bob can openly compare the cases in which their choices of applying HADs (or not) correctly matched up. If they randomly happened to agree in both applying (or not applying) a HAD (this will be about half the time), their value bits should match; i.e., Bob will have correctly decoded Alice's message. If in these *correctly decoded messages* their values *don't* agree, they can conclude that the spy must have READ their message and sent on an *incorrect* replacement qubit to Bob, messing up his decoding.

Conclusion

In this chapter we introduced a way to describe single qubits, as well as a variety of QPU instructions to manipulate them. The random property of the READ operation was used to construct a quantum random number generator, and control over the relative phase in a qubit was used to perform basic quantum cryptography.

The circle notation used to visualize the state of a qubit is also used extensively in the chapters ahead. In Chapter 3, we will extend circle notation to deal with the behavior of multi-qubit systems, and introduce new QPU operations used to work with them.

Multiple Qubits

As useful as single qubits can be, they're much more powerful (and intriguing) in groups. We've already seen in Chapter 2 how the distinctly quantum phenomenon of superposition introduces the new parameters of magnitude and relative phase for computation. When our QPU has access to more than one qubit, we can make use of a second powerful quantum phenomenon known as *entanglement*. Quantum entanglement is a very particular kind of interaction between qubits, and we'll see it in action within this chapter, utilizing it in complex and sophisticated ways.

But to explore the abilities of multiple qubits, we first need a way to visualize them.

Circle Notation for Multi-Qubit Registers

Can we extend our circle notation to multiple qubits? If our qubits *didn't* interact with one another, we could simply employ multiple versions of the representation we used for a single qubit. In other words, we could use a pair of circles for the $|0\rangle$ and $|1\rangle$ states of each qubit. Although this naive representation allows us to describe a superposition of any one *individual* qubit, there are superpositions of *groups* of qubits that it cannot represent.

How else might circle notation represent the state of a *register* of multiple qubits? Just as is the case with conventional bits, a register of N qubits can be used to represent one of 2^N different values. For example, a register of three qubits in the states $|0\rangle|1\rangle|1\rangle$ can represent a decimal value of 3. When talking about multi-qubit registers we'll often describe the decimal value that the register represents in the same quantum notation that we used for a single qubit, so whereas a single qubit can encode the states $|0\rangle$ and $|1\rangle$, a two-qubit register can encode the states $|0\rangle$, $|1\rangle$, $|2\rangle$, and $|3\rangle$. Making use of the quantum nature of our qubits, we can also create superpositions of these different values. To represent these kinds of superpositions of N qubits, we'll use a separate circle for each of the 2^N different values that an N-bit number can assume, as shown in Figure 3-1.

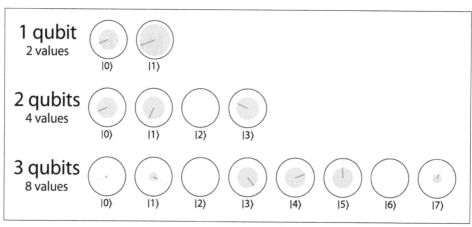

Figure 3-1. Circle notation for various numbers of qubits

In Figure 3-1, we see the familiar two-circle $|0\rangle$, $|1\rangle$ representation for a single qubit. For two qubits we have circles for $|0\rangle$, $|1\rangle$, $|2\rangle$, $|3\rangle$. This is not "one pair of circles per qubit"; instead, it is one circle for each possible two-bit number you may get by reading these qubits. For three qubits, the values of the QPU register are $|0\rangle$, $|1\rangle$, $|2\rangle$, $|3\rangle$, $|4\rangle$, $|5\rangle$, $|6\rangle$, $|7\rangle$, since upon readout we can get any three-bit value. In Figure 3-1, this means that we can now associate a magnitude and relative phase with each of these 2^N values. In the case of the three-qubit example, the magnitude of each of the circles determines the probability that a specific three-bit value will be observed when *all three* qubits are read.

You may be wondering what such a superposition of a multi-qubit register's value looks like in terms of the states of the individual qubits making it up. In some cases we can easily deduce the individual qubit states. For example, the three-qubit register superposition of the states $|0\rangle$, $|2\rangle$, $|4\rangle$, $|6\rangle$ shown in Figure 3-2 can easily be expressed in terms of each individual qubit's state.

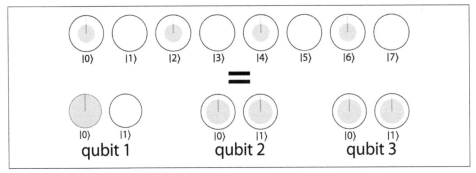

Figure 3-2. Some multi-qubit quantum states can be understood in terms of single-qubit states

To convince yourself that these single-qubit and multi-qubit representations are equivalent, write down each decimal value in the multi-qubit state in terms of the three-bit binary values. In fact, this multi-qubit state can be generated simply using two single-qubit HAD operations, as shown by Example 3-1.

Sample Code

Run this sample online at *http://oreilly-qc.github.io?p=3-1*.

Example 3-1. Creating a multi-qubit state that can be expressed in terms of its qubits

```
qc.reset(3);
qc.write(0);
var qubit1 = qint.new(1, 'qubit 1');
var qubit2 = qint.new(1, 'qubit 2');
var qubit3 = qint.new(1, 'qubit 3');
qubit2.had();
qubit3.had();
```

Example 3-1 introduces some new QCEngine notation for keeping track of larger numbers of qubits. The qint object allows us to label our qubits and treat them more like a standard programming variable. Once we've used qc.reset() to set up our register with some qubits, qint.new() allows us to assign them to qint objects. The first argument to qint.new() specifies how many qubits to assign to this qint from the stack created by qc.reset(). The second argument takes a label that is used in the circuit visualizer. qint objects have many methods allowing us to apply QPU operations directly to qubit groupings. In Example 3-1, we use qint.had().

Although the state in Figure 3-2 can be understood in terms of its constituent qubits, take a look at the three-qubit register state shown in Figure 3-3.

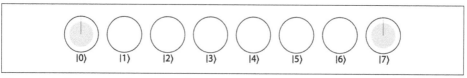

Figure 3-3. Quantum relationships between multiple qubits

This represents a state of three qubits in equal superposition of $|0\rangle$ and $|7\rangle$. Can we visualize this in terms of what each individual qubit is doing like we could in Figure 3-2? Since 0 and 7 are 000 and 111 in binary, we have a superposition of the three qubits being in the states $|0\rangle|0\rangle|0\rangle$ and $|1\rangle|1\rangle|1\rangle$. Surprisingly, in this case, there is no way to write down circle representations for the individual qubits! Notice that reading out the three qubits always results in us finding them to have the *same* values (with 50% probability that the value will be 0 and 50% probability it will be 1). So clearly there must be some kind of link between the three qubits, ensuring that their outcomes are the same.

This link is the new and powerful *entanglement* phenomenon. Entangled multi-qubit states cannot be described in terms of individual descriptions of what the constituent qubits are doing, although you're welcome to try! This entanglement link is only describable in the configuration of the *whole* multi-qubit register. It also turns out to be impossible to produce entangled states from only *single-qubit* operations. To explore entanglement in more detail, we'll need to introduce multi-qubit operations.

Drawing a Multi-Qubit Register

We now know how to describe the configuration of N qubits in circle notation using 2^N circles, but how do we draw multi-qubit quantum circuits? Our multi-qubit circle notation considers each qubit to take a position in a length N bitstring, so it's convenient to label each qubit according to its binary value.

For example, let's take another look at the random eight-qubyte circuit we introduced in Chapter 2. We can collectively refer to a register of eight qubits as a *qubyte* in analogy with a conventional eight-bit byte. In our previous encounter with a qubyte, we simply labeled the eight qubits as qubit 1, qubit 2, etc. Figure 3-4 shows how that circuit looks if we properly label each qubit with the binary value it represents.

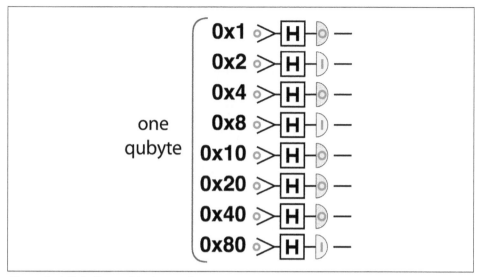

Figure 3-4. Labeling qubits in a qubyte

Naming Qubits

In Figure 3-4 we write our qubit values in hexadecimal (*http://bit.ly/2YmZJtX*), using notation such as 0x1 and 0x2. This is standard programmer notation for hexadecimal values, and we'll use this throughout the book as a convenient notation to clarify when we're talking about a specific qubit—even in cases when we have large numbers of them.

Single-Qubit Operations in Multi-Qubit Registers

Now that we're able to draw multi-qubit circuits and represent them in circle notation, let's start making use of them. What happens (in circle notation) when we apply single-qubit operations such as NOT, HAD, and PHASE to a multi-qubit register? The only difference from the single-qubit case is that the circles are operated on in certain *operator pairs* specific to the qubit that the operation acts on.

To identify a qubit's operator pairs, match each circle with the one whose value differs by the qubit's bit-value, as shown in Figure 3-5. For example, if we are operating on qubit 0x4, then each pair will include circles whose values differ by exactly 4.

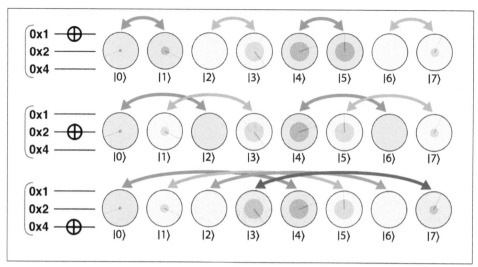

Figure 3-5. The NOT operation swaps values in each of the qubit's operator pairs; here, its action is shown on an example multi-qubit superposition

Once these operator pairs have been identified, the operation is performed on *each pair*, just as if the members of a pair were the $|0\rangle$ and $|1\rangle$ values of a single-qubit register. For a NOT operation, the circles in each pair are simply swapped, as in Figure 3-5.

For a single-qubit PHASE operation, the righthand circle of each pair is rotated by the phase angle, as in Figure 3-6.

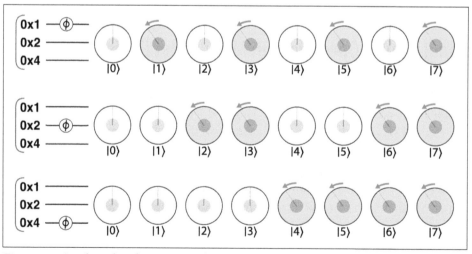

Figure 3-6. Single-qubit phase in a multi-qubit register

Thinking in terms of operator pairs is a good way to quickly visualize the action of single-qubit operations on a register. For a deeper understanding of why this works, we need to think about the effect that an operation on a given qubit has on the binary representation of the whole register. For example, the circle-swapping action of a NOT on the second qubit in Figure 3-5 corresponds to simply flipping the second bit in each value's binary representation. Similarly, a single-qubit PHASE operation acting on (for example) the third qubit rotates each circle for which the third bit is 1. A single-qubit PHASE will always cause exactly half of the values of the register to be rotated, and *which* half just depends on which qubit is the target of the operation.

The same kind of reasoning helps us think about the action of any other single-qubit operation on qubits from larger registers.

 Occasionally we'll colorfully highlight certain circles in circle notation, such as in Figures 3-5 and 3-6. This is only to highlight which states have been involved in operations.

Reading a Qubit in a Multi-Qubit Register

What happens when we perform a READ operation on a single qubit from a multi-qubit register? READ operations also function using operator pairs. If we have a multi-qubit circle representation, we can determine the probability of obtaining a 0 outcome for one single qubit by adding the squared magnitudes of all of the circles on the $|0\rangle$ (lefthand) side of that qubit's operator pairs. Similarly, we can determine the probability of 1 by adding the squared magnitudes of all of the circles on the $|1\rangle$ (righthand) side of the qubit's operator pairs.

Following a READ, the state of our multi-qubit register will change to reflect which outcome occurred. All circles that do not agree with the result will be eliminated, as shown in Figure 3-7.

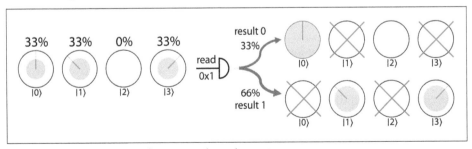

Figure 3-7. Reading one qubit in a multi-qubit register

Note that both states $|1\rangle$ and $|3\rangle$ are compatible with reading an outcome of 1 in the first (0x1) qubit. This is because the binary representations of 1 and 3 both contain a 1 in the first bit. Note also that following this elimination, the state has the remaining values *renormalized* so that their areas (and hence the associated probabilities) add up to 100%. To read more than one qubit, each single-qubit READ operation can be performed individually according to the operator pair prescription.

Visualizing Larger Numbers of Qubits

N qubits require 2^N circles in circle notation, and therefore each additional qubit we might add to our QPU doubles the number of circles we must keep track of. As Figure 3-8 shows, this number quite quickly increases to the point where our circle-notation circles become vanishingly small.

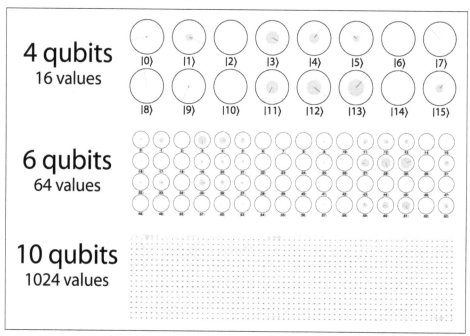

Figure 3-8. Circle notation for larger qubit counts

With so many tiny circles, the circle-notation visualization becomes useful for seeing *patterns* instead of individual values, and we can zoom in to any areas for which we want a more quantitative view. Nevertheless, we can improve clarity in these situations by exaggerating the relative phases, making the line showing a circle's rotation bold, and using differences in color or shading to emphasize differences in phase, as shown in Figure 3-9.

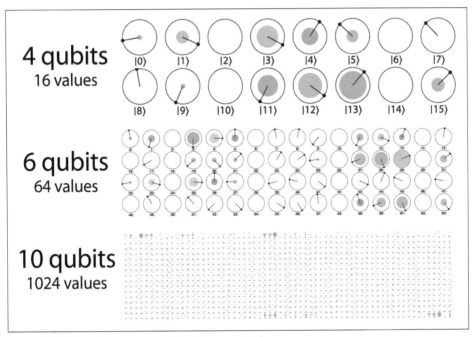

4 qubits
16 values

6 qubits
64 values

10 qubits
1024 values

Figure 3-9. Sometimes exaggeration is warranted

In coming chapters, we'll make use of these techniques. But even these "eyeball hacks" are only useful to a point; for a 32-qubit system there are 4,294,967,296 circles—too much information for most displays and eyes alike.

In your own QCEngine programs you can add the line `qc_options.color_by_phase = true;` at the very beginning to enable the *phase coloring* shown in Figure 3-9. The *bold phase lines* can also be toggled using `qc_options.book_render = true;`.

QPU Instruction: CNOT

It's finally time to introduce some definitively multi-qubit QPU operations. By *multi-qubit* operations we mean ones that *require* more than one qubit to operate. The first we'll consider is the powerful CNOT operation. CNOT operates on *two* qubits and can be thought of as an "if" programming construct with the following condition: *"Apply the NOT operation to a target qubit, but only if a condition qubit has the value 1."* The circuit symbol used for CNOT shows this logic by connecting two qubits with a line. A filled dot represents the control qubit, while a NOT symbol shows the target qubit to be conditionally operated on.[1]

The idea of using *condition* qubits to selectively apply actions is used in many other QPU operations, but CNOT is perhaps the prototypical example. Figure 3-10 illustrates the difference between applying a NOT operation to a qubit within a register versus applying CNOT (conditioned on some other *control* qubit).

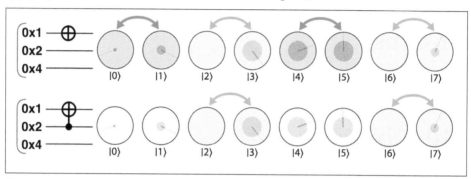

Figure 3-10. NOT versus CNOT in operation

The arrows in Figure 3-10 show which operator pairs have their circles swapped in circle notation. We can see that the essential operation of CNOT is the same as that of NOT, only more selective—applying the NOT operation only to values whose binary representations (in this example) have a 1 in the second bit (010=2, 011=3, 110=6, and 111=7).

Reversibility: Like the NOT operation, CNOT is its own inverse—applying the CNOT operation twice will return a multi-qubit register to its initial state.

On its own there's nothing particularly quantum about CNOT; conditional logic is, of course, a fundamental feature of conventional CPUs. But armed with CNOT we can now ask an interesting and distinctly quantum question. What would happen if the control qubit of a CNOT operation is in a superposition, as exemplified in Figure 3-11?

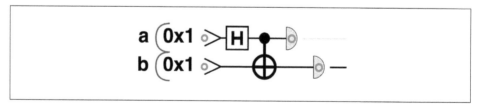

Figure 3-11. CNOT with a control qubit in superposition

---

[1] Operations can also be controlled upon the value 0. To achieve this, we simply use a pair of NOT gates on the control register, one before and one after the operation.

For ease of reference, we've temporarily labeled our two qubits as a and b (rather than using hexadecimal). Starting with our register in the $|0\rangle$ state, let's walk through the circuit and see what happens. Figure 3-12 shows the circuit and the state at the beginning of the program, before instructions have been executed.

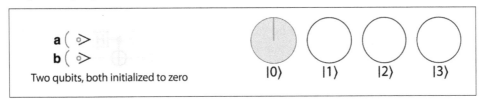

Two qubits, both initialized to zero

Figure 3-12. Bell pair step 1

First we apply HAD to qubit a. Since a is the lowest-weight qubit in the register, this creates a superposition of the values $|0\rangle$ and $|1\rangle$, visualized in Figure 3-13 in circle notation.

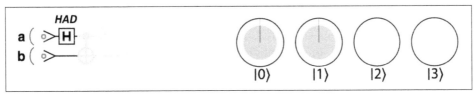

Figure 3-13. Bell pair step 2

Next we apply the CNOT operation such that qubit b is *conditionally* flipped, dependent on the state of qubit a, as shown in Figure 3-14.

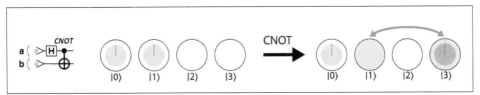

Figure 3-14. Bell pair step 3

The result is a superposition of $|0\rangle$ and $|3\rangle$. This makes sense, since *if* qubit a had taken value $|0\rangle$, then no action would occur on b, and it would remain in the state $|0\rangle$ —leaving the register in a total state of $|0\rangle|0\rangle=|0\rangle$. However, *if* a had been in state $|1\rangle$, then a NOT would be applied to b and the register would have a value of $|1\rangle|1\rangle=|3\rangle$. Another way to understand the operation of CNOT in Figure 3-14 is that it simply follows the CNOT circle-notation rule, which implies swapping the states $|1\rangle$ and $|3\rangle$ (as is shown by the red arrow in Figure 3-14). In this case, one of these circles just so happens to be in superposition.

The result in Figure 3-14 turns out to be a very powerful resource. In fact, it's the two-qubit equivalent of the *entangled state* we first saw in Figure 3-3. We've already noted that these entangled states demonstrate a kind of interdependence between qubits—if we read out the two qubits shown in Figure 3-14, although the outcomes will be random, they will always agree (i.e., be either 00 or 11, with 50% chance for each).

The one exception we've made so far to our mantra of "avoid physics at all costs" was to give a slightly deeper insight into superposition. The phenomenon of entanglement is equally important, so—for one final time—we'll indulge ourselves in a few sentences of physics to give you a better feel for *why* entanglement is so powerful.[2]

 If you prefer code samples over physics insight, you can happily skip the next couple of paragraphs without any adverse side effects.

Entanglement might not necessarily strike you as strange. Agreement between the values of conventional bits certainly isn't cause for concern, even if they *randomly* assume correlated values. In conventional computing, if two otherwise random bits are always found to agree on readout, then there are two entirely unremarkable possibilities:

1. Some mechanism in the past has coerced their values to be equal, giving them a common cause. If this is the case, their randomness is actually illusory.

2. The two bits truly assume random values at the very moment of readout, but they are able to communicate to ensure their values correlate.

In fact, with a bit of thought it is possible to see that these are the *only* two ways we could explain random agreement between two conventional bits.

Yet through a clever experiment initially proposed by the great Irish physicist John Bell, it's possible to conclusively demonstrate that entanglement allows such agreement without either of these two reasonable explanations being responsible! This is the sense in which you may hear it said that entanglement is a kind of distinctly quantum link between qubits that is *stronger than could ever be conventionally possible*. As we start programming more complex QPU applications, entanglement will begin popping up everywhere. You won't need these kinds of philosophical insights to make practical use of entanglement, but it never hurts to have a little insight into what's going on under the hood.

---

2 Honestly, this is for *reals* the absolute, 100%, last mention of physics. Pinky promise.

Hands-on: Using Bell Pairs for Shared Randomness

The entangled state we created in Figure 3-14 is commonly referred to as a Bell pair.[3] Let's see a quick and easy way to put the powerful link within these states to use.

In the previous chapter we noted that measuring a single qubit's superposition provides us with a Quantum Random Number Generator. Similarly, the reading out of a Bell pair acts like a QRNG, only now we will obtain *agreeing* random values on two qubits.

A surprising fact about entanglement is that the qubits involved remain entangled no matter how far apart we may move them. Thus, we can easily use Bell pairs to generate *correlated random bits* at different locations. Such bits can be the basis for establishing secure shared randomness—something that critically underlies the modern internet.

The code snippet in Example 3-2 implements this idea, generating shared randomness by creating a Bell pair and then reading out a value from each qubit, as shown in Figure 3-15.

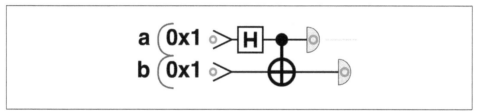

Figure 3-15. Bell pair circuit

Sample Code

Run this sample online at *http://oreilly-qc.github.io?p=3-2*.

Example 3-2. Make a Bell pair

```
qc.reset(2);
var a = qint.new(1, 'a');
var b = qint.new(1, 'b');
qc.write(0);
a.had();              // Place into superposition
b.cnot(a);            // Entangle
var a_result = a.read();
var b_result = b.read();
```

---

3 This and several other states carry that name because they were the states used by John Bell in his demonstration of the inexplicable correlations of entangled states.

```
qc.print(a_result);
qc.print(b_result);
```

QPU Instructions: CPHASE and CZ

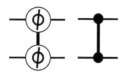 Another very common two-qubit operation is CPHASE(θ). Like the CNOT operation, CPHASE employs a kind of entanglement-generating conditional logic. Recall from Figure 3-6 that the single-qubit PHASE(θ) operation acts on a register to rotate (by angle θ) the $|1\rangle$ values in that qubit's operator pairs. As CNOT did for NOT, CPHASE restricts this action on some target qubit to occur only when another control qubit assumes the value $|1\rangle$. Note that CPHASE only acts when its control qubit is $|1\rangle$, and when it does act, it only affects target qubit states having value $|1\rangle$. This means that a CPHASE(θ) applied to, say, qubits 0x1 and 0x4 results in the rotation (by θ) of all circles for which *both* these two qubits have a value of $|1\rangle$. Because of this particular property, CPHASE has a symmetry between its inputs not shared by CNOT. Unlike with most other controlled operations, it's irrelevant which qubit we consider to be the target and which we consider to be the control for CPHASE.

In Figure 3-16 we compare the operation of a CPHASE between the 0x1 and 0x4 qubits with individual PHASE operations on these qubits.

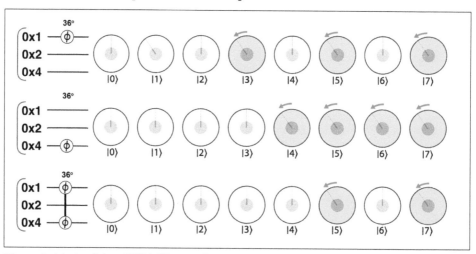

Figure 3-16. Applying CPHASE in circle notation

On their own, single-qubit PHASE operations will rotate the relative phases of *half* of the circles associated with a QPU register. Adding a condition further cuts the number of rotated circles in half. We can continue to add conditional qubits to our CPHASE, each time halving the number of values we act on. In general, the more we *condition* QPU operations, the more selective we can be with which values in a QPU register we manipulate.

QPU programs frequently employ the CPHASE(θ) operation with a phase of $\theta = 180°$, and consequently this particular implementation of CPHASE is given its own name, CZ, along with its own simplified symbol, shown in Figure 3-17. Interestingly, CZ can be constructed from HAD and CNOT very easily. Recall from Figure 2-14 that the phase(180) (Z) operation can be made from two HAD operations and a NOT. Similarly, CZ can be made from two HAD operations and a CNOT, as shown in Figure 3-17.

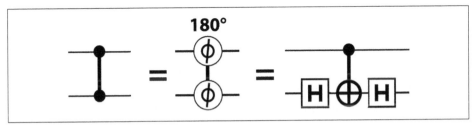

Figure 3-17. Three representations of CPHASE(180)

QPU Trick: Phase Kickback

Once we start thinking about altering the phase of one QPU register *conditioned* on the values of qubits in some other register, we can produce a surprising and useful effect known as *phase kickback*. Take a look at the circuit in Figure 3-18.

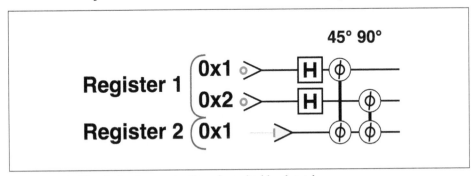

Figure 3-18. Circuit for demonstrating phase-kickback trick

One way to think of this circuit is that, after placing register 1 in a superposition of all of its $2^2 = 4$ possible values, we've rotated the phase of register 2, conditional on the values taken by the qubits of register 1. However, looking at the resulting individual states of *both* registers in circle notation, we see that something interesting has also happened to the state of Register 1, as shown in Figure 3-19.

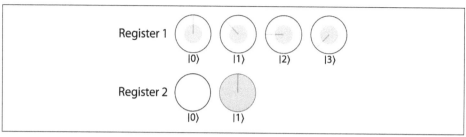

Figure 3-19. States of both registers involved in phase kickback

The phase rotations we tried to apply to the second register (conditioned on qubits from the first) have also affected different values from the first register! More specifically, here's what we're seeing happen in the preceding circle-notation representations:

- The 45° rotation we performed on register 2 conditioned on the lowest-weight qubit from register 1 has *also* rotated every value in register 1 for which this lowest-weight qubit is activated (the $|1\rangle$ and $|3\rangle$ values).

- The 90° rotation we performed on register 2 conditioned on the highest-weight qubit from register 1 has also been *kicked back* onto all values in register 1 having this highest-weight qubit activated (the $|2\rangle$ and $|3\rangle$ values).

The net result that we see on register 1 is the combination of these phase rotations that have been kicked back onto it from our intended target of register 2. Note that since register 2 is *not* in superposition, its (global) phase remains unchanged.

Phase kickback is a very useful idea, as we can use it to apply phase rotations to specific values in a register (register 1 in the preceding example). We can do this by performing a phase rotation on some *other* register conditioned on qubits from the register we really care about. We can choose these qubits to specifically pick out the values we want to rotate.

 For phase kickback to work, we always need to initialize the second register in the $|1\rangle$ value. Notice that although we are applying two-qubit operations between the two registers, we are not creating any entanglement; hence, we can fully represent the state as separate registers. Two-qubit gates do not always generate entanglement between registers; we will see why in Chapter 14.

If this phase-kickback trick initially strikes you as a little mind-bending, you're in good company—it can take a while to get used to. The easiest way to get a feel for it is to play around with some examples to build intuition. To get you started,

Example 3-3 contains QCEngine code for reproducing the two-register example described previously.

Sample Code

Run this sample online at *http://oreilly-qc.github.io?p=3-3*.

Example 3-3. Phase kickback

```
qc.reset(3);
// Create two registers
var reg1 = qint.new(2, 'Register 1');
var reg2 = qint.new(1, 'Register 2');
reg1.write(0);
reg2.write(1);
// Place the first register in superposition
reg1.had();
// Perform phase rotations on second register,
// conditioned on qubits from the first
qc.phase(45, 0x4, 0x1);
qc.phase(90, 0x4, 0x2);
```

Phase kickback will be of great use in Chapter 8 to understand the inner workings of the *quantum phase estimation* QPU primitive, and again in Chapter 13 to explain how a QPU can help us solve systems of linear equations. The wide utility of phase kickback stems from the fact that it doesn't only work for CPHASE operations, but any conditional operation that generates a change in a register's phase. This is as good a reason as any to understand how we might construct more general conditional operations.

QPU Instruction: CCNOT (Toffoli)

We've previously noted that multi-qubit conditional operations can be made more selective by performing operations conditioned on more than one qubit. Let's see this in action and generalize the CNOT operation by adding multiple conditions. A CNOT with two condition qubits is commonly referred to as a CCNOT operation. The CCNOT is also sometimes called a Toffoli gate, after the identically titled equivalent gate from conventional computing.

With each condition added, the NOT operation stays the same, but the number of operator pairs affected in the register's circle notation is reduced by half. We show this in Figure 3-20 by comparing a NOT operation on the first qubit in a three-qubit register with the associated CNOT and CCNOT operations.

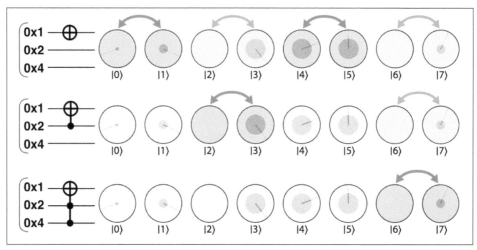

Figure 3-20. Adding conditions makes NOT operations more selective

In a sense, CCNOT can be interpreted as an operation implementing "if A AND B then flip C." For performing basic logic, the CCNOT gate is arguably the single most useful QPU operation. Multiple CCNOT gates can be combined and cascaded to produce a wide variety of logic functions, as we will explore in Chapter 5.

QPU Instructions: SWAP and CSWAP

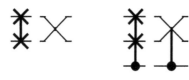 Another very common operation in quantum computation is SWAP (also called *exchange*), which simply exchanges two qubits. If the architecture of a QPU allows it, SWAP may be a truly fundamental operation in which the physical objects representing qubits are actually moved to swap their positions. Alternatively, a SWAP can be performed by exchanging the *information* contained in two qubits (rather than the qubits themselves) using three CNOT operations, as shown in Figure 3-21.

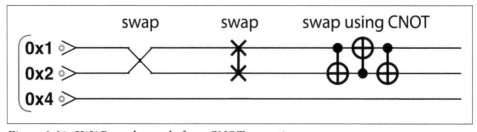

Figure 3-21. SWAP can be made from CNOT operations

In this book, we have two ways to indicate SWAP operations. In the general case we use a pair of connected Xs. When the swapped qubits are adjacent to one another, it is often simpler and more intuitive to cross the qubit lines. The operation is identical in both cases.

You may be wondering why SWAP is a useful operation. Why not simply rename our qubits instead? On a QPU, SWAP comes into its own when we consider generalizing it to a conditional operation called CSWAP, or *conditional exchange*. CSWAP can be implemented using three CCNOT gates, as shown in Figure 3-22.

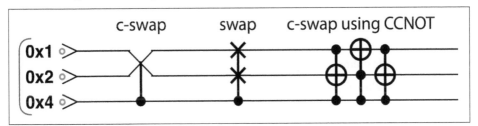

Figure 3-22. CSWAP constructed from CCNOT gates

If the condition qubit for a CSWAP operation is in superposition, we end up with a superposition of our two qubits being exchanged, and also being not exchanged. In Chapters 5 and 12, we'll see how this feature of CSWAP allows us to perform multiplication-by-2 in quantum superposition.

The Swap Test

SWAP operations allow us to build a very useful circuit known as a *swap test*. A swap test circuit solves the following problem: if you're given two qubit registers, how do you tell if they are in the *same* state? By now we know only too well that in general (if either register is in superposition), we can't use the destructive READ operation to completely learn the state of each register in order to make the comparison. The SWAP operation does something a little sneakier. Without telling us what either state is, it simply lets us determine whether or not they're equal.

In a world where we can't necessarily learn precisely what's in an output register, the swap test can be an invaluable tool. Figure 3-23 shows a circuit for implementing a swap test, as demonstrated in Example 3-4.

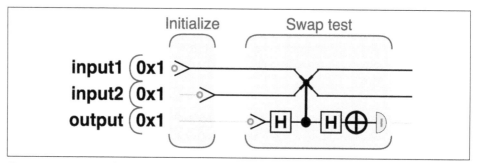

Figure 3-23. Using the swap test to determine whether two registers are in the same state

---

Sample Code

Run this sample online at *http://oreilly-qc.github.io?p=3-4.*

Example 3-4. The swap test

```
// In this example the swap test should reveal
// the equality of the two input states
qc.reset(3);
var input1 = qint.new(1, 'input1');
var input2 = qint.new(1, 'input2');
var output = qint.new(1, 'output');

// Initialize to any states we want to test
input1.write(0);
input2.write(0);

// The swap test itself
output.write(0);
output.had();
// Now exchange the two inputs conditional on the output qubits
input1.exchange(input2, 0x1, output.bits());
output.had();
output.not();
var result = output.read();
// result is 1 if inputs are equal
```

Example 3-4 uses the swap test to compare the states of two single-qubit registers, but the same circuit can easily be extended to compare multi-qubit registers. The result of the swap test is found when we READ the extra single-qubit output register that we introduced (no matter how large the input registers are, the output remains a single qubit). By changing the lines `input1.write(0)` and `input2.write(0)`, you can experiment with inputs that differ to varying extents. You should find that if the two input states are equal, the output register always results in a state of $|1\rangle$, so we definitely obtain a 1 outcome when applying a READ to this register. However, as the two inputs become increasingly more different, the probability of READing a 1 outcome in the output register decreases, eventually becoming 50% in the case where input1 is $|0\rangle$ and input2 is $|1\rangle$. Figure 3-24 shows precisely how the outcome probability in the output register changes as the similarity between the two input registers is increased.

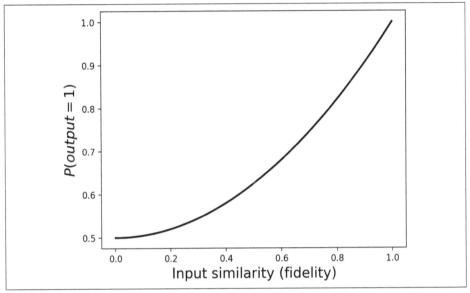

Figure 3-24. How output of swap test varies as input states are made increasingly similar

The x-axis on this plot uses a numerical measure of the difference between two register states known as the *fidelity*. We won't go into the mathematical detail of how the fidelity is calculated between QPU register states, but it mathematically encapsulates a way of comparing two superpositions.

By running the swap test circuit multiple times we can keep track of the outcomes we obtain. The more runs for which we observe a 1 outcome, the more convinced we can be that the two input states were identical. Precisely how many times we would need to repeat the swap test depends on how confident we want to be that the two inputs are identical, and how close we would allow them to be in order to be called identical. Figure 3-25 shows a lower bound for the number of swap tests where we would need to observe 1 outcomes to be 99% confident that our inputs are identical. The plot's y-axis shows how this number changes as we relax the requirement for inputs being identical (varied along the x-axis). Note that the moment we obtain a 0 outcome in a swap test, we know for sure that the two input states are not identical.[4]

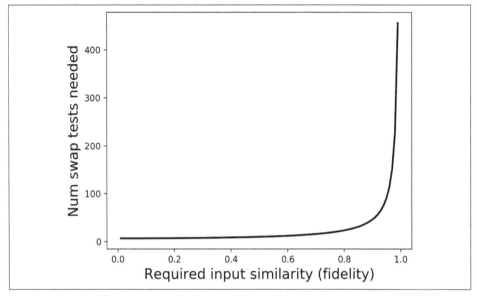

Figure 3-25. Number of swap tests that would need to return an outcome of 1 for us to be 99% confident inputs are identical

Rather than looking at the swap test as a yes/no way of ascertaining whether two states are equal, another useful interpretation is to note that Figure 3-25 shows us that the *probability* that we get a 1 outcome is a measure of just *how* identical the two inputs are (their fidelity). If we repeat the swap test enough times, we can estimate this probability and therefore the fidelity—a more quantitative measure of how close the two states are. Estimating precisely how close two quantum states are in this way is something we'll find useful in quantum machine-learning applications.

Constructing Any Conditional Operation

We've introduced CNOT and CPHASE operations, but is there such thing as a CHAD (conditional HAD), or a CRNOT (conditional RNOT)? Indeed there is! Even if a conditional version of some single-qubit operation is missing from the instruction set of a particular QPU, there's a process by which we can "convert" single-qubit operations into multi-qubit conditional ones.

---

4 In reality we would want to allow for *some* 0 occurrences if we were genuinely content with close but not identical states—and also perhaps to allow for the possibility of errors in the computation. For this simple analysis we have ignored such considerations.

The general prescription for *conditioning* a single-qubit operation involves a little more mathematics than we want to cover here, but seeing an example will help you feel more comfortable with it. The key idea is that we break our single-qubit operation into smaller steps. It turns out that it's always possible to break a single-qubit operation into a set of steps such that we can use CNOTs to conditionally *undo* the operation. The net result is that we can conditionally choose whether or not to effect its action.

This is much easier to see with a simple example. Suppose we are writing software for a QPU that can perform CNOT, CZ, and PHASE operations, but has no instruction to perform CPHASE. This is actually a very common case with current QPUs, but fortunately we can easily create our own CPHASE from these ingredients.

Recall that the desired effect for a two-qubit CPHASE is to rotate the phase for any value of the register for which *both* qubits take the value $|1\rangle$. This is shown in Figure 3-26 for the case of PHASE(90).

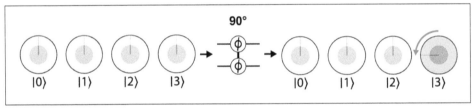

Figure 3-26. Desired operation of a CPHASE(90) operation

We can easily break down a PHASE(90) operation into smaller pieces by rotating through smaller angles. For example, PHASE(90)=PHASE(45)PHASE(45). We can also "undo" a rotation by rotating in the opposite direction; for example, the operation PHASE(45)PHASE(-45) is the same as doing nothing to our qubit. With these facts in mind, we can construct the CPHASE(90) operation described in Figure 3-26 using the operations shown in Figure 3-27 and Example 3-5.

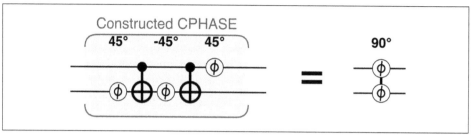

Figure 3-27. Constructing a CPHASE operation

Sample Code

Run this sample online at *http://oreilly-qc.github.io?p=3-5.*

Example 3-5. Custom conditional phase

```
var theta = 90;

qc.reset(2);
qc.write(0);
qc.hadamard();

// Using two CNOTs and three PHASEs...
qc.phase( theta / 2, 0x2);
qc.cnot(0x2, 0x1);
qc.phase(-theta / 2, 0x2);
qc.cnot(0x2, 0x1);
qc.phase( theta / 2, 0x1);

// Builds the same operation as a 2-qubit CPHASE
qc.phase(theta, 0x1, 0x2);
```

Following this circuit's operation on different possible inputs we see that it works to apply PHASE(90) only when both qubits are $|1\rangle$ (an input of $|1\rangle|1\rangle$). To see this, it helps to recall that PHASE has no effect on a qubit in the state $|0\rangle$. Alternatively, we can follow the action of Figure 3-27 using circle notation, as shown in Figure 3-28.

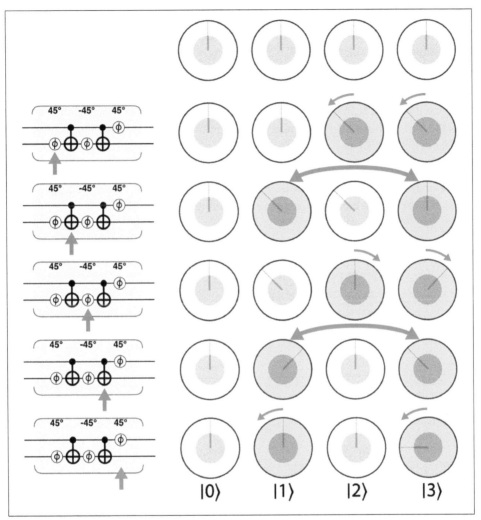

Figure 3-28. Walthrough of the constructed CPHASE operation

While this circuit works correctly to build a `CPHASE(90)` gate, the general case of conditioning an arbitrary operation is slightly more complicated. For a complete recipe and explanation, see Chapter 14.

Hands-on: Remote-Controlled Randomness

Armed with multi-qubit operations, we can explore some interesting and nonobvious properties of entanglement using a small QPU program for *remote-controlled* random number generation. This program will generate two qubits, such that reading out one instantly affects the probabilities for obtaining a random bit READ from the other. Moreover, this effect occurs over any distance of space or time. This seemingly impossible task, enabled by a QPU, is surprisingly simple to implement.

Here's how the remote control works. We manipulate a pair of qubits such that reading one qubit (either one) returns a 50/50 random bit telling us the "modified" probability of the other. If the result is 0, the other qubit will have 15% probability of being READ to be 1. Otherwise, if the qubit we READ returns 1, the other will have 85% probability of being READ as 1.

The sample code in Example 3-6 shows how to implement this remote-controlled random number generator. As in Example 3-1, we make use of QCEngine qint objects to be able to easily address groups of qubits.

Sample Code

Run this sample online at *http://oreilly-qc.github.io?p=3-6.*

Example 3-6. Remote-controlled randomness

```
qc.reset(2);
var a = qint.new(1, 'a');
var b = qint.new(1, 'b');
qc.write(0);
a.had();
// now prob of a is 50%
b.had();
b.phase(45);
b.had();
// now prob of b is 15%
b.cnot(a);
// Now, you can read *either*
// qubit and get 50% prob.
// If the result is 0, then
// the prob of the *remaining*
// qubit is 15%, else it's 85%.
var a_result = a.read();
var b_result = b.read();
qc.print(a_result + ' ');
qc.print(b_result + '\n');
```

We follow the effect of each operation within this program using circle notation in Figure 3-29.

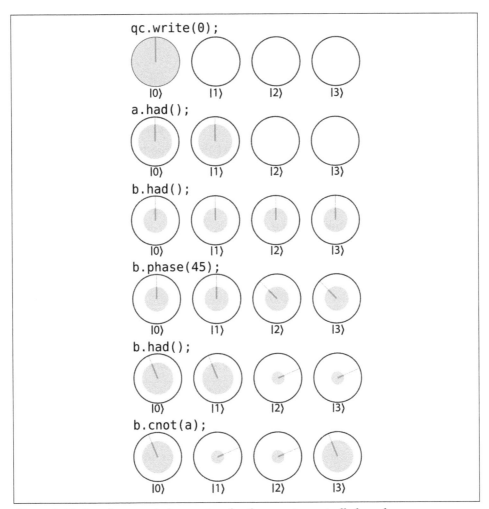

Figure 3-29. Step-by-step circle notation for the remote-controlled randomness program

After these steps are completed we're left with an entangled state of two qubits. Let's consider what would happen if we were to READ qubit a from the state at the end of Figure 3-29. If qubit a were READ to have value 0 (as it will with 50% probability), then only the circles compatible with this state of affairs would remain. These are the values for $|0\rangle|0\rangle = |0\rangle$ and $|1\rangle|0\rangle = |2\rangle$, and so the state of the two qubits becomes the one shown in Figure 3-30.

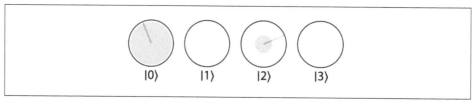

Figure 3-30. The state of one qubit in the remote control after the other is READ to be 0

The two values in this state have nonzero probabilities, both for obtaining 0 and for obtaining 1 when reading out qubit b. In particular, qubit b has 70%/30% probabilities of reading out 0/1.

However, suppose that our initial measurement on qubit a had yielded 1 (which also occurs with 50% probability). Then only the $|0\rangle|1\rangle=|1\rangle$ and $|1\rangle|1\rangle=|3\rangle$ values will remain, as shown in Figure 3-31.

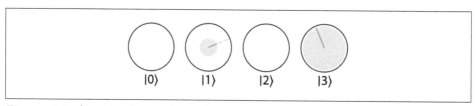

Figure 3-31. The state of one qubit in the remote control after the other is READ to be 1

Now the probabilities for reading out the 0/1 outcomes on qubit b are 30%/70%.

Although we're able to change the probability distribution of readout values for qubit b instantaneously, we're unable to do so with any intent—we can't choose whether to cause the 70%/30% or the 30%/70% distribution—since the measured outcome of qubit a is obtained randomly. It's a good job, too, because if we could make this change deterministically we could send *signals* instantaneously using entanglement; i.e., faster than light. Although sending signals faster than light sounds like fun, were this possible, bad things would happen.[5] In fact, one of the strangest things about entanglement is that it allows us to change the states of qubits instantaneously across arbitrary distances, but always conspires to do so in a way that precludes us from sending intelligible, predetermined information. It seems that the universe isn't a big fan of sci-fi.

---

5 Sending-information-back-in-time-causality-violating kinds of bad things. The venerated work of Dr. Emmett Brown attests to the dangers of such hijinks.

Conclusion

We've seen how single- and multi-qubit operations can allow us to manipulate the properties of superposition and entanglement within a QPU. Having these at our disposal, we're ready to see how they allow us to *compute* with a QPU in new and powerful ways. In Chapter 5 we'll show how fundamental digital logic can be reimagined, but first in the next chapter we conduct a hands-on exploration of quantum teleportation. Not only is quantum teleportation a fundamental component of many quantum applications, but exploring it also consolidates everything we've covered so far about describing and manipulating qubits.

CHAPTER 4

Quantum Teleportation

In this chapter we introduce a QPU program allowing us to immediately teleport an object across a distance of 3.1 millimeters! The same code would work over interstellar distances, given the right equipment.

Although teleportation might conjure up images of magician's parlor tricks, we'll see that the kind of *quantum* teleportation we can perform with a QPU is equally impressive, yet far more practical—and is, in fact, an essential conceptual component of QPU programming.

Hands-on: Let's Teleport Something

The best way to learn about teleportation is to try to do it. Keep in mind that throughout all of human history up until the time of writing, only a few thousand people have actually performed physical teleportation of any kind, so just running the following code makes you a pioneer.

For this example, rather than a simulator, we will use IBM's five-qubit actual QPU, as seen in Figure 4-1. You'll be able to paste the sample code from Example 4-1 into the IBM Q Experience website, click a button, and confirm that your teleportation was successful.

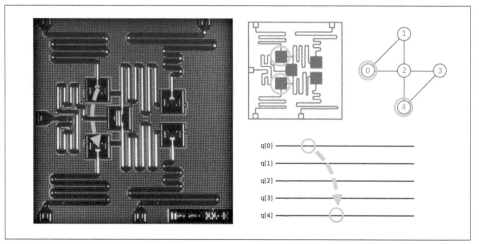

Figure 4-1. The IBM chip is very small, so the qubit does not have far to go; the image and schematics show the regions on the QPU we will teleport between[1]

The IBM Q Experience can be programmed using OpenQASM,[2] and also Qiskit.[3] Note that the code in Example 4-1 is *not* JavaScript to be run on QCEngine, but rather OpenQASM code to be run online through IBM's cloud interface, shown in Figure 4-2. Doing so allows you to not just simulate, but actually *perform* the teleportation of a qubit currently at IBM's research center in Yorktown Heights, New York. We'll walk you through how to do this. Following through the code in detail will also help you understand precisely how quantum teleportation works.

---

1 Courtesy of International Business Machines Corporation, © International Business Machines Corporation.

2 OpenQASM is the quantum assembly language supported by IBM Q Experience.

3 Qiskit is an open-source software development kit for working with the IBM Q quantum processors.

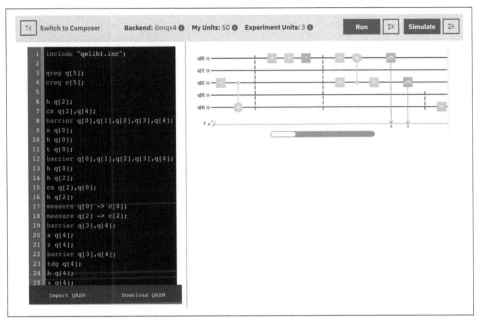

Figure 4-2. The IBM Q Experience (QX) OpenQASM online editor[4]

Sample Code

Run this sample online at *http://oreilly-qc.github.io?p=4-1*.

Example 4-1. Teleport and verify

```
include "qelib1.inc";
qreg q[5];
creg c[5];

// Step 1: Create an entangled pair
h q[2];
cx q[2],q[4];
barrier q[0],q[1],q[2],q[3],q[4];

// Step 2: Prepare a payload
x q[0];
h q[0];
t q[0];
barrier q[0],q[1],q[2],q[3],q[4];

// Step 3: Send
h q[0];
```

---

4 Courtesy of International Business Machines Corporation, © International Business Machines Corporation.

```
h q[2];
cx q[2],q[0];
h q[2];
measure q[0] -> c[0];
measure q[2] -> c[2];
barrier q[3],q[4];

// Step 4: Receive
x q[4];
z q[4];
barrier q[3],q[4];

// Step 5: Verify
tdg q[4];
h q[4];
x q[4];
measure q[4] -> c[4];
```

Before getting to the details, first some clarifying points. By *quantum teleportation* we mean the ability to transport the precise state (i.e., magnitudes and relative phase) of one qubit to another. Our intention is to take all the information contained in the first qubit and put it in the second qubit. Recall that quantum information cannot be replicated; hence the information on the first qubit is necessarily destroyed when we teleport it to the second one. Since a quantum description is the most complete description of a physical object, this is actually precisely what you might colloquially think of as teleportation—only at the quantum level.[5]

With that out of the way, let's teleport! The textbook introduction to quantum teleportation begins with a story that goes something like this: A pair of qubits in an *entangled* state are shared between two parties, Alice and Bob (physicists have an obsession with anthropomorphizing the alphabet). These entangled qubits are a resource that Alice will use to teleport the state of some *other* qubit to Bob. So teleportation involves three qubits: the *payload* qubit that Alice wants to teleport, and an entangled pair of qubits that she shares with Bob (and that acts a bit like a quantum Ethernet cable). Alice prepares her payload and then, using HAD and CNOT operations, she entangles this payload qubit with her other qubit (which is, in turn, *already* entangled with Bob's qubit). She then destroys both her payload and the entangled qubit using READ operations. The results from these READ operations yield two conventional bits of information that she sends to Bob. Since these are *bits*, rather than qubits, she can use a conventional Ethernet cable for this part. Using those two bits,

---

5 The caveat, of course, is that humans are made up of many, many quantum states, and so teleporting qubit states is far removed from any idea of teleportation as a mode of transportation. In other words, although teleportation is an accurate description, Lt. Reginald Barclay doesn't have anything to worry about just yet.

Bob performs some single-qubit operations on his half of the entangled pair originally shared with Alice, and lo and behold, it *becomes* the payload qubit that Alice intended to send.

Before we walk through the detailed protocol of quantum operations described here,[6] you may have a concern in need of addressing. "Hang on…" (we imagine you saying), "if Alice is sending Bob conventional information through an Ethernet cable…" (you continue), "then surely this isn't that impressive at all." Excellent observation! It is certainly true that quantum teleportation crucially relies on the transmission of conventional (digital) bits for its success. We've already seen that the magnitudes and relative phases needed to fully describe an arbitrary qubit state can take on a continuum of values. Crucially, the teleportation protocol works even in the case when Alice does not know the state of her qubit. This is particularly important since it is impossible to determine the magnitude and relative phase of a single qubit in an unknown state. And yet—with the help of an entangled pair of qubits—only two conventional bits were needed to effectively transmit the precise configuration of Alice's qubit (whatever its amplitudes were). This configuration will be correct to a potentially infinite number of bits of precision!

So how do we engineer this magic? Here's the full protocol. Figure 4-3 shows the operations that we must employ on the three involved qubits. All these operations were introduced in Chapters 2 and 3.

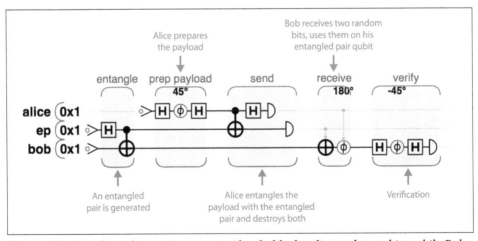

Figure 4-3. Complete teleportation circut: Alice holds the alice and ep qubits, while Bob holds bob

---

6 The complete source code for both the QASM and QCEngine versions of this example can be seen at *http://oreilly-qc.github.io?p=4-1*.

If you paste the code for this circuit from Example 4-1 into the IBM QX system, the IBM user interface will display the circuit shown in Figure 4-4. Note that this is exactly the same program as we've shown in Figure 4-3, just displayed slightly differently. The quantum gate notation we've been using is standardized, so you can expect to find it used outside this book.[7]

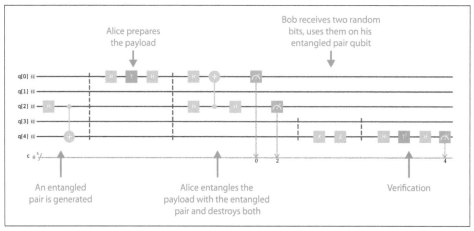

Figure 4-4. Teleportation circuit in IBM QX[8]

When you click Run, IBM will run your program 1,024 times (this number is adjustable) and then display statistics regarding all of these runs. After running the program, you can expect to find something similar (although not identical) to the bar chart shown in Figure 4-5.

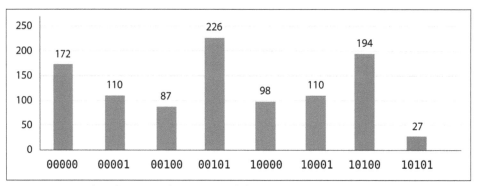

Figure 4-5. Results of running the program (teleportation success?)

---

7 Gates such as CNOTs and HADs can be combined in different ways to produce the same result. Some operations have different decompositions in IBM QX and QCEngine.

8 Courtesy of International Business Machines Corporation, © International Business Machines Corporation.

Success? Maybe! To demonstrate how to read and interpret these results, let's walk through each step in the QPU program in a little more detail, using circle notation to visualize what's happening to our qubits.[9]

At the time of writing, the circuits and results displayed by IBM QX show what's happening with all *five* qubits available in the QPU, even if we're not using them all. This is why there are two empty qubit lines in the circuit shown in Figure 4-4, and why the bars showing results for each output in Figure 4-5 are labeled with a five-bit (rather than three-bit) binary number—even though only the bars corresponding to the $2^3 = 8$ possible configurations of the three qubits we used are actually shown.

Program Walkthrough

Since we use three qubits in our teleportation example, their full description needs $2^3 = 8$ circles (one for each possible combination of the 3 bits). We'll arrange these eight circles in two rows, which helps us to visualize how operations affect the three constituent qubits. In Figure 4-6 we've labeled each row and column of circles corresponding to a given qubit having a particular value. You can check that these labels are correct by considering the binary value of the register that each circle corresponds to.

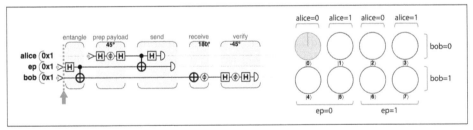

Figure 4-6. The complete teleport-and-verify program

When dealing with multi-qubit registers we'll often arrange our circle notation in rows and columns as we do in Figure 4-6. This is always a useful way of more quickly spotting the behavior of individual qubits: it's easy to pick out the relevant rows or columns.

---

9 The complete source code for this example can be seen at *http://oreilly-qc.github.io?p=4-1*.

At the beginning of the program, all three qubits are initialized in state $|0\rangle$, as indicated in Figure 4-6—the only possible value is the one where `alice=0` and `ep=0` and `bob=0`.

Step 1: Create an Entangled Pair

The first task for teleportation is establishing an entangled link. The `HAD` and `CNOT` combination achieving this is the same process we used in Chapter 3 to create the specially named *Bell pair* entangled state of two qubits. We can readily see from the circle notation in Figure 4-7 that if we read `bob` and `ep`, the values are 50/50 random, but guaranteed to match each other, à la entanglement.

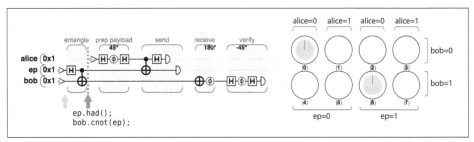

Figure 4-7. Step 1: Create an entangled pair

Step 2: Prepare the Payload

Having established an entanglement link, Alice can prepare the payload to be sent. How she prepares it depends, of course, on the nature of the (quantum) information that she wants to send to Bob. She might write a value to the payload qubit, entangle it with some other QPU data, or even receive it from a previous computation in some entirely separate part of her QPU.

For our example here we'll disappoint Alice by asking her to prepare a particularly simple payload qubit, using only `HAD` and `PHASE` operations. This has the benefit of producing a payload with a readily decipherable circle-notation pattern, as shown in Figure 4-8.

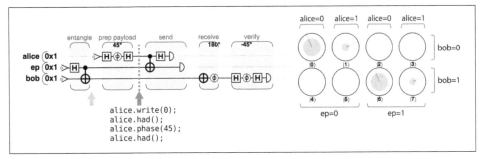

Figure 4-8. Step 2: Prepare the payload

We can see that the bob and ep qubits are still dependent on one another (only the circles corresponding to the bob and ep qubits possessing equal values have nonzero magnitudes). We can also see that the value of alice is not dependent on either of the other two qubits, and furthermore that her payload preparation produced a qubit that is 85.4% |0⟩ and 14.6% |1⟩, with a relative phase of –90° (the circles corresponding to alice=1 are at 90° *clockwise* of the alice=0 circles, which is negative in our convention).

Step 3.1: Link the Payload to the Entangled Pair

In Chapter 2 we saw that the conditional nature of the CNOT operation can entangle the states of two qubits. Alice now uses this fact to entangle her payload qubit with her half of the entangled pair she already shares with Bob. In terms of circle notation, this action swaps circles around as shown in Figure 4-9.

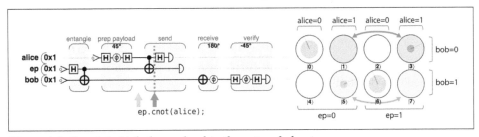

Figure 4-9. Step 3.1: Link the payload to the entangled pair

Now that we have *multiple* entangled states, there's the potential for a little confusion —so let's be clear. Alice and Bob *already* each held one of two entangled qubits (produced in step 1). Now Alice has entangled *another* (payload) qubit onto her half of this (already entangled) pair. Intuitively we can see that in some sense Alice has, by proxy, now linked her payload to Bob's half of the entangled pair—although her payload qubit is still unchanged. READ results on her payload will now be logically linked with those of the other two qubits. We can see this link in circle notation since the

QPU register state in Figure 4-9 only contains entries where the XOR of all three qubits is 0. Formerly this was true of ep and bob, but now it is true for all three qubits forming a *three-qubit* entangled group.

Step 3.2: Put the Payload into a Superposition

To make the link that Alice has created for her payload actually useful, she needs to finish by performing a HAD operation on her payload, as shown in Figure 4-10.

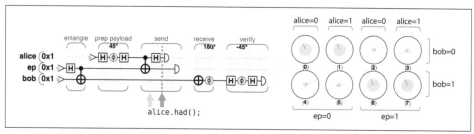

Figure 4-10. Step 3.2: Put the payload into a superposition

To see why Alice needed this HAD, take a look at the circle-notation representation of the state of the three qubits shown in Figure 4-10. In each *column* there is a pair of circles, showing a qubit that Bob might receive (we'll see shortly that precisely which one he *would* receive depends on the results of the READs that Alice performs). Interestingly, the four potential states Bob could receive are all different variations on Alice's original payload:

- In the first column (where alice=0 and ep=0), we have Alice's payload, exactly as she prepared it.

- In the second column, we have the same thing, except with a PHASE(180) applied.

- In the third column, we see the correct payload, but with a NOT having been applied to it ($|0\rangle$ and $|1\rangle$ are flipped).

- Finally, the last column is both phase-shifted and flipped (i.e., a PHASE(180) followed by a NOT).

If Alice hadn't applied HAD, she would have destroyed magnitude and phase information when applying her READ operations that she will shortly use (try it!). By applying the HAD operation, Alice was able to maneuver the state of Bob's qubit closer to that of her payload.

Step 3.3: READ Both of Alice's Qubits

Next, Alice performs a READ operation on her two qubits (the payload and her half of the entangled pair she shares with Bob). This READ irrevocably destroys both these qubits. You may wonder why Alice bothers to do this. As we'll see, it turns out that the results of this unavoidably destructive READ operation are crucial for the teleportation protocol to work. Copying quantum states is not possible, even when using entanglement. The only option to communicate quantum states is to teleport them, and when teleporting, we *must* destroy the original.

In Figure 4-11, Alice performs the prescribed READ operations on her payload and her half of the entangled pair. This operation returns two bits.

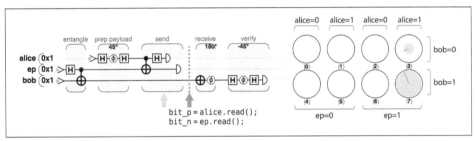

Figure 4-11. Step 3.3: READ both of Alice's qubits

In terms of circle notation, Figure 4-11 shows that by reading the values of her qubits Alice has selected one column of circles (which one she gets being dependent on the random READ results), resulting in the circles outside this column having zero magnitude.

Step 4: Receive and Transform

In "Step 3.2: Put the Payload into a Superposition" on page 76 we saw that Bob's qubit could end up in one of four states—each of which is simply related to Alice's payload by HAD and/or PHASE(180) operations. If Bob could learn which of these four states he possessed, he could apply the necessary inverse operations to convert it back to Alice's original payload. And the two bits Alice has from her READ operations are precisely the information that Bob needs! So at this stage, *Alice picks up the phone and transmits two bits of conventional information to Bob.*

Based on which two bits he receives, Bob knows which column from our circle-notation view represents his qubit. If the first bit he receives from Alice is 1, he performs a NOT operation on the qubit. Then, if the second bit is 1 he also performs a PHASE(180), as illustrated in Figure 4-12.

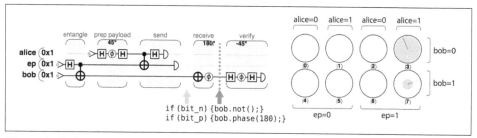

Figure 4-12. Step 4: Receive and transform

This completes the teleportation protocol—Bob now holds a qubit indistinguishable from Alice's initial payload.

The current IBM QX hardware does not support the kind of *feedforward* operation we need to allow the (completely random) bits from Alice's READ to control Bob's actions. This shortcoming can be circumvented by using *post-selection*—we have Bob perform the same operation no matter what Alice sends. This behavior may exasperate Alice, as shown in Figure 4-13. Then we look at all of the outputs, and discard all but the results where Bob did what he would have with the benefit of information from Alice.

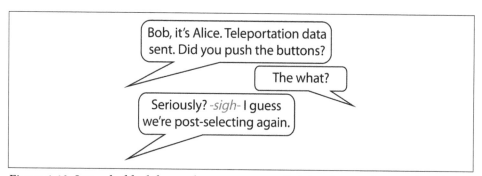

Figure 4-13. Instead of feed-forward, we can assume Bob is asleep at the switch and throw away cases where he makes wrong decisions

Step 5: Verify the Result

If Alice and Bob were using this teleportation in serious work, they'd be finished. Bob would take the teleported qubit from Alice and continue to use it in whatever larger quantum application they were working on. So long as they trust their QPU hardware, they can rest assured that Bob has the qubit Alice intended.

But, what about cases where we'd like to *verify* that the hardware has teleported a qubit correctly (even if we don't mind destroying the teleported qubit in the process)?

Our only option is to READ Bob's final qubit. Of course, we can never expect to learn (and therefore verify) the state of his qubit from a single READ, but by repeating the whole teleportation process and doing multiple READs we can start to build up a picture of Bob's state.

In fact, the easiest way for us to verify the teleportation protocol's success on a physical device would be for Bob to run the "prep the payload" steps that Alice performs on a $|0\rangle$ state to create her payload, on his final qubit, only in reverse. If the qubit Bob has truly matches the one Alice sent, this should leave Bob with a $|0\rangle$ state, and if Bob then performs a final verification READ, it should only ever return a 0. If Bob ever READs this test qubit as nonzero, the teleportation has failed. This additional step for verification is shown in Figure 4-14.

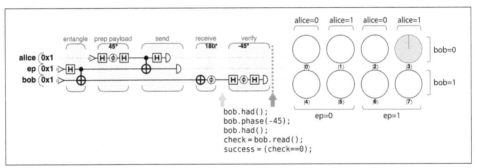

Figure 4-14. Step 5: Verify the result

Even if Alice and Bob are doing serious teleporter work, they will probably want to intersperse their actual teleportations with many verification tests such as these, just to be reassured that their QPU is working correctly.

Interpreting the Results

Armed with this fuller understanding of the teleportation protocol and its subtleties, let's return to the results obtained from our physical teleportation experiment on the IBM QX. We now have the necessary knowledge to decode them.

There are three READ operations performed in the entire protocol: two by Alice as part of the teleportation, and one by Bob for verification purposes. The bar chart in Figure 4-5 enumerates the number of times each of the 8 possible combinations of these outcomes occurred during 1,024 teleportation attempts.

As noted earlier, we'll be *post-selecting* on the IBM QX for instances where Bob happens to perform the right operations (as if he had acted on Alice's READ results). In the example circuit we gave the IBM QX in Figure 4-4, Bob always performs both a HAD and a PHASE(180) on his qubit, so we need to post-select on cases where Alice's two

READ operations gave 11. This leaves two sets of actually useful results where Bob's actions happened to correctly match up with Alice's READ results, as shown in Figure 4-15.

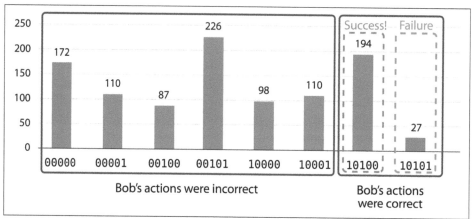

Figure 4-15. Interpreted teleportation results

Of the 221 times where Bob did the correct thing, the teleportation succeeded when Bob's verification READ gave a value of 0 (since he uses the verification step we discussed previously). This means the teleportation succeeded 194 times, and failed 27 times. A success rate of 87.8% is not bad, considering Alice and Bob are using the best available equipment in 2019. Still, they may think twice before sending anything important.

 If Bob receives an erroneously teleported qubit that is *almost* like the one Alice sent, the verification is likely to report success. Only by running this test many times can we gain confidence that the device is working well.

How Is Teleportation Actually Used?

Teleportation is a surprisingly fundamental part of the operation of a QPU—even in straight computational applications that have no obvious "communication" aspect at all. It allows us to shuttle information between qubits while working around the "*no-copying*" constraint. In fact, most practical uses of teleportation are over very short distances within a QPU as an integral part of quantum applications. In the upcoming chapters, you'll see that most quantum operations for two or more qubits function by forming various types of entanglement. The use of such quantum links to perform computation can usually be seen as an application of the general concept of teleportation. Though we may not explicitly acknowledge teleportation in the algorithms and applications we cover, it plays a fundamental role.

Fun with Famous Teleporter Accidents

As science fiction enthusiasts, our personal favorite use of teleportation is the classic film *The Fly*. Both the 1958 original and the more modern 1986 Jeff Goldblum version feature an error-prone teleportation experiment. After the protagonist's cat fails to teleport correctly, he decides that the next logical step is to try it himself, but without his knowledge a fly has gotten into the chamber with him.

We feel a little guilty for bringing the crushing news that actual quantum teleportation doesn't live up to what's promised in *The Fly*. To try to make it up to you, we've put together some sample code to teleport a quantum *image* of a fly—even including the small amount of error called for in the movie's plot. The code sample can be run online at *http://oreilly-qc.github.io?p=4-2*, and the horrifying result it produces is shown in Figure 4-16.

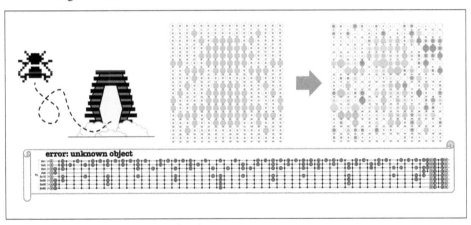

Figure 4-16. Be afraid. Be very afraid.

PART II

QPU Primitives

Now that you know how to describe and manipulate qubits at a basic level, we can introduce some higher-level *QPU primitives*. These primitives form a toolbox, ultimately allowing us to build full-blown applications.

Very roughly speaking, quantum applications tend to have the structure shown in Figure II-1.

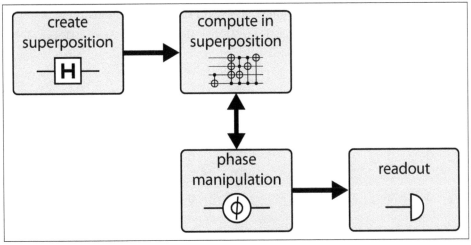

Figure II-1. A high-level view of the structure of quantum applications

QPU primitives help us to fill out this structure. Primitives associated with the second of these four steps (*compute in superposition*) allow us to compute using the implicit parallelism of superposition, while primitives realizing the third step (*phase manipulation*) ensure that our results can actually be READ in a practical way.

These steps are usually implemented together and many times in iteration, in a manner dependent on the particular application. Rather than there being one all-purpose primitive for each step, we'll actually need an arsenal. The next five chapters introduce the primitives listed in Table II-1.

Table II-1. Quantum primitives covered

Primitive	Type	Chapter
Digital logic	Compute in superposition	5
Amplitude amplification	Phase manipulation	6
Quantum Fourier Transform	Phase manipulation	7
Phase estimation	Phase manipulation	8
Quantum data types	Superposition creation	9

In each chapter we first give a "hands-on" introduction to the primitive, then outline ways of *using* that primitive in practical applications. Finally, each chapter ends with a section entitled "Inside the QPU" giving more *intuition* into how the primitive works, often with a breakdown in terms of the fundamental QPU operations we've seen in Chapters 2 and 3.

The art of programming a QPU is to determine which combination of primitives from Table II-1 works to construct a structure like Figure II-1 for a given application. In Part III of the book we show some examples of such constructions.

Now that we know where we're headed, let's start collecting our QPU primitives!

CHAPTER 5

Quantum Arithmetic and Logic

QPU applications often gain an advantage over their conventional counterparts by performing a large number of logical operations *in superposition*.[1]

A key aspect of this is the ability to apply simple arithmetic operations on a qubit register in superposition. In this chapter, we will look in detail at how to do this. Initially, we'll discuss arithmetic operations at the more abstracted level we're used to in conventional programming, dealing with integers and variables rather than qubits and operations. But toward the end of the chapter we'll also take a closer look at the logical operations making these up (akin to the elementary gates of digital logic).

Strangely Different

Conventional digital logic has plenty of well-optimized approaches for performing arithmetical operations—why can't we just replace bits with qubits and use those in our QPU?

The problem, of course, is that conventional operations are expected to operate on a *single* set of inputs at a time, whereas we will often have input registers that are in superposition, for which we want *quantum* arithmetic operations to affect *all* values in the superposition.

Let's start with a simple example demonstrating how we want logic to work on a superposition. Suppose we have three single-qubit QPU registers, a, b, and c, and we want to implement the following logic: if (a and b) then invert c. So if a is $|1\rangle$

---

[1] As we noted in the introduction to this part of the book, superposition alone is not enough; a critical second step must ensure that the (effectively) parallel computations we perform can be read out, rather than remaining hidden in the quantum states of our qubits.

and b is $|1\rangle$, then the value of c will be flipped. We saw in Figure 3-20 that we can implement this logic directly with a single Toffoli operation. Visualizing this in circle notation, the Toffoli operation swaps the $|3\rangle$ and $|7\rangle$ values, regardless of what's in them. If b is $|0\rangle$ and a is $|1\rangle$, as in Figure 5-1, the exchanged circles are both empty, so the gate has no effect on c.

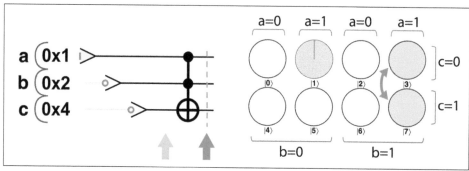

Figure 5-1. When b=0, this operation has no effect

Now suppose that we use a HAD operation (introduced in Chapter 2) to prepare b in a superposition of $|0\rangle$ and $|1\rangle$—what do we want c to do? Properly implemented, this operation should *both* invert and not invert c in superposition, as in Figure 5-2. Toffoli gates also exist for conventional computation, but they certainly couldn't pull off this trick. We need a definitively quantum implementation of the Toffoli gate acting on quantum registers to make this work. The circle notation in Figure 5-2 helps us see what a properly quantum Toffoli gate should do to our superposition input.

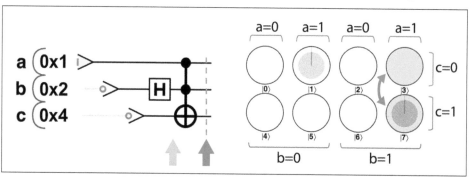

Figure 5-2. A single gate performs two operations at the same time

There are also a few other requirements we will have of operations in order for them to be able to properly operate on qubits within a QPU. Although some of these might not be as obviously necessary as our preceding example, they are worth bearing in mind as we construct a variety of arithmetic and logical operations for QPUs:

Moving and copying data

As we have already learned, qubits cannot be copied. This is a *huge* difference between quantum and conventional logic. Moving or copying bits is the most common operation a conventional CPU performs. A QPU can move qubits using *exchange* instructions to swap them with other qubits, but no QPU will ever implement a COPY instruction. As a result, the = operator, so common for manipulating digital values, cannot be used to assign one qubit-based value to another.

Reversibility and data loss

Unlike many conventional logic operations, our basic non-READ QPU operations *are* reversible (due to details of the laws of quantum mechanics). This imposes significant constraints on the logic and arithmetic we can perform with a QPU, and often drives us to think creatively when trying to reproduce conventional arithmetic operations. READ is the only irreversible operation, and you might be tempted to make heavy use of it to build nonreversible operations. Beware! This will make your computation so conventional that it will most likely rob you of any quantum advantage. The simplest way of implementing *any* conventional circuit in our QPU is to replace it with an equivalent conventional circuit only using *reversible* operations, such as Toffoli. We can then implement it virtually as is on a quantum register.[2]

Arithmetic on a QPU

In conventional programming, we rarely use individual logic gates to write programs. Instead, we trust the compiler and CPU to convert our program into the gates needed to perform our desired operations.

Quantum computation is no different. In order to write serious QPU software, we primarily need to learn how to work with *qubytes* and *quantum integers* rather than *qubits*. In this section we'll lay out the intricacies of performing arithmetical operations on a QPU. Just as classical digital logic can be built up from NAND gates (a single gate which performs NOT(b AND b)), the quantum integer operations we need can be built from the elementary QPU operations we covered in Chapters 2 and 3.

For simplicity, we will diagram and demonstrate the arithmetic operations that follow using four-qubit integers (quantum nibbles, or *qunibbles*, for those who remember the early microcomputer days). However, all of these examples can be extended to larger QPU registers. The size of integers that our arithmetic can handle will depend on the number of qubits available in our QPU or simulator.

---

2 Any conventional operation implemented with reversible logic using N Toffoli gates can be implemented using $O(N)$ single- and two-qubit operations.

Hands-on: Building Increment and Decrement Operators

Two of the simplest useful integer arithmetic operations we can perform are those for incrementing and decrementing a number. Try running Example 5-1, and stepping through the gates one by one to observe the operation shown in Figure 5-3.

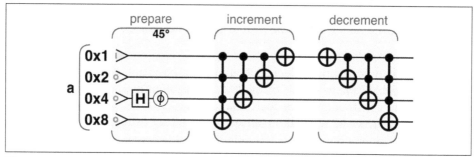

Figure 5-3. Operations performing increment-by-1 and decrement-by-1

 The prepare step and initialization value in Figure 5-3 are not part of the actual increment operation, but chosen simply to provide a nonzero input state, so that we can follow the action of operations.

Sample Code

Run this sample online at *http://oreilly-qc.github.io?p=5-1*.

Example 5-1. Integer increment-by-one operation

```
// Initialize
var num_qubits = 4;
qc.reset(num_qubits);
var a = qint.new(num_qubits, 'a');

// prepare
a.write(1);
a.hadamard(0x4);
a.phase(45, 0x4);

// increment
a.add(1);

// decrement
a.subtract(1);
```

In Example 5-1, we've implemented the increment and decrement operations using an argument of 1 in the QCEngine add() and subtract() functions.

These implementations satisfy all the requirements we have for them being truly quantum—in particular:

Reversibility
> First, and most obviously, the decrement operation is simply the increment with its constituent operations reversed. This makes sense, but may not be obvious if you're used to conventional logic. In conventional logic devices gates tend to have dedicated inputs and outputs, and simply running a device in reverse is likely to damage it, or at least fail to provide a useful result. As we've noted, for quantum operations reversibility is a critical requirement.

Superposition operation
> Crucially, this implementation of increment also works on inputs in superposition. In Example 5-1, the preparation instructions write the value $|1\rangle$ to a quantum integer and then call HAD and PHASE(45) on the 0x4 qubit, resulting in our register containing a superposition[3] of $|1\rangle$ and $|5\rangle$, as shown in Figure 5-4.

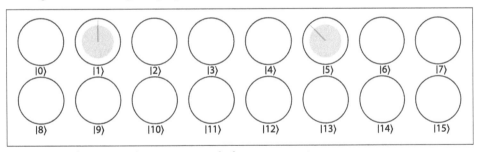

Figure 5-4. The prepared superposition, before incrementing

Now let's try running the increment operation on this input. Doing so transforms the state into a superposition of $|2\rangle$ and $|6\rangle$, where the phase of each value matches its pre-increment counterpart. This is shown in Figure 5-5.

---

3 We include the 45° phase difference between the two values just so that we can tell them apart.

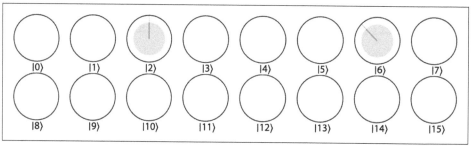

Figure 5-5. The resulting superposition, after incrementing

 How does incrementing work? Looking carefully at the operations involved, we can see that it starts by using a three-condition CNOT gate to apply "if *all* of the lower bits in the integer are 1, then flip the top bit." This is essentially the same as a conventional arithmetic carry operation. We then repeat the process for each bit in the integer, resulting in a complete "add and carry" operation on all qubits, performed using only multicondition CNOT gates.

We can go beyond simple incrementing and decrementing. Try changing the integer values passed to add() and subtract() in Example 5-1. Any integer will work, though different choices result in different configurations of QPU operations. For example, add(12) produces the circuit in Figure 5-6.

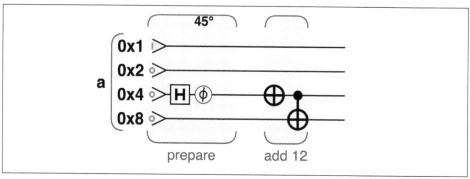

Figure 5-6. A program to add 12 to a quantum integer

In this case, Figure 5-7 shows that the input values $|1\rangle$ and $|5\rangle$ will become $|13\rangle$ and $|1\rangle$, since this program will wrap on overflow (just like conventional integer math).

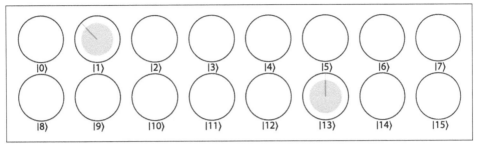

Figure 5-7. add(12) applied to a superposition of 1 and 5 states

The fact that these functions will take any integer brings up an interesting point: this program is performing arithmetic on a conventional digital and a quantum value. We're always adding a *fixed* integer to a quantum register, and have to change the set of gates used to be specific to the particular integer we want to add. What about going a step further—can we perform addition between two *quantum* values?

Adding Two Quantum Integers

Suppose we have two QPU registers a and b (bearing in mind that each of these could potentially store a superposition of integer values), and we ask for a simple + operation that would store the result of their addition in a new register c. This is analogous to how a CPU performs addition with conventional digital registers. However, there's a problem—this approach violates *both* the reversibility and the no-copying restrictions on QPU logic:

- Reversibility is violated by c = a + b because the prior contents of c are lost.
- No copying is violated because we could be sneaky and perform b = c - a to ultimately end up with two copies of whatever superposition might have been in a.

To get around this, we will instead implement the += operator, adding one number directly onto another. The code sample in Example 5-2, shown in Figure 5-8, adds two quantum integers together in a reversible manner, whatever superposition they happen to be in. Unlike the previous approach for adding a conventional digital integer to a quantum register, here the gates don't need to be reconfigured every time the input values change.

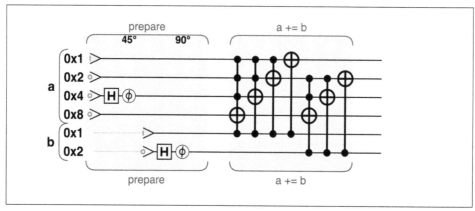

Figure 5-8. Operations assembled to perform a += operation

 How does the circuit in Figure 5-8 work? A close look at the gates of this program will reveal that they are simply the integer addition operations from Figure 5-3 and Figure 5-6 applied to a, but performed *conditional* on the corresponding qubits of b. This allows the values in b, even in superposition, to determine the effect of the addition.

Sample Code

Run this sample online at *http://oreilly-qc.github.io?p=5-2.*

Example 5-2. Adding two quantum integers

```
// a += b
a.add(b);
```

As was the case in Example 5-1, the prepare step in Figure 5-8 is just there to provide test input, and is not part of the operation. Also, we can implement a -= b by simply running the a += b gates in reverse order.

Negative Integers

So far we've dealt only with adding and subtracting positive integers. How can we represent and manipulate negative integers in a QPU register? Fortunately, we can employ a *two's-complement* binary representation, as used by all modern CPUs and programming languages. We provide a quick review of two's complement here, with qubits specifically in mind.

For a given number of bits, we simply associate half the values with negative numbers, and half with positive numbers. For example, a three-bit register allows us to represent the integers −4, −3, −2, −1, 0, +1, +2, and +3 as shown in Table 5-1.

Table 5-1. Two's complement for binary representation of negative integers

0	1	2	3	−4	−3	−2	−1
000	001	010	011	100	101	110	111

If you've never encountered two's complement before, the association between negative and binary values may seem a bit haphazard, but this particular choice has the surprising benefit that methods for performing elementary arithmetic developed for positive integers will also work out of the box with the two's-complement representations. We can also see from Table 5-1 that the highest-order bit conveniently functions as an indicator of an integer's sign.

A two's-complement encoding works just as well for a register of qubits as it does for a register of bits. Thus, all of the examples in this chapter work equally well with negative values represented using two's complement. We must, of course, be diligent in keeping track of whether or not we're encoding data in QPU registers with two's complement, so that we interpret their binary values correctly.

To negate a number in two's complement, we simply flip all of the bits, and then add 1.[4] The quantum operations for performing this are shown in Figure 5-9, which bears a very strong resemblance to the increment operator presented back in Figure 5-3.

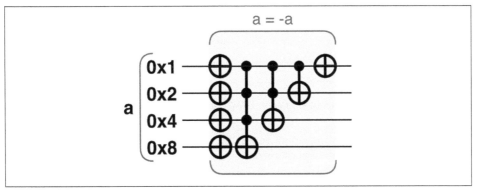

Figure 5-9. Two's complement negation: flip all bits and add 1

---

[4] In this three-bit example, the negation works for all values except −4. As seen in Table 5-1, there is no representation for 4, so the negation leaves it unchanged.

Hands-on: More Complicated Math

Not all arithmetic operations will readily lend themselves to the requirements we demand for QPU operations, such as reversibility and no copying. For example, multiplication is hard to perform reversibly. The code in Example 5-3, shown in Figure 5-10, illustrates a related operation that *can* be constructed to be reversible. Specifically, we square one value and add the result to another.

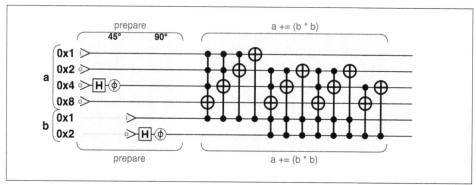

Figure 5-10. Add the square of b to a

Performing a += b * b as in Figure 5-10 will add the squared value of b to a.

How does the circuit in Figure 5-10 work? This implementation performs multiplication by using repeated addition, conditional on bits of b.

Reversibility is an especially interesting consideration for this example. If we try to naively implement b = b * b, we'll quickly discover that there's no suitable combination of reversible operations, as we always end up losing the sign bit. Implementing a += b * b, however, is fine, as reversing it simply gives us a -= b * b.

Getting Really Quantum

Now that we're equipped with quantum versions of arithmetic circuits, there are other entirely new tricks we can play.

Quantum-Conditional Execution

On a conventional computer, conditional execution causes logic to be performed *if* a value is set. During execution, the CPU will read the value and decide whether to execute the logic. With a QPU, a value can be both *set* and *not set* in superposition, so an operation conditional on that value will both *execute* and *not execute* in superposition. We can use this idea at a higher level, and conditionally execute large pieces of digital logic in superposition.

For example, consider the program in Example 5-4, shown in Figure 5-11, which increments a register of three qubits labeled b—but only if another three-qubit register, a, holds an integer value in a certain range. By initializing a in a superposition of $|1\rangle$ and $|5\rangle$, b ends up in a superposition of being *both* incremented and not incremented.

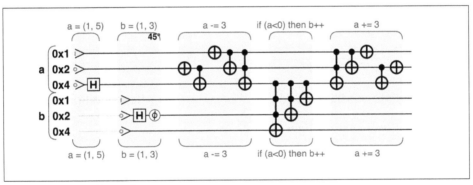

Figure 5-11. Conditional execution

Sample Code

Run this sample online at *http://oreilly-qc.github.io?p=5-4*.

Example 5-4. Conditional execution

```
a.subtract(3);
// if high bit of a is set then b += 1
b.add(1, a.bits(0x4));
a.add(3);
```

Note that for some values of a, subtracting 3 from a will cause its lowest-weight qubit to be set. We can use this top bit as a condition for our increment operation. After incrementing b *conditional* on that qubit's value we need to add 3 back to a, in order to restore it to its original state.

Running Example 5-4, circle notation reveals that only parts of the quantum state where a is less than 3 or greater than 6 are incremented.

Only circles in columns 0, 1, 2, *and* 7 in Figure 5-12 are affected by the incrementing logic.

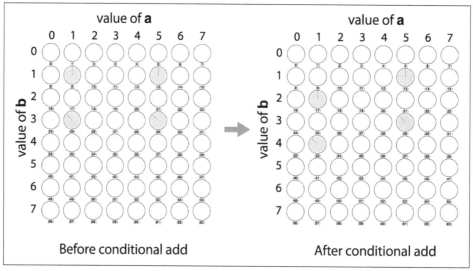

Figure 5-12. *Conditional addition*

Phase-Encoded Results

Our QPU versions of arithmetic operations can also be modified to encode the output of a calculation in the *relative phases* of the original input qubit register—something completely impossible using conventional bits. Encoding calculation results in a register's relative phases is a crucial skill for programming a QPU, and can help us produce answers able to survive READ operations.

Example 5-5, shown in Figure 5-13, modifies Example 5-4 to flip the *phase* in an input register if a is less than 3 and b is equal to 1.

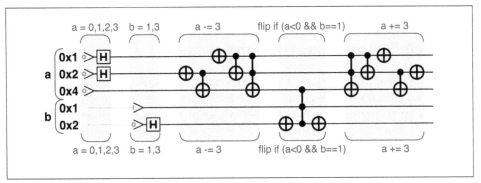

Figure 5-13. Phase-encoding the result

When this operation is complete, the *magnitudes* of the register are unchanged. The probabilities of READing each value remain just as they were, unable to show that this operation was ever performed. However, Figure 5-14 shows that we have used the phases in our input register to "mark" specific states in the superposition as a result of a calculation. We can see this effect most readily in circle notation.

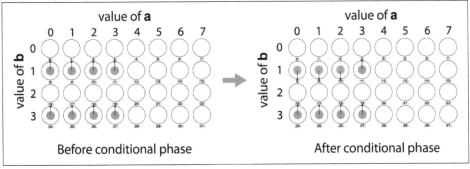

Figure 5-14. The effect of phase encoding

We'll make heavy use of this ability to compute in a register's phases in Chapter 10.

Reversibility and Scratch Qubits

During this chapter we've noted again and again that QPU operations need to be reversible. Naturally, you might ask, "How can I make sure that the arithmetic operations I want to perform are reversible?" Although there's no hard-and-fast way to convert an arithmetical operation into a form that is reversible (and therefore more likely to work on a QPU), a helpful technique is the use of *scratch qubits*.

Scratch qubits are not necessary for encoding the input or output we're interested in, but rather play a temporary role enabling the quantum logic connecting them.

Here's a specific example of an otherwise irreversible operation that can be made reversible with a scratch qubit. Consider trying to find a QPU implementation of abs(a), a function computing the absolute value of a signed integer, as shown in Figure 5-15.

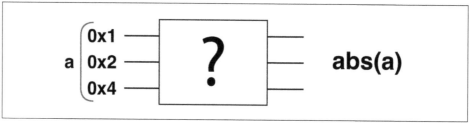

Figure 5-15. What QPU operations can compute the absolute value?

Since we've already seen in Figure 5-9 how to easily negate integers in QPU registers, you might think that implementing abs(a) is simple—negate our QPU register dependent on its own sign bit. But any attempt to do this will fail to be reversible (as we might expect, since the mathematical abs(a) function itself destroys information about the input's sign). It's not that we'll receive a QPU compile or runtime error; the problem is that no matter how hard we try, we won't ever find a configuration of reversible QPU operations able to produce the desired results.

Enter our scratch qubit! This is used to stash the sign of the integer in a. We begin with it initialized to $|0\rangle$, and then use a CNOT to flip the scratch qubit dependent on the highest-weight qubit in register a. We then perform the negation conditional on the scratch qubit's value (rather than directly on the sign of the a register itself), as shown in Figure 5-16.

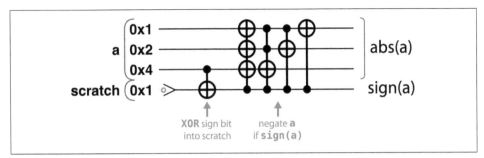

Figure 5-16. Scratch qubits can make an irreversible operation reversible

With the scratch qubit involved, we now *can* find a set of gates that will ultimately implement abs on our a register. But before we verify in detail that the circuit in Figure 5-16 achieves this, note that the CNOT operation we use between our scratch qubit and the 0x4 qubit of a (which tells us the sign of its integer value in two's complement) does not *copy* the sign qubit exactly. Instead, the CNOT *entangles* the scratch qubit with the sign qubit. This is an important distinction to note, since we also know that QPU operations cannot copy qubits.

Figure 5-17 follows the progression of these operations using an illustrative sample state that has varying relative phases, simply so that we can easily keep track of which circle moves where during the various QPU operations.

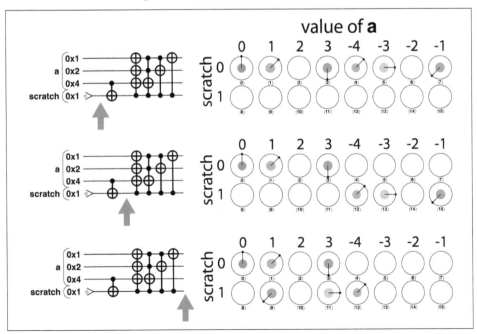

Figure 5-17. Circle notation steps for the absolute value

Note that each value in the superposition that corresponds to a starting with a positive or zero value is left unchanged throughout. However, values for which a has a negative value are moved first into the second row of circles (corresponding to the scratch qubit having been conditionally flipped), and then into the corresponding positive values (as required by abs), *while remaining in the "scratch = 1" row.*[5]

Following the action of the scratch qubit in circle notation visually demonstrates how it solves our irreversibility issues. If we tried to perform abs *without* a scratch qubit, our circle notation in Figure 5-17 would only have a single row, and trying to move the negative-value circles into the corresponding positive values would obliterate the magnitudes and phases already held there—such that we could never later figure out what the original state was (i.e., we would have an irreversible operation). The scratch qubit gives us an extra row we can move into and then across in, leaving everything from the original state untouched and recoverable.[6]

Uncomputing

Although scratch qubits are frequently a necessity, they do tend to get tangled up with our QPU registers. More precisely, they tend to get *entangled*. This introduces two related problems. First, scratch qubits rarely end up back in an all-zero state. This is bad news, since we now need to reset these scratch qubits to make them usable again further down the line in our QPU.

"No problem!" you may think, "I'll just READ and NOT them as necessary, like we learned in Chapter 1." But this would lead you to encounter the second problem. Because using scratch qubits almost always results in them becoming entangled with the qubits in our output register (this is certainly the case in Figure 5-17), performing a READ on them can have a disastrous effect on the output state they helped us create. Recall from Chapter 3 that when qubits are entangled, any operations you perform on one have unavoidable effects on the others. In the case of Figure 5-17, attempting to reset the scratch qubit to $|0\rangle$ (as we must if we ever want to use it again in our QPU) destroys half of the quantum state of a!

Fortunately, there's a trick that solves this problem: it's called *uncomputing*. The idea of uncomputing is to reverse the operations that entangled the scratch qubit, returning it to its initial, disentangled $|0\rangle$ state. In our abs example, this means reversing all the abs(a) logic involving a and the scratch qubit. Brilliant! We have our scratch

---

[5] Note that in this case –4 is unchanged, which is correct for a three-bit number in a two's-complement encoding.

[6] This is quite a remarkable feat. Keeping track of the original state using conventional bits would require an exponentially vast number of bits, but just adding one scratch qubit allows us to do so perfectly.

qubit back in a $|0\rangle$ state. Unfortunately, we will, of course, also have completely undone all the hard work of our absolute-value calculation.

What good is getting back our scratch qubit if we've also undone our answer? Thanks to the no-copying constraints faced by qubits, we can't even copy the value stored in a to another register before uncomputing it. However, the reason uncomputing is not completely self-defeating is that *we will often make use of our answer within register a before we uncompute*. In most cases, functions such as abs are used as part of a larger arithmetic computation. For example, we might *actually* want to implement "add the absolute value of a to b." We can make this operation reversible and save our scratch qubit with the circuit shown in Figure 5-18.

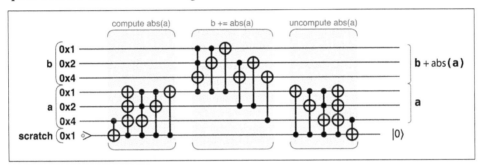

Figure 5-18. Using uncomputation to perform b += abs(a)

After these operations, a and b are likely entangled with one another; however, the scratch qubit has been returned to its disentangled $|0\rangle$ state, ready to be used in some other operation. The larger operation *is* reversible, even though abs itself is not. In quantum computation, this trick is extremely common: use temporary scratch qubits to perform an otherwise-irreversible computation, perform other operations conditional on the result, and then uncompute.

In fact, although we cannot just simply "copy" the absolute value into another register before uncomputing its action, we can do something similar by initializing b to 0 before the addition in Figure 5-18. We can actually achieve the same result more simply using a CNOT operation instead of addition, as shown in Figure 5-19.

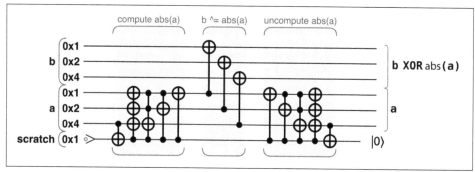

Figure 5-19. Using uncomputation to produce b xor abs(a)

Another extremely common application of uncomputation involves performing a computation (potentially using scratch qubits), storing the results in the relative phases of the output register, and then uncomputing the result. So long as the initial computation (and thus also the final uncomputation step) does not interfere with the relative phases of the output registers, they will survive the process intact. We make use of this trick in Chapter 6.

As an example, the circuit in Figure 5-20 performs the operation "flip the phase of any value where abs(a) equals 1." We compute the absolute value using a scratch qubit, flip the phase of the output register only if the value is 1, and then uncompute.

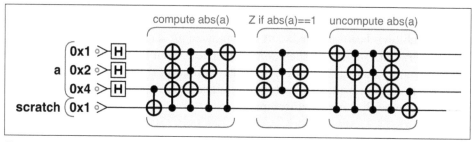

Figure 5-20. Using uncomputation to perform phase(180) if abs(a)==1

In Figure 5-21 we follow this program step by step in circle notation.

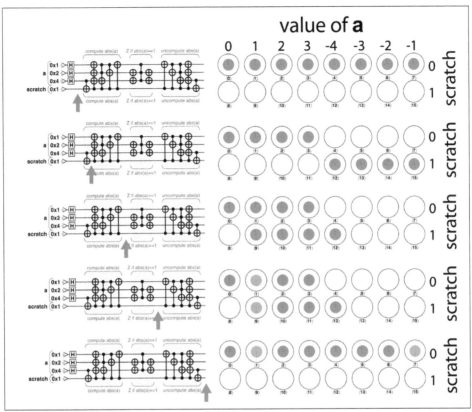

Figure 5-21. Step-by-step walkthrough of using uncompute for conditional phase inversion

Mapping Boolean Logic to QPU Operations

Just as digital arithmetic is built from digital logic gates, to see in detail how the circuits for our basic QPU arithmetic work we rely on a toolbox of programmable quantum logic. In this section we'll highlight the quantum analogs of some low-level digital logic gates.

Basic Quantum Logic

In digital logic, there are a few basic logic gates that can be used to build all of the others. For example, if you have just a NAND gate, you can use it to create AND, OR, NOT, and XOR, which can be combined into any logical function you wish.

Note that the NAND gates in Figure 5-22 can have any number of inputs. With a single input (the simplest case), NAND performs a NOT.

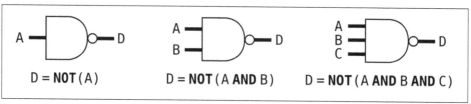

Figure 5-22. Digital NAND gates in different sizes

In quantum computation we can similarly start with one versatile gate, as in Figure 5-23, and build our quantum digital logic from it. To accomplish this, we'll use a multiple-condition `CNOT` gate: the Toffoli gate. As with the `NAND` gate, we can vary the number of condition inputs to expand the logic performed, as shown in Example 5-6.

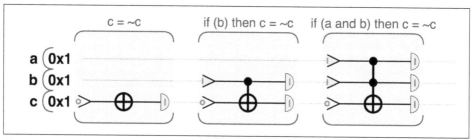

Figure 5-23. Quantum CNOT gates in different sizes

Sample Code

Run this sample online at *http://oreilly-qc.github.io?p=5-6*.

Example 5-6. Logic using CNOT gates

```
// c = ~c
c.write(0);
c.not();
c.read();

// if (b) then c = ~c
qc.write(2, 2|4);
c.cnot(b);
qc.read(2|4);

// if (a and b) then c = ~c
qc.write(1|2);
qc.cnot(4, 1|2);
qc.read(1|2|4);
```

Note that this performs *almost* the same operation as NAND. We can express its digital-logic equivalent using AND and XOR, as shown in Figure 5-24.

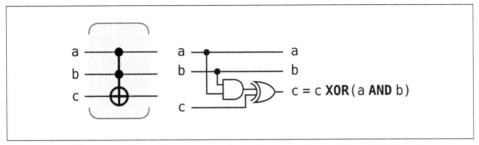

Figure 5-24. The exact digital logic equivalent of our multicondition CNOT gate

Armed with this gate, we can produce QPU equivalents of a wide variety of logical functions, as shown in Figure 5-25.

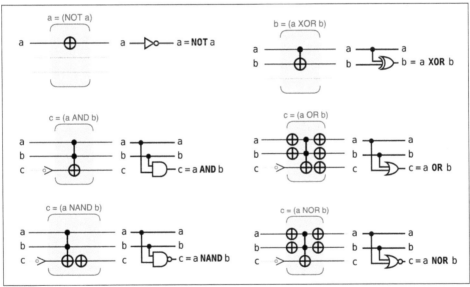

Figure 5-25. Some basic digital logic gates, built from multiple conditioned CNOT gates

Notice that in some cases in order to get the desired logic function we need to add an extra scratch qubit, initialized to $|0\rangle$. One substantial challenge in quantum computation is reducing the number of scratch qubits needed to perform a specific computation.

Conclusion

The ability to perform digital logic in superposition is a core part of most QPU algorithms. In this chapter, we have taken a close look at ways to manipulate quantum data and even to perform conditional operations within superpositions.

Performing digital logic in superposition is of limited use unless we can extract information from the resulting state in a useful way. Recall that if we try to READ a superposition of solutions to an arithmetic problem, we'll randomly obtain just one of them. In the next chapter, we will explore a QPU primitive allowing us to reliably extract output from quantum superpositions, known as *amplitude amplification*.

CHAPTER 6

Amplitude Amplification

In the previous chapter we showed how to build conventional arithmetic and logical operations that utilize the power of superposition. But when using a QPU, being able to perform computations in superposition is useless if we don't have something clever up our sleeves to make sure that we're actually able to READ out a solution.

In this chapter we introduce the first *quantum primitive* allowing us to manipulate superpositions into a form that we can reliably READ. We've already noted that there are many such primitives, each suited to different kinds of problems. The first we will cover is *amplitude amplification.*[1]

Hands-on: Converting Between Phase and Magnitude

Very simply, amplitude amplification is a tool that converts inaccessible *phase* differences inside a QPU register into READable *magnitude* differences (and vice versa). As a QPU tool, it's simple, elegant, powerful, and very useful.

 Given that amplitude amplification converts phase differences into magnitudes, you might think that *magnitude* amplification would be a better name. However, "amplitude amplification" is commonly used in the wider literature to refer to the kind of primitive we describe here.

For example, suppose we have a four-qubit QPU register containing one of the three quantum states (A, B, or C), shown in Figure 6-1, but we don't know which one.

---

1 In this book, we use the term *amplitude amplification* in a slightly different way than the term is used in the academic literature. We cover the exact difference in Chapter 14.

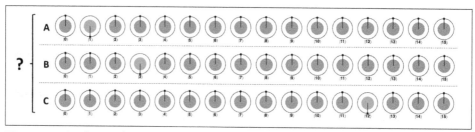

Figure 6-1. Each state has a single flipped value

These three states are clearly distinct in that each one has a different certain value phase-flipped. We'll call that the *marked value*. However, as all of the values in the register have the same magnitude, reading a QPU register in any of these states will return an evenly distributed random number, revealing nothing about which of the three states we started with. At the same time, such READs will destroy the phase information in the register.

But with a single QPU subroutine we can reveal the hidden phase information. We call this subroutine the `mirror` operation (we'll see why later), and you can see its action for yourself by running the sample code in Example 6-1, shown in Figure 6-2.

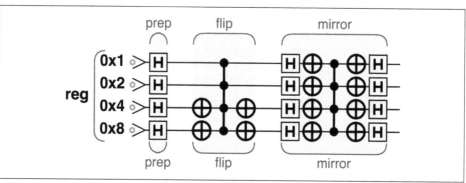

Figure 6-2. Applying the mirror subroutine to a flipped phase

Sample Code

Run this sample online at *http://oreilly-qc.github.io?p=6-1*.

Example 6-1. Applying the mirror subroutine to a flipped phase

```
var number_to_flip = 3; // The 'marked' value

var num_qubits = 4;
qc.reset(num_qubits);
var reg = qint.new(num_qubits, 'reg')
reg.write(0);
```

```
reg.hadamard();

// Flip the marked value
reg.not(~number_to_flip);
reg.cphase(180);
reg.not(~number_to_flip);

reg.Grover();
```

Note that before applying the mirror subroutine we first flip, which takes our register initially in state $|0\rangle$ and *marks* one of its values. You can alter which value is flipped in the preceding code sample by changing the number_to_flip variable.

Applying the mirror subroutine to the A, B, and C states from Figure 6-1, we obtain the results in Figure 6-3.

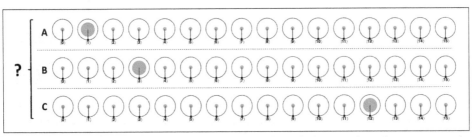

Figure 6-3. After applying the mirror subroutine, phase differences have been converted into magnitude differences

The magnitudes within each state are now very different, and performing a READ on the QPU register is very likely (though not certain) to reveal which value had its phase flipped, and hence which of the three states our register had been in. Instead of all values having the same probability of 6.25%, the marked value now has a READ probability of about 47.3%, with the nonmarked values being at about 3.5%. At this point, READing the register gives us an almost 50% chance of obtaining the value that had its phase flipped. That's still not great.

Notice that although the mirror subroutine changed the magnitude of the marked value, its *phase* is now the same as the rest of the register. In a sense, mirror has *converted* the phase difference into a magnitude difference.

The `mirror` operation is commonly called the "Grover iteration" in the quantum computing literature. Grover's algorithm for an unstructured database search was the first algorithm implementing the `flip-mirror` routine, and in fact, the amplitude amplification primitive that we cover here is a generalization of Grover's original algorithm. We've chosen to call the operation `mirror` to make it easier for the reader to recall its effect.

Can we repeat the operation again to try to further improve our probability of success? Suppose we have the B state from Figure 6-1 (i.e., `flip` acted on the $|3\rangle$ value). Applying the `mirror` subroutine again simply leaves us where we started, converting the magnitude differences back into differences of phase. However, suppose that before reapplying `mirror` we also reapply the `flip` subroutine (to re-flip the marked value). This starts us out with another phase difference before our second `mirror` application. Figure 6-4 shows what we get if we apply the *whole* `flip-mirror` combination twice.

Figure 6-4. After applying flip-mirror a second time on state B

Following two applications of `flip-mirror`, the probability of finding our marked value has jumped from 47.3% to 90.8%!

The Amplitude Amplification Iteration

Together, the `flip` and `mirror` subroutines are a powerful combination. `flip` allows us to target a value of the register and distinguish its phase from the others. `mirror` then converts this phase difference into a magnitude difference. We'll refer to this combined operation, shown in Figure 6-5, as an amplitude amplification (AA) iteration.

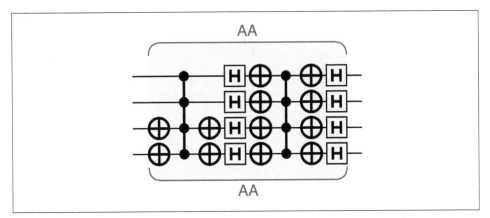

Figure 6-5. A single AA iteration

You've probably noticed that the AA operation assumes that we know which value we want to amplify—it's hardwired into which value the flip subroutine affects. This may seem to defeat the whole point of amplitude amplification—if we already know which values we should amplify, why do we need to find them? We've used the flip subroutine as the simplest possible example of a subroutine flipping the phase of selected values within our QPU register. In a real application, flip would be replaced with some more complex subroutine performing a combination of phase flips representing logic specific to that application. In Chapter 10 we'll show in more detail how computations can be performed purely on the phases of a QPU register. When applications make use of this kind of *phase logic* they can take the place of flip, and amplitude amplification becomes an extremely useful tool.

The key point is that although we discuss using flip alongside the mirror subroutine, compounding more complex phase-altering subroutines with mirror still converts phase alterations into magnitude differences.

More Iterations?

In Figure 6-4 we've applied two AA iterations to the B state, leaving us with a 90.8% success probability of observing the marked value. Can we continue applying AA iterations to bring that even closer to 100%? This is easy to try. The sample code in Example 6-2 repeats the AA steps a specified number of times. By varying the number_of_iterations variable in the sample code, we can run as many AA iterations as we like.

Example 6-2. Repeated amplitude amplification iterations

```
var number_to_flip = 3;
var number_of_iterations = 4;

var num_qubits = 4;
qc.reset(num_qubits);
var reg = qint.new(num_qubits, 'reg')
reg.write(0);
reg.hadamard();

for (var i = 0; i < number_of_iterations; ++i)
{
    // Flip the marked value
    reg.not(~number_to_flip);
    reg.cphase(180);
    reg.not(~number_to_flip);

    reg.Grover();

    // Peek at the probability
    var prob = reg.peekProbability(number_to_flip);
}
```

Figure 6-6 shows the result of running this code with `number_of_iterations=4`, so that we `flip` and then `mirror` our register four consecutive times.

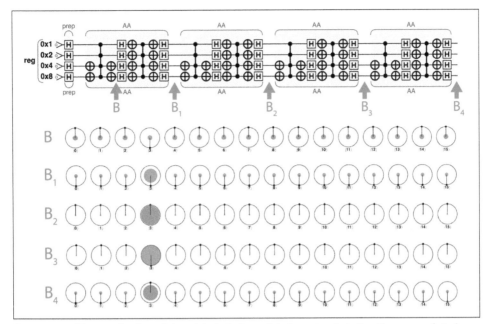

Figure 6-6. The result of applying AA 1, 2, 3, and 4 times to state B—the rows of circles show the state of our QPU register at the positions marked in the circuit

Let's follow the action of each successive AA iteration. After the `flip` of the first AA we begin with the state B from Figure 6-1. As we've already seen, B_1 has a success probability of 47.3%, while after two iterations, B_2 has a probability of 90.8%.

The third iteration brings us to 96.1%, but notice that in B_3 the marked state is out of phase with the others, so our next `flip` subroutine will cause all phases to be *in alignment*. At that point, we will have a magnitude difference but no phase difference, so further AA iterations will start diminishing magnitude differences until we end up with the original state.

Sure enough, by the time we get to B_4 our chances of successfully reading out the marked state are way down to 58.2%, and they'll continue to drop if we apply more AA iterations.

So how many AA iterations should we apply to maximize the chances of READing out our marked value correctly?

The plot in Figure 6-7 shows that as we continually loop through our iterations, the probability of reading the marked value oscillates in a predictable way. We can see that to maximize the chance of getting the correct result, we're best off waiting for the 9th or 15th iteration, giving a probability of finding the marked value of 99.9563%.

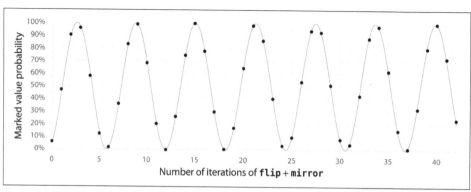

Figure 6-7. Probability of reading the marked value versus the number of AA iterations

On the other hand, if each iteration is expensive to perform (we'll see some cases of this later), we can stop after three and attempt to harvest the answer at 96.1%. Even if we fail and need to repeat the entire QPU program, we'll have a 99.848% chance that one of the two attempts will succeed, only costing us at most six total iterations.

In general, there's a simple and useful equation allowing us to determine the number of AA iterations, N_{AA}, that we should perform to get the highest probability *within the first oscillation* made by the success probability (this would be the 96.1% success probability at $N_{AA} = 3$ in our previous example). This is shown in Equation 6-1, where n is the number of qubits.

Equation 6-1. Optimal number of iterations in amplitude amplification

$$N_{AA} = \left\lfloor \frac{\pi \sqrt{2^n}}{4} \right\rfloor$$

We now have a tool that can convert a single phase difference within a QPU register into a detectable magnitude difference. But what if our register has several values with different phases? It's easy to imagine that subroutines more complicated than flip might alter the phases of multiple values in the register. Fortunately, our AA iterations can handle this more general case.

Multiple Flipped Entries

With a small modification to the circuit in Example 6-1 we can try running multiple AA iterations on a register having any number of phase-flipped values. In Example 6-3 you can use the n2f variable to set which values in the register should be flipped by the flip subroutine inside each AA operation. As before, you can also adjust the number of AA iterations performed using the number_of_iterations variable.

Sample Code

Run this sample online at *http://oreilly-qc.github.io?p=6-3*.

Example 6-3. Amplitude amplification iterations with multiple values flipped

```
var n2f = [0,1,2];              // Which values to flip
var number_of_iterations = 50;  // The number of Grover iterations

var num_qubits = 4;
qc.reset(num_qubits);
var reg = qint.new(num_qubits, 'reg')
reg.write(0);
reg.hadamard();

for (var i = 0; i < number_of_iterations; ++i)
{
    // Flip the marked value
    for (var j = 0; j < n2f.length; ++j)
    {
        var marked_term = n2f[j];
        reg.not(~marked_term);
        reg.cphase(180);
        reg.not(~marked_term);
    }

    reg.Grover();

    var prob = 0;
    for (var j = 0; j < n2f.length; ++j)
    {
        var marked_term = n2f[j];
        prob += reg.peekProbability(marked_term);
    }
    qc.print('iters: '+i+' prob: '+prob);
}
```

By running this sample with a single value flipped (e.g., n2f = [4], as shown in Figure 6-8), we can reproduce our earlier results, where increasing the number of AA iterations causes the probability of READing the "marked" value to vary sinusoidally, as illustrated in Figure 6-9.

Figure 6-8. One value flipped

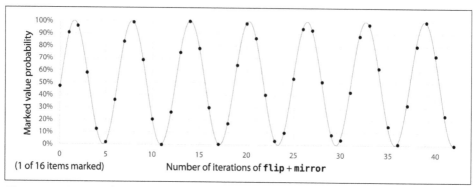

Figure 6-9. Repeated AA iterations with 1 value of 16 flipped

But now let's instead flip *two* values (e.g., n2f=[4,7], as shown in Figure 6-10). In this case we ideally want to end up with the QPU register configured so that we will READ either of the two phase-flipped values, with zero possibility of READing any others. Applying multiple AA iterations just like we did for one marked state (albeit with two flip subroutines run during each iteration—one for each marked state) yields the results shown in Figure 6-11.

Figure 6-10. Two values flipped

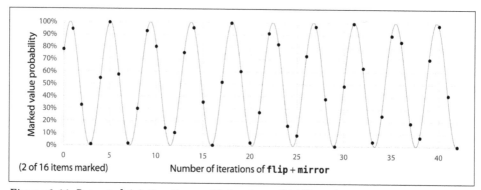

Figure 6-11. Repeated AA iterations with 2 values of 16 flipped

Note that in Figure 6-11 the probability shown on the y-axis is the probability of obtaining *either one of the (two) marked values* if we were to READ our register.

Although we still get a sinusoidally varying chance of success, comparing this with the similar plot for only *one* phase-flipped value in Figure 6-7 you'll notice that the frequency of the sinusoidal wave has increased.

With three values flipped (e.g., n2f=[4,7,8], as shown in Figure 6-12), the wave's frequency continues to increase, as you can see in Figure 6-13.

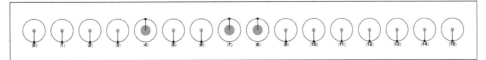

Figure 6-12. Three values flipped

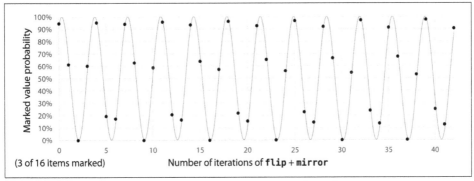

Figure 6-13. Repeated AA iterations with 3 values of 16 flipped

When we have 4 of the 16 values flipped, as shown in Figure 6-14, something interesting happens. As you can see in Figure 6-15, the wave's frequency becomes such that the probability of us READing one of the marked values repeats with every third AA iteration that we apply. This ends up meaning that the very first iteration gives us 100% probability of success.

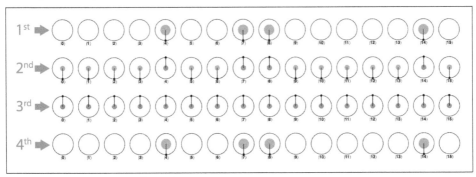

Figure 6-14. Four values flipped

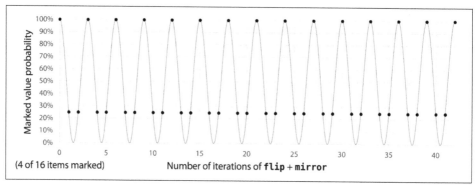

Figure 6-15. Repeated AA iterations with 4 values of 16 flipped

This trend continues for up to seven flipped values, as illustrated in Figures 6-16 and 6-17.

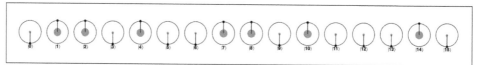

Figure 6-16. Seven values flipped

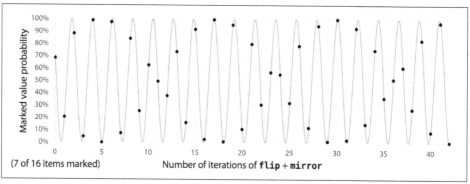

Figure 6-17. Repeated AA iterations with 7 values of 16 flipped

Of course, with 7 of our 16 values being marked, even getting a correct READ value might not provide us with much useful information.

Everything comes to a halt in Figure 6-19, where we have 8 of our 16 values flipped as shown in Figure 6-18. As has been mentioned in previous chapters, only the *relative* phase matters for quantum states. Because of this, flipping half of the values to mark them is physically the same as flipping the other half. The AA iterations fail completely here, and we're left with just as much chance of READing out any value in the register.

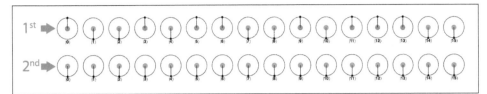

Figure 6-18. Eight values flipped

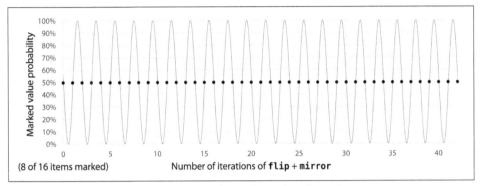

Figure 6-19. Repeated AA iterations with 8 values of 16 flipped

When 50% of the register values are marked, we could continue applying AA operations as much as we liked and we'd never do better than READing out random numbers.

 Note that by symmetry we don't really need to consider what happens if we have more than 50% of our register values phase-flipped. For example, if 12 of our 16 values are marked, attempting to read "success" is identical to what we observed when marking 4 of them, but with what we consider success and failure flipped.

Interestingly, our exploration shows that the frequency with which our chance of success oscillates depends only on the *number* of flipped values, not *which* values are flipped. In fact, we can extend Equation 6-1 to also hold for when we have multiple marked items, as shown in Equation 6-2 (where *n* is the number of qubits and *m* is the number of marked items).

Equation 6-2. Optimal number of iterations for multiple flipped phases

$$N_{AA} = \left\lfloor \frac{\pi}{4} \sqrt{\frac{2^n}{m}} \right\rfloor$$

So long as we know m, we can use this expression to decide how many AA iterations we should apply to amplify the magnitudes of the flipped values to give a high probability of success. This raises an interesting point: if we *don't* know how many states are flipped, then how can we know how many AA iterations to apply to maximize our chance of success? When we come to employ amplitude amplification to applications in Chapter 10, we'll revisit this question and see how other primitives can help.

Using Amplitude Amplification

Hopefully you now have an idea of amplitude amplification's capabilities. Being able to convert unREADable phases into READable magnitudes definitely sounds useful, but how do we actually employ this? Amplitude amplification finds utility in a number of ways, but one strikingly pragmatic use is as part of a *Quantum Sum Estimation* technique.

AA and QFT as Sum Estimation

We've seen that the *frequency* with which probabilities fluctuate in these AA iteration examples depends on the number of flipped values. In the next chapter, we'll introduce the Quantum Fourier Transform (QFT)—a QPU primitive allowing us to READ out the frequency with which values vary in a quantum register.

It turns out that by combining the AA and QFT primitives, we can devise a circuit allowing us to READ not just one of our marked values, but a value corresponding to *how many marked values* in our initial register state were flipped. This is a form of Quantum Sum Estimation. We'll discuss Quantum Sum Estimation fully in Chapter 11, but mention it here to give a feeling for just how useful amplitude amplification can be.

Speeding Up Conventional Algorithms with AA

It turns out that AA can be used as a subroutine on many conventional algorithms, providing a quadratic performance speedup. The problems that AA can be applied to are those invoking a subroutine that repeatedly checks the validity of a solution. Examples of this type of problem are *boolean satisfiability* and finding *global* and *local minima*.

As we have seen, the AA primitive is formed of two parts, flip and mirror. It is in the flip part that we *encode* the equivalent to the classical subroutine that checks the validity of a solution, while the mirror part remains the same for all applications. In Chapter 14 we will cover this aspect of AA fully and learn how to encode classical subroutines in the flip part of AA.

Inside the QPU

So how do the QPU operations making up each AA iteration allow it to undertake its task? Rather than worry about the functioning of every individual operation, we'll try to build an intuitive understanding of an AA iteration's effect. It turns out there's a useful way of understanding amplitude amplification in terms of its geometrical effect on a QPU register's circle notation.

The Intuition

There are two stages to amplitude amplification: flip and mirror. The flip subroutine flips the phase of a marked term in the superposition that we ultimately want to extract from our QPU.

The mirror subroutine, which remains unchanged throughout the AA primitive, turns phase differences into contrasts in magnitude. But another way to understand mirror is that it causes each value in a state to *mirror about the average* of all values.

As well as explaining why we call this subroutine mirror, this alternative interpretation also helps us give a more precise step-by-step account of what mirror achieves.

Suppose we have a two-qubit input state to the mirror subroutine, which is in a superposition of $|0\rangle$ and $|3\rangle$ as shown in Figure 6-20.

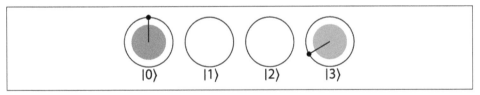

Figure 6-20. Starting state

In terms of circle notation, the mirror subroutine performs the following steps:

1. Find the *average* of all the values (circles). This can be done by numerically averaging the x and y positions of the points within the circles.[2] When calculating the average, the zero values (empty circles) should be included as [0.0, 0.0], as shown in Figures 6-21 and 6-22.

---

2 In terms of the full-blown mathematical description of a QPU register state as a complex vector, this corresponds to averaging the real and imaginary parts of its components.

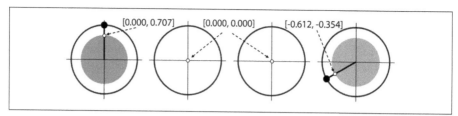

Figure 6-21. Calculating the average

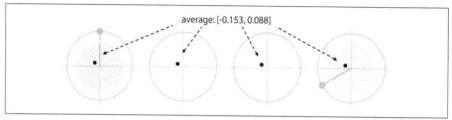

Figure 6-22. Plotting the average

2. Flip each value about the common average. Visually, this is simply a reflection, as shown in Figure 6-23.

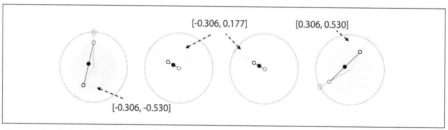

Figure 6-23. Flipping about the average

That's all there is to it. The result, as shown in Figure 6-24, is that the phase differences in our original state have been converted into magnitude differences. It's worth noting that the common average of the circles is still the same. This means that applying the transform again will simply return the initial state.

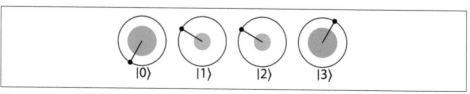

Figure 6-24. The resulting state

How is it that this "mirror about the average" operation ends up converting phase and magnitude differences? Imagine that there are many states with similar phases, but one oddball state with a very different phase, as shown in Figure 6-25.

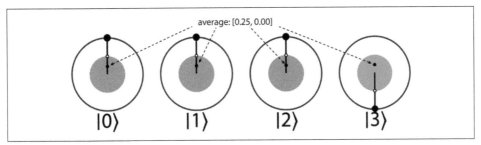

Figure 6-25. State with one oddball phase

Given that most values are the same, the average will lie closer to the value of most of the states, and very far from the state that has the opposite phase. This means that when we mirror about the average, the value with the different phase will "slingshot" over the average and stand out from the rest, as shown in Figure 6-26.

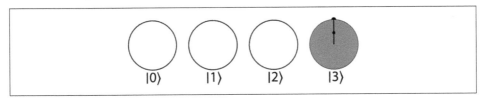

Figure 6-26. Final state

For most applications of AA that we discuss in Chapter 10, the replacements for `flip` will introduce a phase difference of 180° between the marked and unmarked states, so the preceding "slingshotting" example is particularly relevant.

 In practice, it's actually simpler to implement *mirror about the average + flip all phases* rather than simply *mirror about the average*. Since only the *relative* phases in a register are actually important, this is entirely equivalent.

Conclusion

This chapter introduced one of the core operations in many QPU applications. By converting phase differences into magnitude differences, amplitude amplification allows a QPU program to provide useful output relating to phase information from a state that would otherwise remain invisible. We explore the full power of this primitive in Chapters 11 and 14.

CHAPTER 7

QFT: Quantum Fourier Transform

The *Quantum Fourier Transform* (QFT) is a primitive allowing us to access hidden patterns and information stored inside a QPU register's relative phases and magnitudes. While amplitude amplification allowed us to turn relative-phase differences into READable differences in magnitudes, we'll see that the QFT primitive has its own distinct way of manipulating phases. In addition to performing *phase manipulation*, we'll also see that the QFT primitive can help us *compute in superposition* by easily preparing complex superpositions of a register. This chapter begins with some straightforward QFT examples, and then dives into subtler aspects of the tool. For the curious, "Inside the QPU" on page 146 will examine the QFT operation by operation.

Hidden Patterns

Let's make our state guessing game from Chapter 6 a little harder. Suppose we have a four-qubit quantum register containing one of the three states (A, B, or C) shown in Figure 7-1, but we don't know which one.

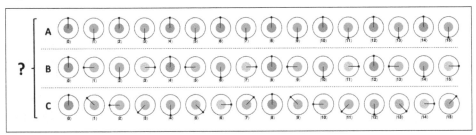

Figure 7-1. Three different states, before applying QFT

Note that these are *not* the same A, B, and C states that we discussed in the previous chapter.

Visually we can tell that these states are different from each other, but since the magnitudes of all values in each of these states are the same, reading the register returns an evenly distributed random value, regardless of which state it was actually in.

Even amplitude amplification isn't much help to us here, since no single phase stands out as being different in each state. But the QFT primitive comes to the rescue! (Cue dramatic music.) Applying the QFT to our register before readout would transform each of the states A, B, and C into the results shown in Figure 7-2.

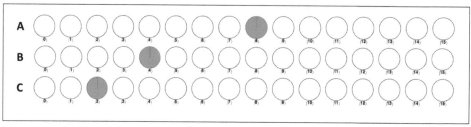

Figure 7-2. The same three states, after applying QFT

Reading the register now lets us immediately and unambiguously determine which state we started with, using only a single set of READs. These QFT results have an intriguing relationship to the input states from Figure 7-1. In state A, the relative phase of the input state returns to 0 eight times, and the QFT allows us to READ the value 8. In state B the relative phase rotates back to its starting value four times, and the QFT allows us to READ 4. State C continues the trend. In each case, the QFT has actually revealed a *signal frequency* contained in our QPU register.

The sample code in Example 7-1 allows you to generate the states A, B, and C to experiment with yourself. By altering the value of which_signal you can select which state to prepare.

Sample Code

Run this sample online at *http://oreilly-qc.github.io?p=7-1*.

Example 7-1. Using QFT to distinguish between three states

```
var num_qubits = 4;
qc.reset(num_qubits);
var signal = qint.new(num_qubits, 'signal')
var which_signal = 'A';

// prepare the signal
signal.write(0);
signal.hadamard();
if (which_signal == 'A') {
    signal.phase(180, 1);
```

```
    } else if (which_signal == 'B') {
        signal.phase(90, 1);
        signal.phase(180, 2);
    } else if (which_signal == 'C') {
        signal.phase(45, 1);
        signal.phase(90, 2);
        signal.phase(180, 4);
    }

    signal.QFT()
```

 If you want to apply the QFT primitive to the states produced by Example 7-1 you can do so in QCEngine using the built-in QFT() function. This can either be implemented using the global method qc.QFT(), which takes a set of qubits as an argument, or as a method of a qint object—qint.QFT()—which performs the QFT on all qubits in the qint.

The QFT, DFT, and FFT

Understanding the QFT's ability to reveal signal frequencies is best achieved by examining its very strong similarity to a classic signal-processing mechanism called the *Discrete Fourier Transform* (DFT). If you've ever fiddled with the graphical equalizer on a sound system, you'll be familiar with the idea of the DFT—like the QFT, it allows us to inspect the different *frequencies* contained within a signal. While the DFT is used to inspect more conventional signals, under the hood the transformation it applies is essentially identical to the QFT's mathematical machinery. It's easier to build intuition with the more tangible DFT, so we'll familiarize ourselves with its core concepts as we move through the chapter.

A widely used fast implementation of the DFT is the *Fast Fourier Transform* (FFT). The FFT is the fastest known method for determining Discrete Fourier Transforms, so we'll generally use the FFT as the point of comparison when talking about our quantum variant. The FFT also conveniently shares a similarity with the QFT in that it is restricted to power-of-two signal lengths.

Since there'll be a lot of *-FT* acronyms floating around, here's a quick glossary:

DFT
    The conventional *Discrete Fourier Transform*. Allows us to extract frequency information from conventional signals.

FFT

The *Fast Fourier Transform*. A specific algorithm for implementing the DFT. Performs precisely the same transformation as the DFT, but is significantly faster in practice. The one to beat for our QFT.

QFT

The *Quantum Fourier Transform*. Performs the same transformation as the DFT, only it operates on signals encoded *in quantum registers* rather than conventional streams of information.

Frequencies in a QPU Register

Thinking of the magnitudes and relative phases in quantum registers as signals is a very powerful idea, but one that warrants some clarification. Given the idiosyncrasies of the QPU, let's be a little more explicit about what it means for a quantum register to contain frequencies at all. Suppose that we have the four-qubit register state shown in Figure 7-3.

Figure 7-3. Example QFT input state

This is state C from our previous example. Notice that if we look along the register from left to right, the relative phases of the $2^4 = 16$ values go through two full anti-clockwise rotations. Thus, we can think of the relative phases in our register as representing a *signal* that repeats with a frequency of *twice per register*.

That gives us an idea of how a quantum register might encode a signal having some frequency associated with it—but since that signal is tied up in the relative phases of our qubits, we know only too well that we won't be able to extract it by simply reading the register. As with the example at the beginning of this chapter, the information is *hidden* in the phases, but can be revealed by applying the QFT (see Figure 7-4).

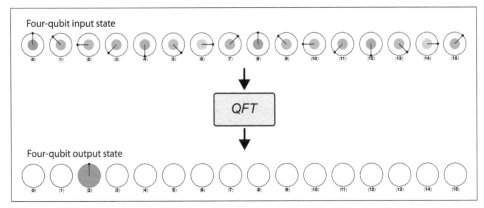

Figure 7-4. QFT example 2

In this simple case, reading out our register after the QFT allows us to determine that the frequency of repetition it contained was 2 (i.e., the relative phase makes two rotations per register). This is the key idea of the QFT, and we'll learn next to more accurately use and interpret it. To reproduce this, see Example 7-2, shown in Figure 7-5.

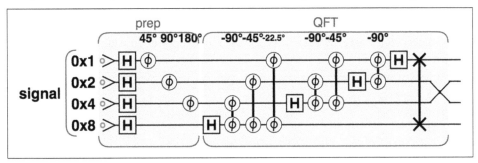

Figure 7-5. QFT of simple QPU register signal

Sample Code

Run this sample online at *http://oreilly-qc.github.io?p=7-2*.

Example 7-2. QFT of simple QPU register signal

```
var num_qubits = 4;
qc.reset(num_qubits);
var signal = qint.new(num_qubits, 'signal')

// prepare the signal
signal.write(0);
signal.hadamard();
signal.phase(45, 1);
signal.phase(90, 2);
```

```
signal.phase(180, 4);

// Run the QFT
signal.QFT()
```

 Example 7-2 demonstrates an important property of the QFT. Although we saw in Chapter 5 that operations implemented on a QPU often need to use distinct input and output registers (for reversibility), the QFT's output occurs on the same register that provided its input—hence the suffix *transform*. The QFT can operate *in-place* because it is an inherently reversible circuit.

You may be wondering why we care about a tool that helps us find frequencies in a QPU register. How can this help us solve practical problems? Surprisingly, the QFT turns out to be a versatile tool in QPU programming, and we'll give some specific examples toward the end of the chapter.

So, is that all there is to the QFT? Pop in a register, get back its frequency? Well, yes and no. So far the signals we've looked at have, after applying the QFT, given us a single well-defined frequency (because we cherry-picked them). But many other periodic signals don't give us such nice QFTs. For example, consider the four signals shown in Figure 7-6.

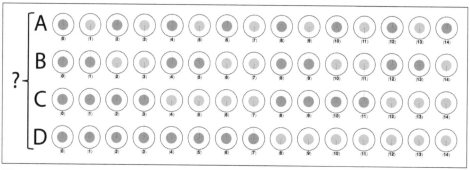

Figure 7-6. Four square-wave signals before applying QFT

 A value in a QPU register's state having a phase of 180° (shown in circle notation as a south-pointing line) is equivalent to its amplitude having a negative value.

These are the square-wave equivalents of the examples we first considered in Figure 7-1. Though oscillating at the same frequency as these previous examples, their relative phases abruptly flip-flop between two positive and negative values, rather than varying continuously. Consequently, their QFTs are a little harder to interpret, as you can see in Figure 7-7.

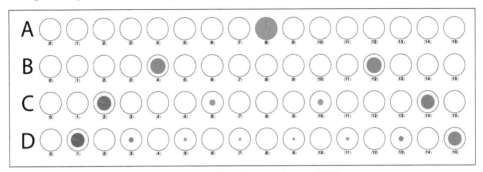

Figure 7-7. The same square-wave signals, after applying QFT

Note that we can produce the square-wave input states shown in these examples using HAD and carefully chosen PHASE QPU operations. The sample code in Example 7-3, shown in Figure 7-8, generates these square-wave states and then applies the QFT. Changing the wave_period variable allows us to select which state from Figure 7-6 we want to produce.

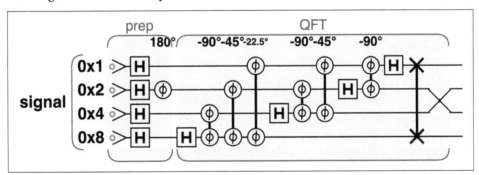

Figure 7-8. The quantum operations used by the QFT

<hr>

Sample Code

Run this sample online at *http://oreilly-qc.github.io?p=7-3*.

Example 7-3. Square-wave QFT

```
var num_qubits = 4;
qc.reset(num_qubits);
var signal = qint.new(num_qubits, 'signal')
var wave_period = 2; // A:1 B:2 C:4 D:8

// prepare the signal
signal.write(0);
```

```
signal.hadamard();
signal.phase(180, wave_period);

signal.QFT()
```

If you're familiar with the conventional DFT, the results in Figure 7-7 may not be quite so perplexing. Since the QFT really just applies the DFT to QPU register signals, we'll begin by recapping this more conventional cousin.

The DFT

The DFT acts on discrete samples taken from a signal, whether it be a musical waveform or a digital representation of an image. Although conventional signals are normally thought of as lists of more tangible real values, the DFT will also work on complex signal values. This is especially reassuring for us, since (although we try our best to avoid it) the full representation the state of a QPU register is most generally described by a list of complex numbers.

 We've used circle notation to intuitively visualize the mathematics of complex numbers wherever we can. Whenever you see "complex number," you can always think of a single circle from our notation, with a magnitude (size of circle) and phase (rotation of circle).

Let's try out the conventional DFT on a simple sine-wave signal, one for which the samples are real numbers and there is one well-defined frequency (if we were dealing with a sound signal, this would be a pure tone). Furthermore, let's suppose that we have taken 256 samples of the signal. Each sample is stored as a complex floating-point number (with magnitude and phase, just like our circle notation). In our particular example the imaginary part will be zero for all samples. Such an example signal is shown in Figure 7-9.

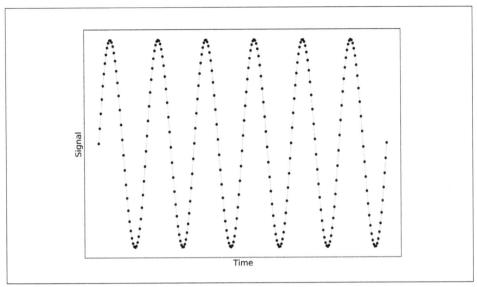

Figure 7-9. Sampling 256 points from a simple sine wave

If each sample is stored as a 16-byte complex float (8 bytes for real, and 8 for imaginary), then this signal will fit in a 4,096-byte buffer. Note that we still need to keep track of the imaginary parts of our samples (even though in this example we used only real input values), since the *output* of the DFT will be 256 complex values.

The *magnitudes* of the complex output values from the DFT tell us how significantly a given frequency contributes to making up our signal. The *phase* parts tell us how much these different frequencies are *offset* from each other in the input signal. Figure 7-10 shows what the magnitudes of the DFT look like for our simple real sine-wave signal.

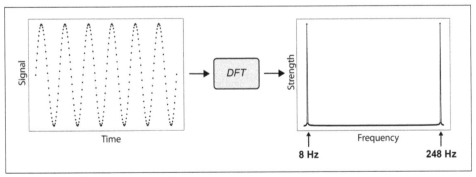

Figure 7-10. The DFT of a simple, single-frequency sine wave

Looking carefully around the base of the two peaks in Figure 7-10, you'll notice that they are surrounded by small nonzero values. Since the DFT output is limited to a finite number of bits, we can see peaks of nonzero width, even in cases where a signal truly contains only a single frequency. It's worth being aware that the same can be true for the QFT.

The DFT has transformed the signal into *frequency space*, where we can see all the frequency components present inside a signal. Since the input signal completes eight full oscillations within the sample time (1s), we expect it to have a frequency of 8 Hz, and this is precisely what the DFT returns to us in the output register.

Real and Complex DFT Inputs

Looking at our example DFT output, you may notice the 248 Hz elephant in the room. Alongside the expected 8 Hz frequency, the DFT also produces a conspicuous second *mirror-image* peak in frequency space.

This is a property of the DFT of any real signal (one where the samples are all real numbers, as is the case for most conventional signals). In such cases, only the first half of the DFT result is actually useful. So in our example, we should only take note of the first 256/2 = 128 points that the DFT returns. Everything else in the DFT after that point will be the mirror image of the first half (which is why we see the second peak symmetrically at 256 – 8 = 248 Hz). Figure 7-11 shows a few more examples of the DFTs of real signals, further highlighting this symmetry.

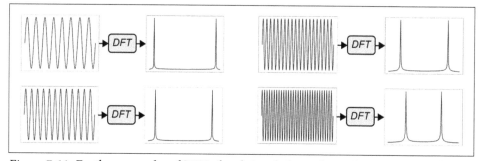

Figure 7-11. Further examples of DFT of real signals (actual sample points omitted for clarity)

Had we used a *complex* input signal, we wouldn't see this symmetry effect, and each of the 256 data points in the DFT's output would contain distinct information.

The same caveat on interpreting the output of real versus complex input signals also holds true for the QFT. Looking back at the QFT examples we first gave in Figures 7-2 and 7-4, you'll notice that there was no such symmetry effect—we only observed a single "peak" in the output registers corresponding to precisely the frequency of the input. This is because the signal, being encoded in the relative phases of our input register's states, was complex, so no symmetrical redundancy was seen.

It is nevertheless possible to prepare entirely real signals in our QFT register. Suppose that the signal we planned to QFT was encoded in the magnitudes of our input QPU register, instead of the relative phases, as shown in Figure 7-12.[1]

Figure 7-12. Quantum register with signal encoded in terms of magnitudes

This input signal is entirely real. Don't be fooled by the fact that the relative phases change across the state—recall that a phase of 180° is the same as a negative sign, so all we ever have are real positive and negative numbers.

Applying the QFT to this *real* input state we find that the output register exhibits precisely the mirror-image effect that we saw with the conventional DFT (see Figure 7-13).

Figure 7-13. Output register after QFT for signal encoded in magnitudes only

Consequently, we need to take care of how we interpret QFT results dependent on whether our input register is encoding information in phases or magnitudes.

DFT Everything

So far we've vaguely talked about the DFT (and QFT) showing us what frequencies a signal contains. To be slightly more specific, these transforms are actually telling us the frequencies, proportions, and offsets of simple *sinusoidal* components that we could combine to produce the input signal.

Most of the example input signals we considered have actually been simple sinusoids themselves, with single well-defined frequencies. As a consequence, our DFTs and QFTs have yielded single well-defined peaks in frequency space (effectively saying, "You can build that from just one sine function having a certain frequency!"). One of the most useful things about the DFT is that we can apply it to much more complex signals that aren't obviously sinusoidal. Figure 7-14 shows the magnitudes from a

---

1 We will shortly show a QPU circuit that allows us to produce a register having such magnitude-encoded oscillatory signals.

conventional DFT performed on an input signal containing sinusoidal oscillations at three different frequencies.

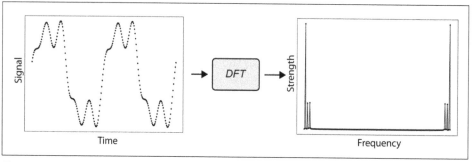

Figure 7-14. DFT on a signal consisting of a mixture of frequencies

 It's always worth taking note of the value of a DFT (or QFT) corresponding to *zero* frequency. This is sometimes known as the *DC bias*, and it reveals the baseline value that the signal oscillates above and below. Since our examples have all oscillated about zero, they've had no DC bias component in their DFTs.

Not only does this DFT show us that three sinusoidal frequencies make up our signal, but the relative heights of the peaks in frequency space also tell us how significantly each frequency contributes to the signal (by inspecting the phase of the fully complex values returned by the DFT we could also learn how the sinusoids should be offset from each other). Don't forget, of course, that since our input signal here is real, we can ignore the second (mirror-image) half of the DFT.

One particularly common and useful class of input signals that don't look at all sinusoidal are square waves. We actually saw the QFT of a few square waves already, in Figure 7-7. In Figure 7-15 we show what the magnitudes look like for the conventional DFT of a square wave.

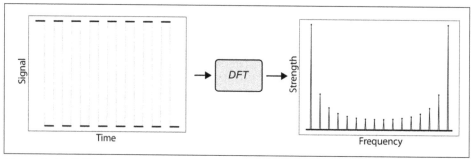

Figure 7-15. DFT of a square wave

Although Figure 7-7 already showed us the QFTs of a set of square waves, let's walk through an example more carefully. To make things a bit more interesting, we consider an eight-qubit register (i.e., a qubyte), giving us 256 state values to play with. The sample code in Example 7-4, shown in Figure 7-16, prepares a square wave repeating eight times—the QPU register equivalent to the signal shown in Figure 7-15.

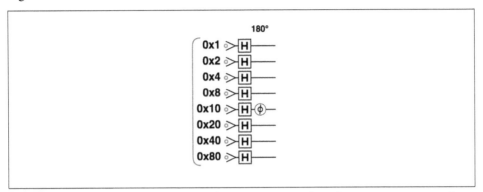

Figure 7-16. The quantum gates needed to prepare an eight-qubit square-wave signal

---

Sample Code

Run this sample online at *http://oreilly-qc.github.io?p=7-4.*

Example 7-4. Square-wave QFT circuit

```
// Setup
qc.reset(8);

// Create equal superposition
qc.write(0);
qc.had();

// Introduce a negative sign with a certain frequency
// (By placing the phase on different qubits we can alter
// the frequency of the square wave)
qc.phase(180, 16);

// Apply the QFT
qc.QFT();
```

The code just before the QFT leaves our QPU input register in the state shown in Figure 7-17.

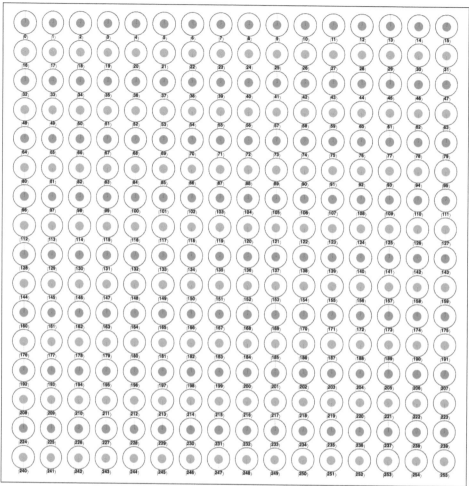

Figure 7-17. Square-wave signal in a qubyte

Recalling that the green circles (with a relative phase of 180°) represent negative signs, you should hopefully be able to convince yourself that this signal is both entirely real and completely analogous to the DFT input signal shown in Figure 7-15.

Applying the QFT to a register in this state (by calling `qc.QFT()` in QCEngine), we obtain the output state shown in Figure 7-18.

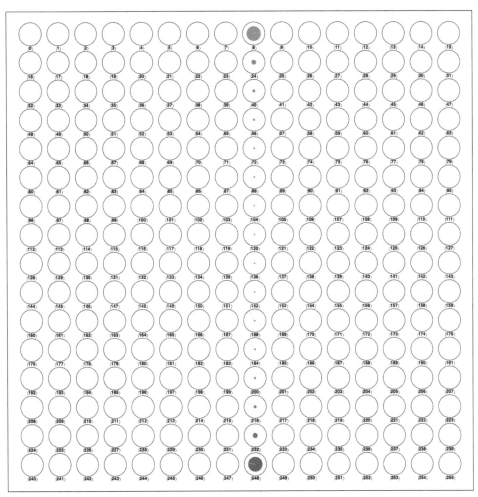

Figure 7-18. QFT output from a square-wave input

This register is precisely the square-wave DFT from Figure 7-15, with each component in frequency space being encoded in the magnitudes and relative phases of the states of our QPU register. This means that the probability of reading out a given configuration of the post-QFT register is now determined by how strongly a given frequency contributes to our signal.

Plotting these probabilities in Figure 7-19, we can see the similarity to the conventional DFT results previously obtained for a square wave in Figure 7-15.

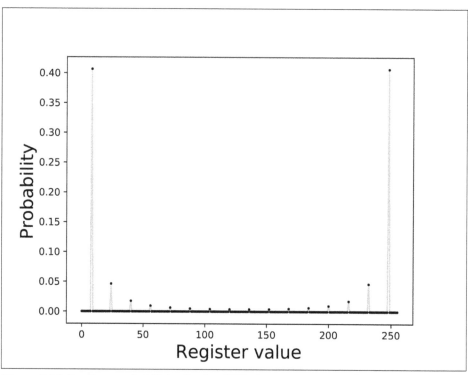

Figure 7-19. Readout probabilities for the QFT of a square-wave qubyte input

Using the QFT

We've gone to some lengths to show that we can think of the QFT as faithfully implementing the DFT on QPU register signals. Given how finicky and expensive a QPU is, this sounds like a lot of trouble just to reproduce a conventional algorithm. It's important to remember that our motivation for using the QFT primitive is primarily to manipulate phase-encoded computation results, rather than to provide a full-blown FFT replacement.

That said, we'd be remiss if we didn't evaluate how the computational complexity of the QFT compares to the FFT—especially since the QFT turns out to be far, *far* faster than the best conventional counterpart.

The QFT Is Fast

When talking about the speed of FFT and QFT algorithms, the figure we're interested in is how the runtime of the algorithm increases as we increase the size of our input signal (in terms of the total number of bits needed to represent it). For all practical purposes, we can think of the number of fundamental operations that an algorithm uses as being equivalent to the time it takes to run, since each operation takes a fixed time to act on a QPU's qubits.

The FFT requires a number of operations that grows with the number of input bits n as $O(n2^n)$. The QFT, however—by leveraging the 2^m states available in an m-qubit register—uses a number of gates that grows only as $O(m^2)$.

Pragmatically, this means that for small signals (less than 22 bits, or about 4 million samples) the conventional FFT will be faster, even using just a laptop. But as the size of the input problem grows, the exponential advantage of the QFT becomes clear. Figure 7-20 shows how the two methods compare as the signal size increases. Note that the x-axis refers to the number of bits (in the case of the FFT) or qubits (for the QFT) making up the input register.

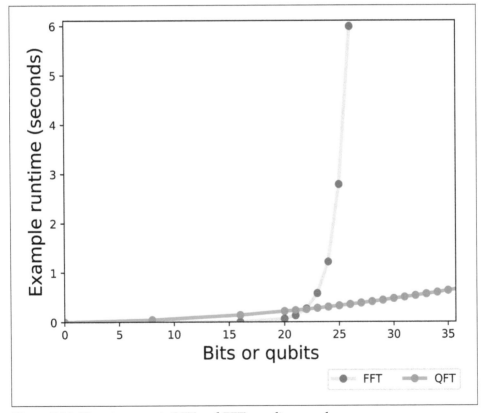

Figure 7-20. Time to compute QFT and FFT on a linear scale

Signal processing with the QFT

Given the importance of the FFT to the wide-ranging field of signal processing, it's very tempting to think that the main use of the QFT is surely to provide an exponentially faster implementation of this signal-processing tool. But whereas the output of the DFT is an array of digital values that we can study at our leisure, the output of the QFT is locked in our QPU's output register.

Let's be a little more methodical in stating the limitations we face anytime we try to make practical use of output from the QFT. Having our input signal and its QFT output encoded in the amplitudes of a quantum state introduces two challenges:

1. How do we get our signal into an input quantum register in the first place?
2. How do we access the result of the QFT when we're done?

The first problem—getting an input signal into a quantum register—is not always easy to solve. The square-wave example we studied in Figure 7-18 could be generated with a fairly simple quantum program, but if we intend to input arbitrary conventional data into a quantum register, such a simple circuit may not exist. For some signals, the cost of initializing the input register may wipe out the QFT's benefit.

 There are techniques for preparing certain kinds of superpositions in a QPU register more easily, although often these require additions to standard QPU hardware. In Chapter 9 we present one such technique.

The second problem we listed is, of course, the fundamental challenge of QPU programming—how do we READ out an answer from our register? For simple single-frequency QFTs like those we saw in Figure 7-2, reading out the register gives an unambiguous answer. But the QFT of more complex signals (such as those in Figure 7-18) produces a superposition of frequency values. When READing this out we only randomly obtain one of the present frequencies.

However, the final state after a QFT can still be useful to us under certain circumstances. Consider the output from the square-wave signal input in Figure 7-17:

1. If an application (the one calling the QFT) is okay with randomly getting an answer that is "the dominant frequency or a multiple of it," we're all set. There are eight correct answers in our square-wave example, and we'll always get one of them.
2. If an application can verify a desired answer, we can quickly detect whether a random outcome from a READing the QFT output state is suitable. If not, we can run the QFT again.

In these ways, the signal-processing capabilities of the QFT can still offer a valuable phase manipulation primitive; in fact, we'll see it play just such a role in Shor's factoring algorithm in Chapter 12.

Preparing superpositions with the inverse QFT

So far we've thought of the QFT as a *phase manipulation* primitive. Another use of the QFT is to prepare (or alter) periodically varying superpositions in ways that would otherwise be very difficult. Like all non-READ QPU operations, the QFT has an *inverse*. The inverse QFT (invQFT) takes as its input a qubit register representing frequency space, and returns as output a register showing the signal that this corresponds to.

We can use the invQFT to easily prepare periodically varying register superpositions as follows:

1. Prepare a quantum register representing the state you need in frequency space. This is often easier than preparing the state directly with a more complicated circuit.

2. Apply the invQFT to return the required signal in the QPU output's register.

Example 7-5, shown in Figure 7-21, shows how we can create a qubyte register with a relative phase oscillating three times across the register.

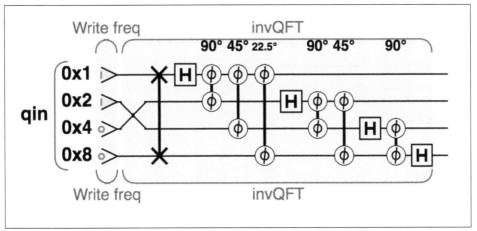

Figure 7-21. The quantum operations needed to produce a signal having periodically varying phase

---

Sample Code

Run this sample online at *http://oreilly-qc.github.io?p=7-5*.

Example 7-5. Converting frequency into state

```
// Setup
var num_qubits = 4;
qc.reset(num_qubits);
```

```
var qin = qint.new(num_qubits, 'qin');

// Write the frequency we want to register
qin.write(3);

// Inverse QFT to turn into a signal
qin.invQFT()
```

The invQFT can also be used to prepare a QPU register that varies periodically in magnitude rather than relative phase, like the example we saw in Figure 7-12. To do this we need only recall that a register with periodically varying magnitudes is a real signal, and so in frequency space we need a symmetric representation for the invQFT to act on. This is demonstrated in Example 7-6, and shown in Figure 7-22.

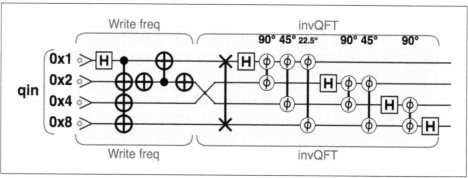

Figure 7-22. The quantum operations needed to produce a signal having periodically varying magnitude

Example 7-6. Prepare a state with invQFT

```
// Setup
var num_qubits = 4;
qc.reset(num_qubits);
var qin = qint.new(num_qubits, 'qin');
qin.write(0);

// Write the frequencies we want to register
qin.had(1);
qc.cnot(14,1);
qin.not(2);
qc.cnot(1,2);
qin.not(2);
```

```
//Inverse QFT to turn into a signal
qin.invQFT()
```

As well as preparing states with given frequencies, the invQFT also allows us to easily *alter* their frequency information. Suppose that at some point during an algorithm we want to increase the frequency with which the relative phases oscillate in our QPU register. We can take the following steps:

1. Apply the QFT to the register, so that we now have the signal represented in frequency space.

2. Add 1 to the value now stored in the register. Since our input signal is complex, this will increase the value of each frequency component.

3. Apply the invQFT to get back our original signal, only now with increased frequencies.

The sample code in Example 7-7, shown in Figure 7-23, provides a simple example of doing this.

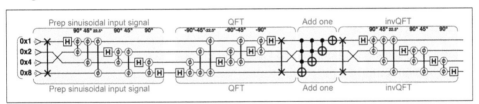

Figure 7-23. Simple example of using the QFT and inverse QFT to manipulate the frequency of a signal

---

Sample Code

Run this sample online at *http://oreilly-qc.github.io?p=7-7*.

Example 7-7. QFT frequency manipulation

```
// Set up input register
var n = 4;

// Prepare a complex sinusoidal signal
qc.reset(n);
var freq = 2;
qc.write(freq);
var signal = qint.new(n, 'signal');
signal.invQFT();

// Move to frequency space with QFT
signal.QFT();
```

```
// Increase the frequency of signal
signal.add(1)

// Move back from frequency space
signal.invQFT();
```

Moving to frequency space can allow us to perform otherwise tricky manipulations on a state, but there are cases where we need to take care. For example, *real* input signals are harder to manipulate.

If the QPU register contains a state representing a single frequency, or a superposition of frequencies that is not symmetric, after the application of the invQFT we will have a QPU register that varies periodically in *relative phase*. If, on the other hand, prior to the application of the invQFT, the register contains a symmetric superposition of frequencies, the output QPU register will contain a state that varies periodically in *magnitude*.

Inside the QPU

Figure 7-24 shows the fundamental QPU operations used for performing the QFT on a qubyte signal.

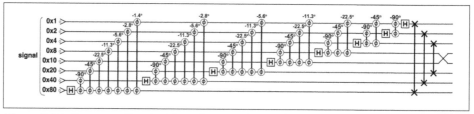

Figure 7-24. Quantum Fourier Transform, operation by operation

Our challenge is to understand how the arrangement of simple QPU operations in Figure 7-24 can extract the frequency components from a signal in the input register.

Explaining the QFT would require thinking about how this circuit acts on an input state looking something like Figure 7-6, where phases vary periodically across the register. This is quite a mind-bending task. We'll take a handily simpler approach and try to explain how the *inverse* QFT works. If we can understand the invQFT, the QFT is simply the reverse.

In the simple case of a four-qubit input, the invQFT has the decomposition shown in Figure 7-25.

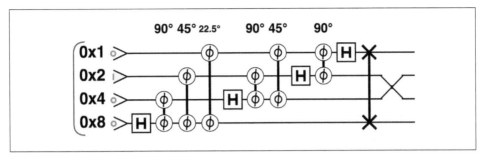

Figure 7-25. Four-qubit inverse QFT

Although this looks very similar to the QFT circuit, crucially the phases are different. Figure 7-26 shows what we get if we apply the preceding circuit to a register containing the value 2.

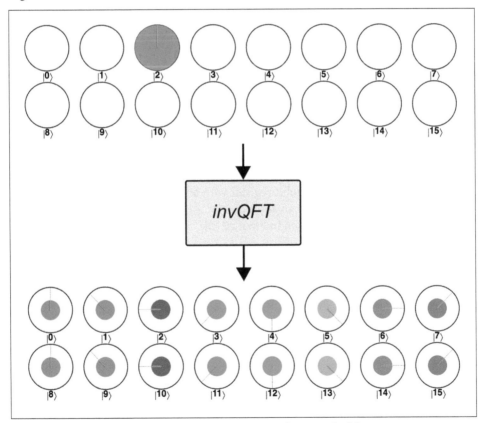

Figure 7-26. The inverse QFT prepares a register with a specified frequency

There's more than one way that the circuits for the QFT and invQFT can be written. We've chosen forms here that are especially convenient for helping us explain the circuit's action. If you see slightly different circuits for these primitives, it's worth checking if they are equivalent.

The Intuition

Suppose we provide the invQFT with an N-qubit input register encoding some integer n. As we imagine scanning along the output register's 2^N values, we need each consecutive value's relative phase to rotate enough to perform a full 360° every $2^N/n$ circles. This means that to produce our desired output state we need each consecutive circle to have its relative phase rotated by an additional $360° \times n/2^N$, as shown in Figure 7-27.

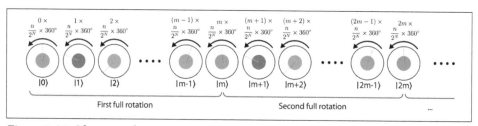

Figure 7-27. Obtaining the inverse QFT output by incrementally rotating the phase of each amplitude in the register

Perhaps this is easier to see in the case of the specific example from Figure 7-26. In this case, since we have a four-qubit register with an input value of 2, we will want to rotate each consecutive value by an angle of $360° \times n/2^N = 360° \times 2/2^4 = 45°$ to get our desired output state. This is shown in Figure 7-28.

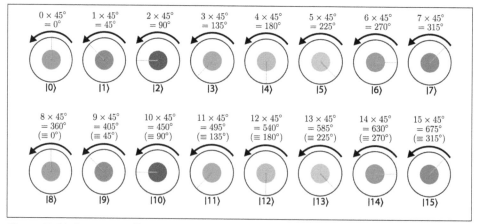

Figure 7-28. Incrementally rotating to get QFT output—a specific example

We see that rotating by this simple rule gets us precisely the required periodicity in the register's relative phases (noting of course that $360° \equiv 0°$, $405° \equiv 45°$, etc.).

Operation by Operation

The invQFT circuit in Figure 7-25 is just a cleverly compact way of implementing this conditional rotation rule. To help see this, we can split the tasks that the circuit in Figure 7-25 must perform into two separate requirements:

1. Determine the value $\theta = n/2 \times 360°$ (where n is the value initially stored in the register).
2. Rotate the phase of each circle in the register by a multiple of the angle θ found in the previous step, *where the multiple is the circle's decimal value.*

The invQFT actually performs both of these steps at once in an ingeniously compact way. However, we'll tease apart how it performs each individual step to see its operation more clearly. Although it might seem a little backward, it will actually be easiest to start with the second step. How can we apply a PHASE where the rotation angle for each value in the register is a multiple of that value?

Rotating each circle's phase by a multiple of its value

When expressing an integer in our QPU register, the 0/1 value of the kth qubit indicates whether there is a contribution of 2^k to the integer's value—just like in a normal binary register. So to perform any given operation on the register *the number of times that is represented in the register*, we need to perform the operation once on the qubit with a weighting of 2^0, twice on the qubit with a weighting of 2^1, and so on.

We can see how this works with an example. Suppose we wanted to perform k lots of $20°$ rotations on a register, where k is the value stored in the register. We could do so as shown in Figure 7-29.

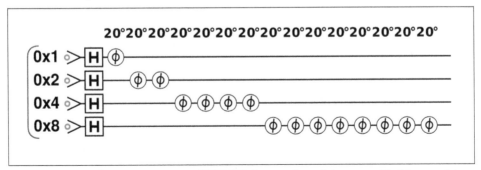

Figure 7-29. Applying an operation (PHASE) the number of times specified in a register

Note that we've performed HAD operations at the start as well, just so that we obtain the result on every possible value of k in superposition. Example 7-8 contains the code we used to generate this circuit.

Example 7-8. QFT rotating phases by different amounts

```
// Rotate kth state in register by k times 20 degrees
var phi = 20;

// Let's consider a 4-qubit register
qc.reset(4);
// First HAD so that we can see the result for all k values at once
qc.write(0);
qc.had();
// Apply 2^k phase operations to kth qubit
for (var i=0; i<4; i++) {
    var val = 1<<i;
    for (var j=0; j<val; j++) {
      qc.phase(phi, val);
    }
}
```

Running Example 7-8, we obtain the kth state rotated by $k \times 20°$, as shown in Figure 7-30. Precisely what we wanted!

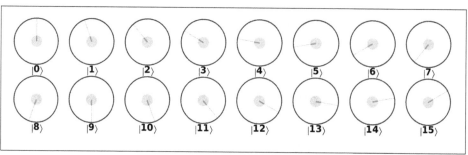

Figure 7-30. Result of applying a number of operations to each qubit given by the qubit's binary weighting

To implement the invQFT we need to perform this trick with the angle we use being $n/2^N \times 360°$ rather than 20° (where n is the initial value in the register).

Conditionally rotating by the angle n/2ᴺ × 360°

Referring back to Figure 7-25, we see that the invQFT consists of four subroutines, shown in Figure 7-31.

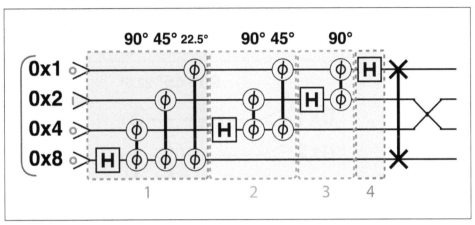

Figure 7-31. The four subroutines of invQFT

Each of these subroutines performs precisely the multiple rotations of increasing weighting that we described in Figure 7-28. The question is, what angle is it that these subcircuits are rotating multiples of? We'll now see that, in fact, the first subcircuit rotates the highest-weight qubit by $n/2^N \times 360°$ while the second rotates the next-highest-weight qubit by 2^1 times this value, and so on, as shown in Figure 7-32—precisely as prescribed by Figure 7-28.

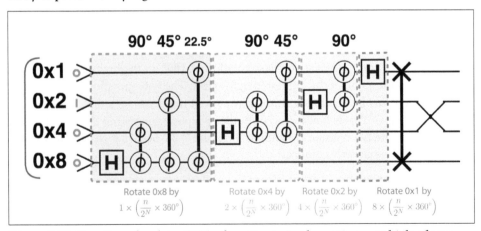

Figure 7-32. Function of each invQFT subroutine in implementing a multiple of rotations specified by input register

If you're following carefully you'll notice that this actually applies the rotations that Figure 7-28 specifies in the reverse order—but we'll see how to simply deal with this problem shortly.

Consider the first subcircuit from Figure 7-32, shown in more detail in Figure 7-33. We can confirm that it performs the stated rotation of $n/2^N \times 360°$ on the highest-weight (0x8) qubit.

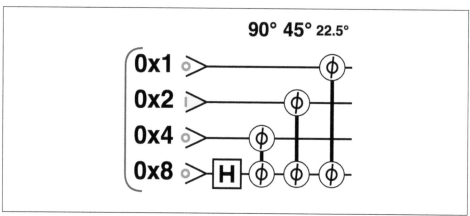

Figure 7-33. First subcircuit of inverse QFT

Each CPHASE in this subroutine conditionally rotates the 0x8 qubit by an angle that is the same proportion of 360° as the condition qubit is of 2^N. For example, the CPHASE acting between the 0x4 and 0x8 qubits in Figure 7-33 rotates the highest-weight qubit by 90°, and $4/2^4 = 90°/360°$. In this way we are building up the rotation $n/2^N \times 360°$ on the 0x8 qubit through each component of its binary expansion.

But what about the highest-weight qubit? This binary expansion should also require performing a conditional relative phase rotation of 180° *on* the highest-weight qubit, *dependent* on the value of the highest-weight qubit. The HAD operation in Figure 7-33 does precisely this for us (to see this, simply recall the defining action of HAD on the $|0\rangle$ and $|1\rangle$ states). This HAD also serves another purpose: generating the superposition of this qubit from the register as required in Figure 7-28. See what we meant when we said this circuit is cleverly compact?

Each subsequent subcircuit from Figure 7-32 effectively performs a *roll left*, shifting up the weight of the angle associated with each qubit (so that, for example, in sub-circuit 2, the 0x2 qubit is associated with a rotation of 90°, rather than 45°). As a result, each subcircuit multiplies the phase of $n/2^N \times 360°$ that it applies by 2 before imparting it to the particular qubit it acts on—just as required in Figure 7-32.

Taken together, this performs the conditional rotations that we need for the invQFT —but with one problem. Everything is upside-down! Subcircuit 1 rotates the 0x8 qubit by a single multiple of the phase, whereas Figure 7-28 shows we should rotate by eight times its value. This is why we need the exchanges at the very end of Figure 7-32.

How clever is that? The inverse QFT circuit performs the multiple steps needed for our desired periodically varying output, all compressed into a small multipurpose set of operations!

To simplify our preceding explanation we restricted ourselves to a single integer input to the invQFT, but the QPU operations we've used work just as well on a superposition of inputs.

Conclusion

In this chapter you have learned about one of the most powerful QPU primitives, the Quantum Fourier Transform. While the AA primitive allowed us to extract information about discrete values encoded in the phases of our register, the QFT primitive enables us to extract information about *patterns* of information encoded in the QPU register. As we will see in Chapter 12, this primitive is at the core of some of the most powerful algorithms that we can run on a QPU, including Shor's algorithm, which first kick-started mainstream interest in quantum computing.

CHAPTER 8

Quantum Phase Estimation

Quantum phase estimation (also referred to simply as phase estimation) is another QPU primitive for our toolbox. Like amplitude amplification and QFT, phase estimation extracts tangible, readable information from superpositions. Phase estimation is also quite possibly the most challenging primitive we've introduced so far, being conceptually tricky for two reasons:

1. Unlike the AA and QFT primitives, phase estimation teaches us an attribute of an *operation* acting on a QPU register, rather than an attribute of the QPU register state itself.

2. The specific attribute that phase estimation teaches us about a QPU operation, despite being hugely important in many algorithms, *appears* to be useless and arbitrary. Revealing its practical use is a challenge without resorting to some relatively advanced mathematics. But we'll give it a shot!

In this chapter we'll discuss what phase estimation is, try some hands-on examples, and then break it down operation by operation.

Learning About QPU Operations

Programming a problem that we want to solve into a QPU inevitably involves acting on some QPU register with the fundamental operations introduced in Chapters 2 and 3. The idea that we would want a primitive that teaches us something might sound strange—surely if we constructed a circuit, then we know everything there is to know about it! But some kinds of input data can be encoded in QPU operations, so learning more about them can potentially get us a long way toward finding the solutions that we're after.

For example, we will see in Chapter 13 that the HHL algorithm for inverting certain matrices encodes these matrices through judiciously chosen QPU operations. The properties of these operations, which are revealed by quantum phase estimation, teach us something critical and nontrivial about the matrix we need to invert.

Eigenphases Teach Us Something Useful

So precisely what property does phase estimation teach us about QPU operations? It's perhaps easiest to answer this question through an example. Let's take a look at our old friend HAD. Recall that when acting on a single qubit register HAD transforms $|0\rangle$ and $|1\rangle$ into entirely new states, as shown in Figure 8-1.

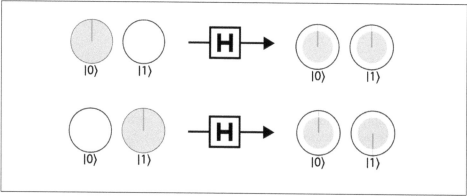

Figure 8-1. Action of HAD on $|0\rangle$ and $|1\rangle$ states

For most other input states HAD similarly produces entirely new output states. However, consider HAD's action on the two special input states shown in Figure 8-2.

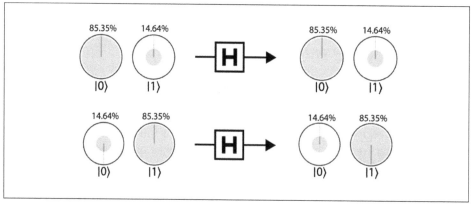

Figure 8-2. Action of HAD on eigenstates

The first input state has both its components in phase with a 14.64% chance of being READ to be in state $|1\rangle$, while the second input has its components 180° out of phase and a 14.64% chance[1] of being in state $|0\rangle$.

Take careful of note how HAD acts on these states. The first is completely unchanged, while the second only acquires a *global* phase of 180° (i.e., the *relative* phase is unchanged). We noted in Chapter 2 that global phases are unobservable, so we can equally say that HAD *effectively* leaves this second state unchanged.

States impervious to a certain QPU's operation in this way (except for global phases) are known as the operation's *eigenstates*. Every QPU operation has a distinct and unique set of such special states for which it will only impart an unimportant global phase.

Although the global phases that eigenstates can acquire are unobservable, they do teach us something revealing about the QPU operation producing them. The global phase acquired by a particular eigenstate is known as that eigenstate's *eigenphase*.

As we've just seen, HAD has two (and in fact only two) eigenstates, with associated eigenphases as shown in Table 8-1.

Table 8-1. Eigenstates and eigenphases of HAD

It's worth reiterating that the particular eigenstates (and associated eigenphases) shown in Table 8-1 are specific to HAD—other QPU operations will have entirely different eigenstates and eigenphases. In fact, the eigenstates and eigenphases of a QPU operation determine the operation entirely, in the sense that no other QPU operation has the same set.

---

[1] The actual value of this probability is $\sin^2(22.5)$.

What Phase Estimation Does

Now that we're well versed in the language of eigenstates and eigenphases, we can describe what the phase estimation primitive achieves. Phase estimation will help determine the eigenphases associated with the eigenstates of a QPU operation, returning us a superposition of all the eigenphases. This is no mean feat, since global phases are usually unobservable artifacts. The beauty of the phase estimation primitive is that it finds a way of moving information about this global phase into another register—in a form that we *can* READ.

Why would we ever *want* to determine the eigenphases of a QPU operation? We'll see in later chapters how useful this can be, but our previous note that they can uniquely characterize a QPU operation should hint that they're powerful things to know.

 For readers with experience in linear algebra: eigenstates and eigenphases are the *eigenvectors* and *complex eigenphases* of the unitary matrices representing QPU operations in the full mathematics of quantum computing.

How to Use Phase Estimation

Having an idea of what quantum phase estimation does, let's get our hands dirty and see how to utilize it in practice. Suppose we have some QPU operation U, which acts on n qubits and has some set of eigenstates, which we'll refer to as u_1, u_2, ..., u_j. Using phase estimation, we wish to learn the eigenphases associated with each of these eigenstates. Don't forget that the eigenphase associated with the jth eigenstate is always a global phase—so we can specify it by the angle θ_j through which the global phase rotates the register state. Using this notation, we can give a slightly more concise description of the task performed by phase estimation:

> Given a QPU operation U and one of its eigenstates u_j, phase estimation returns (to some precision) the corresponding eigenphase angle θ_j.

In QCEngine we can perform phase estimation using the built-in `phase_est()` function (see Example 8-2 for an implementation of this function in terms of more elementary QPU operations). To call this primitive successfully we need to understand what inputs it expects and how its output should be interpreted. These inputs and outputs are summarized in Figure 8-3.

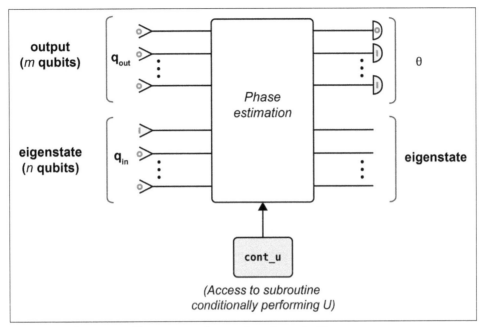

Figure 8-3. Overview of how to use phase estimation primitive

Let's take a more in-depth look at the arguments of `phase_est()`.

Inputs

Phase estimation's signature is:

```
phase_est(qin, qout, cont_u)
```

qin and qout are both QPU registers, while cont_u should be a reference to a function performing the QPU operation we're interested in (although in a particular way, as we'll see shortly):

qin

An *n*-qubit input register prepared in the eigenstate u_j that we wish to obtain the eigenphase for.

qout

A second register of *m* qubits, initialized as all zeros. The primitive will ultimately use this register to return a binary representation of the desired angle θ_j corresponding to the eigenstate we input in qin. In general, the larger we make *m*, the greater the precision with which we obtain a representation of θ_j.

cont_u

An implementation of a *controlled* version of the QPU operation *U* that we are determining the eigenphases of. This should be passed as a function of the form cont_u(in, out), which takes a single qubit in that will control whether *U* is applied to the *n*-qubit register out.

To give a concrete example of using phase estimation, we'll apply the primitive to find an eigenphase of HAD. We saw in Table 8-1 that one of HAD's eigenstates has an eigenphase of 180°—let's see whether phase_est() can reproduce this result using the sample code in Example 8-1.

Sample Code

Run this sample online at *http://oreilly-qc.github.io?p=8-1*.

Example 8-1. Using the phase estimation primitive

```
//Specify the size of output register - determines precision
// of our answer
var m = 4;
// Specify the size of input register that will specify
// our eigenstate
var n = 1;
// Setup
qc.reset(m + n);
var qout = qint.new(m, 'output');
var qin = qint.new(n, 'input');
// Initialize output register all zeros
qout.write(0);

// Initialize input register as eigenstate of HAD
qin.write(0);
qin.roty(-135);
// This state will have an eigenphase of 180.
// For eigenphase 0, we would instead use qin.roty(45);

// Define our conditional unitary
function cont_u(qcontrol, qtarget, control_count) {
    // For Hadamard, we only need to know if control_count
    // is even or odd, as applying HAD an even number of
    // times does nothing.
    if (control_count & 1)
        qtarget.chadamard(null, ~0, qcontrol.bits(control_count));
}
// Operate phase estimation primitive on registers
phase_est(qin, qout, cont_u);
// Read output register
qout.read();
```

We specify the eigenstate of interest with qin, and initialize qout as a four-qubit register of all zeros. When it comes to cont_u, it's worth emphasizing that we don't simply pass HAD, but rather a function implementing a *controlled* HAD operation. As we'll see later in this chapter, the inner workings of phase estimation explicitly require this. Since generating the *controlled* version of any given QPU operation can be non-trivial, phase_est() leaves it up to the user to specify a function achieving this. In this specific example we make use of the controlled version of HAD built into QCEngine, called chadamard().

Figure 8-4 shows an overview in circle notation of what we can expect from running Example 8-1.

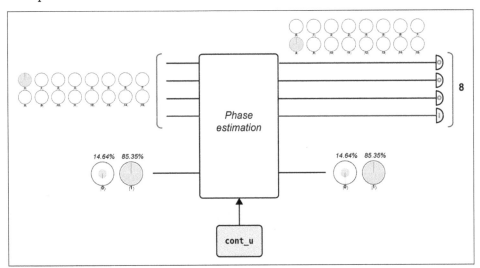

Figure 8-4. Overview of how to use phase estimation primitive

The state of the input register remains the same before and after we apply phase_est(), as expected. But what's going on with the output register? We were expecting 180° and we got 8!

Outputs

We obtain our eigenphase by applying READ operations to the m qubits of the output register. An important point to note is that the inner workings of phase estimation end up expressing θ_j as a *fraction of 360°*, which is encoded in the output register *as a fraction of its size*. In other words, if the output eigenphase was 90°, which is one quarter of a full rotation, then we would expect a three-qubit output register to yield the binary value for 2, which is also a quarter of the $2^3 = 8$ possible values of the register. For the case in Figure 8-4, we were expecting a phase of 180°, which is half of a full rotation. Therefore, in a four-qubit output register with $2^4 = 16$ values, we expect the value 8, since that is exactly half the register size. The simple formula that relates the eigenphase (θ_j) with the register value we will read out (R), as a function of the size of the register, is given by Equation 8-1.

Equation 8-1. Relationship between output register (R), eigenphase (θ_j), and size of the QPU register m

$$R = \frac{\theta_j}{360°} \times 2^m$$

The Fine Print

As is always the case with QPU programming, we should take careful note of any limitations we might face. With phase estimation, there are a few pieces of fine print to keep in mind.

Choosing the Size of the Output Register

In Example 8-1 the eigenphase we sought to reveal could be expressed perfectly in a four-qubit representation. In general, however, the precision with which we can determine an eigenphase will depend on the output register size. For example, with a three-qubit output register we can precisely represent the following angles:

Binary	000	001	010	011	100	101	110	111
Fraction of register	0	$\frac{1}{8}$	$\frac{1}{4}$	$\frac{3}{8}$	$\frac{1}{2}$	$\frac{5}{8}$	$\frac{3}{4}$	$\frac{7}{8}$
Angle	0	45	90	135	180	225	270	315

If we were attempting to use this three-qubit output register to determine an eigenphase that had a value of 150°, the register's resolution would be insufficient. Fully representing 150° would require increasing the number of qubits in the output register.

Of course, endlessly increasing the size of our output register is undesirable. In cases where an output register has insufficient resolution we find that it ends up in a superposition centered around the closest possible values. Because of this superposition, we return the best lower-resolution estimate of our phase only with some probability. For example, Figure 8-5 shows the actual output state we obtain when running phase estimation to determine an eigenphase of 150° with an output register having only three qubits. This complete example can be run online at *http://oreilly-qc.github.io? p=8-2*.

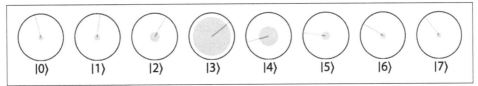

Figure 8-5. Estimating phases beyond the resolution of the output register

The probability of obtaining the best estimate is always greater than about 40%, and we can of course improve this probability by increasing the output register size.

If we want to determine the eigenphase to p bits of accuracy, and we want a probability of error (i.e., not receiving the best possible estimate) of no more than ϵ, then we can calculate the size of output register that we should employ, m, as:

$$m = p + \left\lceil \log \left(2 + \frac{1}{\epsilon} \right) \right\rceil$$

Complexity

The complexity of the phase estimation primitive (in terms of number of operations needed) depends on the number of qubits, m, that we use in our output register, and is given by $O(m^2)$. Clearly, the more precision we require, the more QPU operations are needed. We'll see in "Inside the QPU" on page 164 that this dependence is primarily due to phase estimation's reliance on the invQFT primitive.

Conditional Operations

Perhaps the biggest caveat associated with phase estimation is the assumption that we can access a subroutine implementing a *controlled* version of the QPU operation we want to find the eigenphases of. Since the phase estimation primitive calls this subroutine multiple times, it's critical that it can be performed *efficiently*. How efficiently depends on the requirements of the particular application making use of phase estimation. In general, if our cont_u subroutine has a complexity higher than $O(m^2)$, the overall efficiency of the phase estimation primitive will be eroded. The difficulty of finding such efficient subroutines depends on the particular QPU operation in question.

Phase Estimation in Practice

Phase estimation lets us extract the eigenphase associated with a particular eigenstate, requiring us to specify that eigenstate within an input register. This may sound a little contrived—how often would we happen to know the eigenstate, yet need to know the associated eigenphase?

The real utility of phase estimation is that—like all good QPU operations—we can work it in superposition! If we send a *superposition of eigenstates* as an input to the phase estimation primitive, we'll obtain a superposition of the associated eigenphases. The magnitude for each eigenphase in the output superposition will be precisely the magnitude that its eigenstate had in the input register.

This ability of phase estimation to act on superpositions of eigenstates makes the primitive especially useful, since it turns out that *any* state of a QPU register whatsoever can be thought of as a superposition of the eigenstates of any QPU operation.[2] This means that if we set the `cont_u` input of `phase_est()` to be some QPU operation *U*, and `qin` to be some general register state $|x\rangle$, then the primitive returns details of what eigenphases *characterize* the action of *U* on $|x\rangle$. Such information is useful in many mathematical applications involving linear algebra. The fact that we can effectively extract all these eigenphases *in superposition* raises the possibility of *parallelizing* these mathematical applications on our QPU (although, as always, with some fine print).

Inside the QPU

The inner workings of phase estimation are worth a peek. Not only does it instructively build on the QFT primitive introduced in Chapter 7, but phase estimation also plays a central role in many QPU applications.

Example 8-2 gives a complete implementation of the `phase_est()` function that we first used in Example 8-1.

Sample Code

Run this sample online at *http://oreilly-qc.github.io?p=8-2*.

Example 8-2. Implementation of the phase estimation primitive

```
function phase_est(q_in, q_out, cont_u)
{
    // Main phase estimation single run
    // HAD the output register
    q_out.had();

    // Apply conditional powers of u
    for (var j = 0; j < q_out.numBits; j++)
        cont_u(q_out, q_in, 1 << j);
```

---

[2] This fact is by no means obvious, but is possible to demonstrate with the full mathematical machinery of quantum computing. In Chapter 14 we point to more technical resources that give further insight into why this statement is true.

```
    // Inverse QFT on output register
    q_out.invQFT();
}
```

This code implements the circuit shown in Figure 8-6.

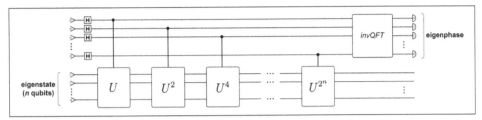

Figure 8-6. Full circuit for implementing phase estimation

Pretty concise! Our task is to explain how this manages to extract the eigenphases of the QPU operation passed to it through the cont_u parameter.

The Intuition

Getting eigenphases from a QPU operation *sounds* pretty simple. Since phase_est() has access to the QPU operation under scrutiny and one (or more) of its eigenstates, why not simply act the QPU operation on the eigenstate, as shown in Figure 8-7?

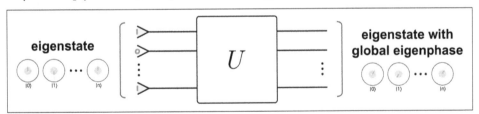

Figure 8-7. Simple suggestion for phase estimation

Thanks to the very definition of eigenstates and eigenphases, this simple program results in our output register being the same input eigenstate, but with the eigenphase applied to it as a global phase. Although this approach *does* represent the eigenphase θ in the output register, we already reminded ourselves earlier that a *global* phase cannot be READ out. So this simple idea falls foul of the all-too-familiar problem of having the information we want trapped inside the phases of a QPU register.

What we need is some way of tweaking Figure 8-7 to get the desired eigenphase in a more READable property of our register. Looking back through our growing toolbox of primitives, the QFT offers some promise.

Recall that the QFT transforms periodic phase differences into amplitudes that can be read out. So *if* we can find a way to cause the relative phases in our output register to vary periodically with a frequency determined by our eigenphase, we're home free—we simply apply the *inverse* QFT to read out our eigenphase.

Using two explicit eigenphase angles as examples, Figure 8-8 shows what we're after.

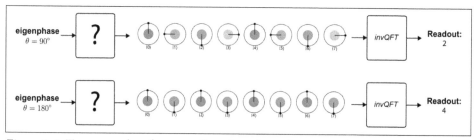

Figure 8-8. Two examples of representing eigenphases in register frequencies

We want to fill in the question marks with a set of QPU operations that produce these results. Say we're trying to determine an eigenphase of 90° (the first example in Figure 8-8), and we want to encode this in our register by having the register's relative phases rotate with a frequency of $\frac{90}{360} = \frac{1}{4}$. Since we have $2^3 = 8$ possible states in our register, this means we want the register to perform two full rotations across its length to give a frequency of $\frac{2}{8} = \frac{1}{4}$. When we perform the invQFT operation on this we, of course, read out a value of 2. From this we could successfully infer the eigenphase: $\frac{2}{8} = \frac{\theta}{360°} \Rightarrow \theta = 90°$.

After ruminating on Figure 8-8, one realizes that we can get the states we need with a few carefully chosen conditional rotations. We simply take an equal superposition of all possible register states and rotate the kth state by k times whatever frequency is desired. That is, if we wanted to encode an eigenphase of θ, we would rotate the kth state by $k\theta$.

This gives just the results we wanted in Figure 8-8, as we show explicitly in Figure 8-9 for the example of wanting to encode a 90° eigenphase in the eight states of a three-qubit register.

Figure 8-9. How to encode a value in the frequency of a register through conditional rotations

So, we've managed to reframe our problem as follows: *if we can rotate the kth state of a register by k times the eigenphase we're after, then (via the inverse QFT) we'll be able to read it out.*

 If this idea of rotating by multiples of a register's value sounds familiar, that's probably because this was precisely the approach that we used to understand the invQFT at the end of Chapter 7. Now, however, we need the register frequencies to be determined by the eigenphase of an operation.

Operation by Operation

As we'll now see, we can build up a circuit to achieve this kind of conditional rotation by combining the cont_u subroutine (providing conditional access to U) with the *phase-kickback* trick that we introduced in Chapter 3.

Every time we act our QPU operation U on its eigenstate we produce a global rotation by its eigenphase. Global phases aren't much good to us as they stand, but we can extend this idea and apply a global phase that is rotated by any integer multiple k (specified in another QPU register) of an eigenphase angle. The circuit shown in Figure 8-10 achieves this.

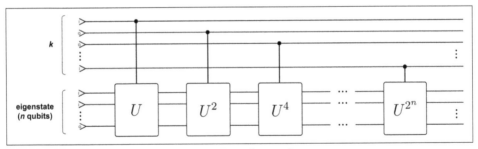

Figure 8-10. Rotating by a specified number of eigenphases

Every time we apply U to the eigenstate in the bottom register we rotate by the eigenphase θ. The choice of conditional operations simply performs the number of rotations required by each bit in the binary representation of k—resulting in us applying U a total of k times on our bottom eigenstate register—thus rotating it by $k\theta$.

This circuit allows us to implement just one global phase, for some single value of k. To perform the trick that we're asking for in Figure 8-9 we really want to implement such a rotation for all values of k in the register in superposition. Instead of specifying a single k value in the top register, let's use a uniform superposition of all 2^n possible values, as shown in Figure 8-11.

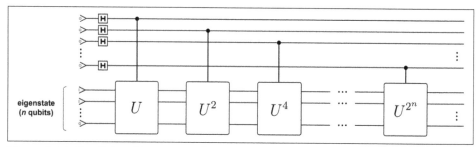

Figure 8-11. Conditionally rotating all states in a register at once

The result of this circuit on the second register is that *if* the first register was in state $|0\rangle$, then the second register would have its global phase rotated by $0 \times \theta = 0°$, whereas if the first register was in state $|1\rangle$, the second would be rotated by $1 \times \theta = \theta$, etc. But after all this, it still seems like we've only ended up with pretty useless (conditional) *global* phases in our *second* register.

What can we say about the state of the *first* register that initially held a superposition of k values? Recall from "QPU Trick: Phase Kickback" on page 51 that at the end of this circuit we can equally think of each state in the first register having its *relative* phase rotated by the specified amount. In other words, the $|0\rangle$ state acquires a relative phase of $0°$, the $|1\rangle$ state acquires a relative phase of $90°$, etc., which is exactly the state we wanted in Figure 8-9. Bingo!

It might take a few runs through the preceding argument to see how we've used cont_u and phase kickback to extract the eigenphase into the first register's frequency. But once we've done this, all we need to do is apply invQFT to the register and READ it to acquire the eigenphase we're after. Hence, the full circuit for implementing phase estimation is as shown in Figure 8-12.

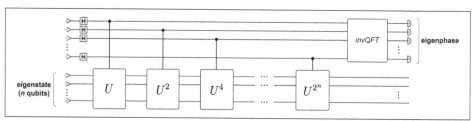

Figure 8-12. Full circuit for implementing phase estimation

We now see why we needed to be able to provide a subroutine for performing a *conditional* version of our QPU operation. Note also that the bottom register will remain in the same eigenstate at the end of the primitive. It's hopefully also now clear why (thanks to invQFT) the size of the upper output register limits the precision of the primitive.

How we perform the powers of cont_u can have a huge effect on the efficiency of phase estimation. Naively performing (for example) U^4 by calling cont_u four consecutive times is massively inefficient. For this reason, we may want to pass phase_est() a subroutine that can also efficiently return the nth power of the QPU operation in question (i.e., cont_u(n)).

Conclusion

In this chapter we have explored a new QPU primitive, *phase estimation*. This primitive uses three previously introduced concepts (phase kickback, construction of controlled unitaries, and the invQFT primitive) to achieve a great feat: it can extract information that QPU operations encode in the *global* phases of a register. It does so by transforming the global phase information into relative phase information in a second quantum register, and then applying invQFT to extract that information in a READable format. This operation will prove crucial for some of the machine-learning operations that we will encounter in Chapter 13.

PART III

QPU Applications

With some essential QPU primitives firmly in place, it's time to graduate from "How do QPUs work?" to "How can we use QPUs to do something useful?"

In Chapter 9, we will begin by demonstrating how useful data structures (rather than simple integers) can be represented and stored inside a QPU. Following this, in Chapter 10 we provide recipes to show how our arithmetic primitives from Chapter 5 can be used in a general class of applications that go under the name *quantum search*. We then move on in Chapter 11 to presenting applications in computer graphics, before introducing Peter Shor's famous factoring algorithm in Chapter 12 and finally turning to applications of our QPU primitives to machine learning in Chapter 13.

The search for useful QPU applications is an ongoing one, the focus of intense research by thousands of specialists around the globe. Hopefully this part of the book will prepare and encourage you to take the first steps toward discovering QPU applications in areas that may not even yet have been explored.

CHAPTER 9

Real Data

Fully fledged QPU applications are built to operate on genuine, unaccommodating data. Real data won't necessarily be as simple to represent as the basic integer inputs we've been satisfied with up until now. Thinking of how to represent more complex data within QPUs is thus well worth our effort, and a good data structure can be just as important as a good algorithm. This chapter sets out to answer two questions that we've previously sidestepped:

1. *How should we represent complicated data types in a QPU register?* A positive integer can be represented with simple binary encoding. What should we do with irrational, or even compound types of data, such as a vectors or matrices? This question takes on more depth when considering that superposition and relative phase might allow entirely *quantum* ways of encoding such data types.

2. *How can we read stored data into a QPU register?* So far we've been initializing our input registers by hand, using WRITE operations to manually set a register's qubits to binary integers of interest. If we're ever to employ quantum applications on large swathes of data we'll need to read that data into QPU registers from memory. This is a nontrivial requirement as we may want to initialize a QPU register with a superposition of values—something that conventional RAM isn't cut out for.

We'll start by addressing the first of these questions. As we describe QPU representations for increasingly complex types of data, we'll be led to introduce some truly *quantum* data structures and the concept of Quantum Random Access Memory (QRAM). QRAM is a crucial resource for many practical QPU applications.

In coming chapters we rely heavily on the data structures introduced here. For example, the so-called *amplitude encoding* we introduce for vector data is at the heart of every quantum machine-learning application mentioned in Chapter 13.

Noninteger Data

How can we encode noninteger numerical data in a QPU register? Two common methods for representing such values in binary are *fixed point* and *floating point*. Although a floating-point representation is more flexible (able to adapt to the range of values we need to express with a certain number of bits), given the premium we place on qubits and our desire for simplicity, fixed point is a more attractive starting point.

Fixed-point representation splits a register into two sections, one of which encodes the integer part of a number and the other of which encodes the fractional part. The integer part is expressed using a standard binary encoding, with higher-weight qubits representing increasing powers of two. However, in the fractional part of the register, qubits of *decreasing* weight represent *increasing* powers of $\frac{1}{2}$.

Fixed-point numbers are often described using *Q notation* (sadly, the Q is not for quantum). This helps take care of the ambiguity about where the fractional bits in a register end and the integer bits begin. The notation Q$n.m$ denotes an n-bit register with m of its bits being fractional (and thus the remaning ($n - m$) being integer). We can, of course, use the same notation to specify how we use a QPU register for fixed-point encodings. For example, Figure 9-1 shows an eight-qubit QPU register encoding a value of 3.640625 in Q8.6 fixed-point encoding.

0x$\frac{1}{64}$ ▷	Qubit 1 ($\frac{1}{2^6}$)
0x$\frac{1}{32}$ ▷	Qubit 2 ($\frac{1}{2^5}$)
0x$\frac{1}{16}$ ▷	Qubit 3 ($\frac{1}{2^4}$)
0x$\frac{1}{8}$ ▷	Qubit 4 ($\frac{1}{2^3}$)
0x$\frac{1}{4}$ ▷	Qubit 5 ($\frac{1}{2^2}$)
0x$\frac{1}{2}$ ▷	Qubit 6 ($\frac{1}{2^1}$)
0x1 ▷	Qubit 7 (2^0)
0x2 ▷	Qubit 8 (2^1)

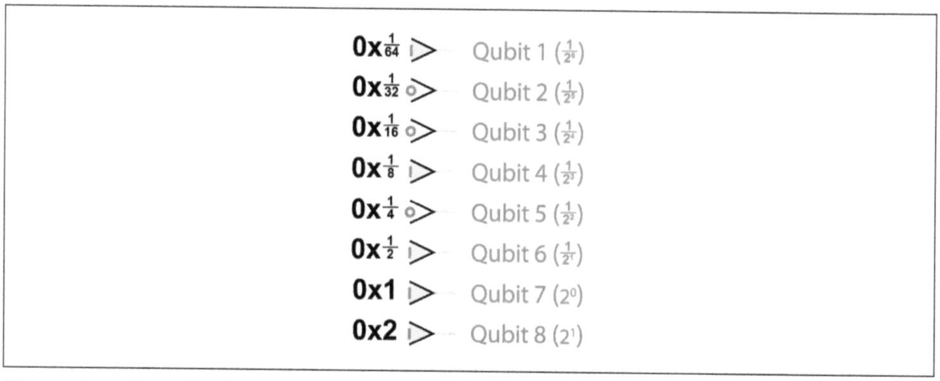

Figure 9-1. Q8.6 fixed-point encoding of the number 3.640625, which in binary reads 11101001

In the preceding example we managed to encode the chosen number precisely in fixed point because $3.640625 = 2^1 + 2^0 + \frac{1}{2^1} + \frac{1}{2^3} + \frac{1}{2^6}$ (how convenient!). Of course, we might not always get so lucky. Whereas increasing the number of bits in the integer side of a fixed-point register increases the *range* of integer values it can encode, increasing the number of bits in the fractional side increases the *accuracy* with which it can represent the fractional component of a number. The more qubits we have in the fractional part, the more chance there is that some combination of $\frac{1}{2^1}, \frac{1}{2^2}, \frac{1}{2^3}, \dots$ can accurately represent a given real number.

Although in the coming chapters we'll only point out when we use fixed-point encodings in passing, they're critical to being able to experiment with real data in small QPU registers and so well worth being aware of. When dealing with the various encodings that we have introduced, we must be diligent in keeping track of which particular encoding we're using for data in a given QPU register, so that we interpret the state of its qubits correctly.

 Take care—operations using two's complement and fixed-point encodings can often be subject to *overflow*, where the result of a calculation is too large to be represented in a register. This effectively scrambles the output into a meaningless number. Sadly, the only real solution to overflow is to add more qubits to your registers.

QRAM

We can now represent various numerical values in our QPU registers, but how do we actually get these values into them? Initializing input data by hand gets old very quickly. What we really need is the ability to read values from memory, where a binary address allows us to locate stored values. A programmer interfaces with *conventional* Random Access Memory (RAM) through two registers: one initialized with a memory address, and the other uninitialized. Given these inputs, the RAM sets the second register to the binary contents stored at the address specified by the first, as shown in Figure 9-2.

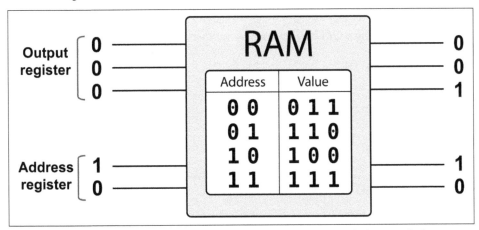

Figure 9-2. Conventional RAM—the table shows the values stored along with the interface used to access them

Can we use conventional RAM to store values for initializing our QPU registers? It's tempting to think so.

If we only want to initialize a QPU register with a single conventional value (whether in two's complement, fixed-point, or just simple binary encoding), RAM works just fine. We simply store the value in question within the RAM, and insert or retrieve it from our QPU register with write() and read() operations. Under the hood, this is precisely the restricted way in which our QCEngine JavaScript has been interfacing with our QPU registers so far.

For example, the sample code shown in Example 9-1, which takes an array a and implements a[2] += 1;, is implicitly drawing that array of values from RAM in order to initialize our QPU register. This is illustrated in Figure 9-3.

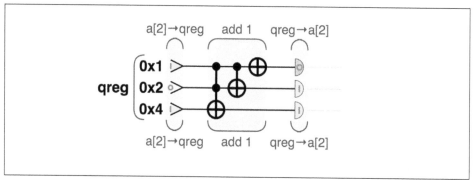

Figure 9-3. Using a QPU to increment a number in RAM

Sample Code

Run this sample online at *http://oreilly-qc.github.io?p=9-1.*

Example 9-1. Using a QPU to increment a number in RAM

```
var a = [4, 3, 5, 1];

qc.reset(3);
var qreg = qint.new(3, 'qreg');

qc.print(a);
increment(2, qreg);
qc.print(a);

function increment(index, qreg)
{
    qreg.write(a[index]);
    qreg.add(1);
```

```
        a[index] = qreg.read();
}
```

A point worth noting is that in this simple case, not only is conventional RAM being used to store the integer, but a conventional CPU is performing the array indexing to select and issue the QPU with the array value that we want.

Although using RAM in this way allows us to initialize QPU registers with simple binary values, it has a serious shortcoming. What if we want to initialize a QPU register in a *superposition* of stored values? For example, suppose our RAM stores a value 3 (110) at address 0x01, and a 5 (111) at address 0x11. How do we prepare an input register in a superposition of these two values?

With RAM and its clumsy conventional write() there's no way to achieve this. Like their vacuum-tube grandparents, QPUs are in need of a new piece of memory hardware—something fundamentally quantum in nature. Enter QRAM, which allows us to read and write data in a truly quantum way. There are already several ideas for how to physically build QRAM, but it's worth noting that history could very well repeat itself, and excitingly powerful QPUs may exist long before they are complemented with working QRAM hardware.

Let's be a little more precise about what QRAM actually does. Like conventional RAM, QRAM takes two registers as input: an *address* QPU register for specifying a memory address, and an *output* QPU register that returns the value stored at that address. Note that for QRAM these are both qubit registers. This means that we can specify a superposition of locations in the address register and consequently receive a superposition of the corresponding values in the output register, as shown in Figure 9-4.

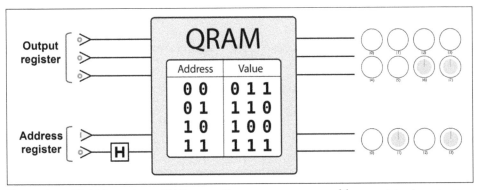

Figure 9-4. QRAM—using a HAD operation we prepare our address register in superposition, and we receive a similar superposition of stored values (shown in circle notation)

Thus, QRAM essentially allows us to read stored values in superposition. The precise amplitudes of the superposition we receive in the output register are determined by the superposition provided in the address register. Example 9-2 illustrates the difference by performing the same increment operation as Example 9-1, as shown in Figure 9-5, but using QRAM to access data instead of a QPU write/read. "A" denotes the register that provides the QRAM with an address (or superposition thereof). "D" denotes the register in which the QRAM returns a corresponding superposition of stored values (data).

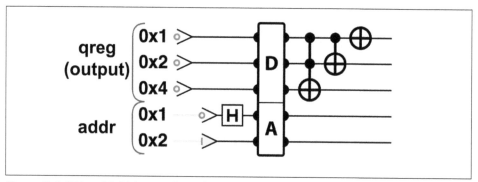

Figure 9-5. Using QRAM to perform the increment

Sample Code

Run this sample online at *http://oreilly-qc.github.io?p=9-2*.

Example 9-2. Using a QPU to increment a number from QRAM—the address register can be accessed in a superposition, resulting in the output register being a superposition of the stored values

```
var a = [4, 3, 5, 1];
var reg_qubits = 3;
qc.reset(2 + reg_qubits + qram_qubits());
var qreg = qint.new(3, 'qreg');
var addr = qint.new(2, 'addr');
var qram = qram_initialize(a, reg_qubits);

qreg.write(0);
addr.write(2);
addr.hadamard(0x1);

qram_load(addr, qreg);
qreg.add(1);
```

Can you *write* superpositions back into QRAM? That's not the purpose of it. QRAM allows us to *access* conventionally written digital values in superposition. A *persistent quantum memory* that could store superpositions indefinitely would be a whole different piece of hardware—one that might be even more challenging to build.

This description of QRAM might seem unsatisfyingly vague—just what *is* a piece of QRAM hardware? In this book we don't give a description of how QRAM can be built in practice (just as most C++ books don't give a detailed description of how RAM works). The code samples, such as Example 9-2, run using a simplified simulator model that mimics QRAM's behavior. However, examples of proposed QRAM technology do exist.[1]

Although QRAM will be a critical component in serious QPUs, like much quantum computing hardware, its implementation details are likely subject to change. What matters to us is the idea of a *fundamental resource* behaving in the manner illustrated in Figure 9-4, and the powerful applications that we can be build using it.

With QRAM at our disposal we can begin to build more sophisticated quantum data structures. Of particular interest are those allowing us to represent vector and matrix data.

Vector Encodings

Suppose we wanted to initialize a QPU register to represent a simple vector such as the one shown in Equation 9-1.

Equation 9-1. Example vector for initializing a QPU register

$$\vec{v} = [0, 1, 2, 3]$$

We'll often encounter data of this form in quantum machine-learning applications.

Perhaps the most obvious approach to encoding vector data is to represent each of its components in the state of a distinct QPU register, using an appropriate binary encoding. We'll refer to this (perhaps most obvious) approach as a *state encoding for vectors*. We could state-encode our preceding example vector into four two-qubit registers, as shown in Figure 9-6.

---

1 See, for example, Giovannetti et al., 2007 (*https://arxiv.org/abs/0708.1879*), and Prakash, 2014 (*http://bit.ly/2IZ3RLn*).

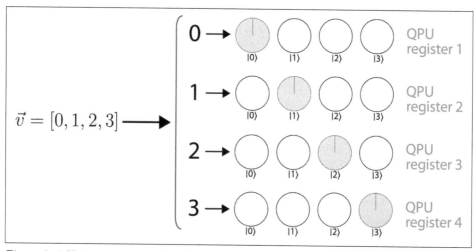

Figure 9-6. Using a state encoding for storing vector data in QPU registers

One problem with this naive state encoding is that it's pretty heavy on qubits—our QPU's scarcest resource. That said, state-encoding conventional vectors does benefit from not requiring any QRAM. We can simply store the vector components in standard RAM and use their individual values to dictate how we prepare each separate QPU register. But this advantage also belies vector state encoding's biggest *drawback*: storing vector data in such a conventional way prevents us from utilizing the unconventional abilities of our QPU. To exploit a QPU's power, we really want to be in the business of manipulating the relative phases of superpositions—something that's hard to do when each component of our vector is essentially treating our QPU as though it were a set of conventional binary registers!

Instead, let's get a little more quantum. Suppose we store the components of a vector in the superposition amplitudes of a *single* QPU register. Since a QPU register of n qubits can exist in a superposition having 2^n amplitudes (meaning we have 2^n circles to play with in circle notation), we can imagine encoding a vector with n components in a QPU register of ceil($\log(n)$) qubits.

For the example vector in Equation 9-1 this approach would require a two-qubit register—the idea being to find appropriate quantum circuitry to encode the vector data as shown in Figure 9-7.

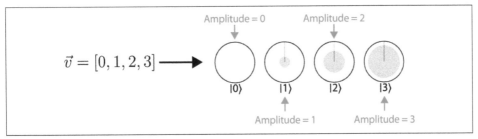

Figure 9-7. The basic idea of amplitude encoding for vectors

We call this uniquely quantum way of encoding vector data an *amplitude encoding for vector data*. It's critical to appreciate the difference between amplitude encoding and the more mundane *state encoding*. Table 9-1 compares these two encodings side by side for various example vector data. In the final example of state encoding, four seven-qubit registers would be needed, each using a Q7.7 fixed-point representation.

Table 9-1. The difference between amplitude and state encoding for vector data

Vector	Amplitude encoding	State encoding
[0, 1, 2, 3]		
[6, 1, 1, 4]		
[0.52, 0.77, 0.26, 0.26]		

We can produce amplitude-encoded vectors in QCEngine using a convenient function called `amplitude_encode()`. Example 9-3 takes a vector of values and a reference to a QPU register (which must be of sufficient size), and prepares that register in an amplitude encoding of the vector.

Sample Code

Run this sample online at *http://oreilly-qc.github.io?p=9-3.*

Example 9-3. Preparing amplitude-encoded vectors in QCEngine

```
// We have ensured that our input vector has a length
// that is a power of two
var vector = [-1.0, 1.0, 1.0, 5.0, 5.0, 6.0, 6.0, 6.0];

// Create register of right size to amplitude-encode vector
var num_qubits = Math.log2(vector.length);
qc.reset(num_qubits);
var amp_enc_reg = qint.new(num_qubits, 'amp_enc_reg');

// Generate amplitude encoding in amp_enc_reg
amplitude_encode(vector, amp_enc_reg);
```

In this example, we simply provide our vector as a JavaScript array stored in conventional RAM—yet we've stated that amplitude encoding depends on QRAM. How does QCEngine manage to amplitude-encode when it only has access to your laptop's RAM? Although it's possible to generate circuits for amplitude encoding *without* QRAM, it's certainly not possible to do so in an efficient way. QCEngine provides us with a slow, but usable simulation of what we could achieve with access to QRAM.

Limitations of Amplitude Encoding

Amplitude encoding seems like a great idea—it uses fewer qubits and gives us a very quantum way of dealing with vector data. However, any application that leverages it comes with two important caveats.

Caveat 1: Beware of quantum outputs

You may have already spotted the first of these limitations: *quantum superpositions are generally unREADable.* Our old nemesis strikes again! If we spread the components of a vector across a quantum superposition, we can't read them out again. Naturally this isn't such a big deal when we're *inputting* vector data to some QPU program from memory—we presumably know all the components anyway. But very often QPU applications that take amplitude-encoded vector data as an input will also produce amplitude-encoded vector data as an output.

Using amplitude encoding therefore imposes a severe limitation on our ability to READ outputs from applications. Fortunately, though, we can still often extract useful information from an amplitude-encoded output. We'll see in later chapters that although we can't learn individual components, we can still learn *global* properties of vectors encoded in this way. Nevertheless, there's no free lunch with amplitude encoding, and its successful use requires care and ingenuity.

 If you read about quantum machine-learning applications that solve some conventional machine-learning problem with a fantastic speedup, always be sure to check whether they return a *quantum* output. Quantum outputs, such as amplitude-encoded vectors, limit the usage of applications, and require additional specification of how to extract practical, useful results.

Caveat 2: The requirement for normalized vectors

The second caveat to amplitude encoding is hidden in Table 9-1. Take a closer look at the amplitude encodings of the first two vectors in that table: [0,1,2,3] and [6,1,1,4]. Can the amplitudes of a two-qubit QPU register *really* take the values [0,1,2,3] or the values [6,1,1,4]? Unfortunately not. In earlier chapters we've generally eschewed numerical discussion of magnitudes and relative phases in favor of our more readily intuitive circle notation. Although building intuition, this has limited your exposure to an important numerical rule about state amplitudes: *the squares of a register's amplitudes must sum to unity*. This requirement, known as *normalization*, makes sense when we recall that the squared magnitudes in a register are the probabilities of reading different outcomes. Since one outcome must occur—these probabilities, and hence the squares of each amplitude, must sum to one. It's easy to forget about normalization from the comfort of circle notation, but it places an important restriction on what vector data we can amplitude-encode. The laws of physics forbid us from ever creating a QPU register that's in a superposition with amplitudes [0,1,2,3] or [6,1,1,4].

To amplitude-encode the two troublesome vectors from Table 9-1 we would first need to normalize them, dividing each component by the summed squares of all components. For example, to amplitude-encode the vector [0,1,2,3], we first divide by 3.74 to yield a normalized vector [0.00, 0.27, 0.53, 0.80]—which is now suitable for encoding in the amplitudes of a superposition.

Does normalizing vector data have any adverse effects? It seems as though we've totally altered our data! Normalization actually leaves most of the important information intact (geometrically it rescales the length of a vector, while leaving its direction unchanged). Whether normalized data is just as good as the real thing depends on the requirements of the particular QPU application we plan to use it in. Keep in mind that we can, of course, always keep track of the normalization factor's numerical value in another register.

Amplitude Encoding and Circle Notation

As we start thinking more concretely about the numerical values of register amplitudes it becomes useful to remind ourselves how amplitudes are represented in circle notation, and highlight a potential pitfall. The filled-in areas in circle notation represent the squared *magnitudes* of the (potentially complex) amplitudes of a quantum state. In cases like amplitude encoding, where we want these amplitudes to assume real-valued vector components, this means that the filled-in areas are given by the *square* of the associated vector component, rather than simply the vector component itself. Figure 9-8 shows how we should properly interpret the circle notation representation of the vector [0,1,2,3] after normalization.

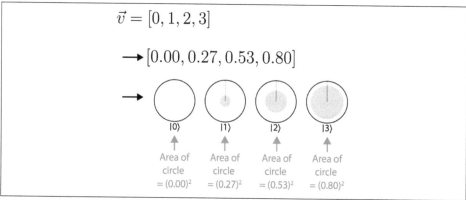

Figure 9-8. Correct amplitude encoding with a properly normalized vector

 When estimating numerical values of amplitudes from circle notation, don't forget that the *square* of a state's magnitude (and hence amplitude for real-valued cases) determines the filled area of its circle. Take care to account for the square!

You now know enough about amplitude-encoded vectors to make sense of the QPU applications we'll introduce. But for many applications, especially those from quantum machine learning, we need to go one step further and use our QPU to manipulate not just vectors, but whole *matrices* of data. How should we encode two-dimensional arrays of numbers?

Although the example vectors we've used so far have all involved real components, since the relative phases of a superposition allow its amplitudes to, in general, be complex numbers, it's worth noting that amplitude encoding can easily represent (normalized) complex vectors in a QPU register. This is why amplitude encoding is not referred to as *magnitude* encoding—we can make use of the full amplitude in a superposition to also encode complex values, though we won't do so explicitly in this chapter.

Matrix Encodings

The most obvious way of encoding an $m \times n$ matrix of values would be to employ m QPU registers, each of length $\log_2(n)$, to amplitude-encode each row of the matrix as if it were a vector. Although this is certainly one way of getting matrix data into our QPU, it doesn't necessarily represent the data *as a matrix* very well. For example, it's not at all obvious how this approach would enable fundamental operations such as transposition, or matrix multiplication with amplitude-encoded vectors in other QPU registers.

The best way for us to encode a matrix in QPU register(s) depends on precisely how we want to later use that matrix within QPU applications, and—at least at the time of writing—there are several kinds of matrix encodings that are commonly utilized.

There is, however, one universal requirement we'll have for encoding matrices. Since acting (multiplying) matrices on vectors of data is so common, and since vector data is encoded in QPU registers, it makes sense to think about encoding matrices as QPU operations able to act on vector-holding registers. Representing a matrix as a QPU operation in a meaningful way is a difficult task, and each existing method for achieving this comes with its own important pros and cons. We'll focus on one very popular approach known as *quantum simulation*. But before we do, let's be clear on exactly what it aims to achieve.

How Can a QPU Operation Represent a Matrix?

What does it even mean to say that a QPU operation correctly *represents* a particular matrix of data? Suppose that we worked out how every possible vector that this matrix might act on would be encoded in a QPU register (according to some scheme such as amplitude encoding). If a QPU operation acting on these registers resulted in output registers encoding precisely the vectors we would expect acting on the *matrix* to give, we would certainly feel confident that the QPU operation captured the behavior of our matrix.

When introducing phase estimation in Chapter 8, we noted that a QPU operation is entirely characterized by its eigenstates and eigenphases. Similarly, the eigendecomposition of a matrix characterizes it completely. So, a simpler way to convince ourselves that a QPU operation faithfully represents a matrix of data is if they both have the same eigendecomposition. By this we mean that the eigenstates of the QPU operation are (the amplitude encodings of) the eigenvectors of the original matrix, and its eigenphases are related to the matrix's eigenvalues. If this is the case, we can be confident that the QPU operation implements the desired matrix's action on amplitude-encoded vectors. Manipulating or studying a QPU operation sharing a matrix's eigendecomposition allows us to reliably answer questions about the encoded matrix.

The term *eigendecomposition* refers to the set of eigenvalues and eigenvectors of a matrix. We can also apply the term to QPU operations, where we mean the set of eigenstates and eigenphases associated with that operation.

Suppose we identify a QPU operation having the same eigendecomposition as a matrix we want to encode. Is that all we need? Almost. When we ask for a *representation of a matrix as a QPU operation*, we don't just want some abstract mathematical description of a suitable QPU operation. Pragmatically speaking, we want a prescription for how to actually perform that operation in terms of the simple single- and multi-qubit operations we introduced in Chapters 2 and 3. Furthermore, we want this prescription to be *efficient*, in the sense that we don't need so many such operations that including matrix data in a QPU application renders it uselessly slow. So for our purposes we can be a little bit more concrete about what we would like:

> A good matrix representation is a procedure for associating a matrix with a QPU operation that can be efficiently implemented through basic single- and multi-qubit operations.

For certain classes of matrices, the procedure of *quantum simulation* provides good matrix representations.

Quantum Simulation

Quantum simulation is actually a catch-all term for a whole class of procedures that can find efficiently implementable QPU operations for representing *Hermitian* matrices.

Hermitian matrices are those for which $H = H^\dagger$, where $\dagger$ denotes the *adjoint*. The adjoint is found by taking the transpose and complex conjugate of a (potentially complex) matrix.

As desired, quantum simulation techniques provide a QPU operation having the same eigendecomposition as the original Hermitian matrix. Each of the many methods for performing quantum simulation produce circuits with different resource requirements, and may even enforce different additional constraints on the kinds of matrices that can be represented. However, at a minimum, all quantum simulation techniques require the encoded matrix to be Hermitian.

But doesn't requiring a matrix of real data to be Hermitian render quantum simulation techniques uselessly niche? Well, it turns out that only being able to represent Hermitian matrices is not as restrictive as it might sound. Encoding an $m \times n$ non-Hermitian matrix X can be achieved by constructing a larger $2m \times 2n$ Hermitian matrix H as follows:

$$H = \begin{bmatrix} \mathbf{0} & X \\ X^\dagger & \mathbf{0} \end{bmatrix}$$

Where the $\mathbf{0}$s on the diagonal represent $m \times n$ blocks of zeros. This constant one-off additional overhead of creating a larger matrix is usually relatively insignificant.

We'll outline the general high-level approach taken by many different quantum simulation techniques, giving a little more detail on one particular approach as an example. This will involve more mathematics than we've dealt with so far, but only the kind of linear algebra that's par for the course when dealing with matrices.

The basic idea

Despite relying on circle notation, we've noted that the full quantum mechanical description of a QPU register's state is a complex-valued vector. It turns out that the full quantum mechanical description of a QPU operation is a matrix. This might make our goal of encoding matrices as QPU operations sound simple. If, deep down, QPU operations are described by matrices, then just find one that has the same matrix as the data to be encoded! Unfortunately, only a subset of matrices correspond to valid (constructable) QPU operations. In particular, valid QPU operations are described by *unitary* matrices.

 A *unitary* matrix U is one for which $UU^\dagger = \mathbb{1}$, where $\mathbb{1}$ is an identity matrix (having ones along the diagonal and zeros elsewhere) of the same size as U. QPU operations need to be described by unitary matrices as this ensures that the circuits realizing them will be reversible (a requirement we noted in Chapter 5).

The good news is that given a Hermitian matrix H, it's possible to construct an associated unitary matrix U through exponentiation: $U = \exp(-iHt)$ is unitary if H is Hermitian. Quantum simulation techniques make use of this fact (hence why they're restricted to representing Hermitian matrices). The t appearing in the exponent is the *time* that we apply the QPU operation $U = \exp(-iHt)$ for. We can, for our purposes, consider choosing t to be a hardware implementation detail that we gloss over for simplicity of exposition.

Quantum simulation's task is therefore to efficiently provide a circuit performing this exponentiation of H.

 Although we're using it to encode matrix data, quantum simulation is so called because it's primarily used as a technique for *simulating* the behavior of quantum mechanical objects (for example, in molecular or materials simulations). When simulating quantum objects, a certain Hermitian matrix (known in physics as the Hamiltonian) mathematically describes the simulation to be performed, and a QPU operation $\exp(-iHt)$ predicts how the quantum object evolves over time. This technique is heavily used in QPU algorithms for quantum chemistry, see "The Promise of Quantum Simulation" on page 305 for more information.

For some particularly simple Hermitian matrices H it turns out that finding a set of simple QPU operations to implement $\exp(-iHt)$ is relatively easy. For example, if H only has elements on its diagonal, or would only act on a very small number of qubits, then a circuit can easily be found.

It's unlikely, however, that a Hermitian data matrix will satisfy either of these simplicity requirements out of the box, and quantum simulation gives us a way to break down such difficult-to-encode matrices into a number easier-to-encode ones. In the next section we'll outline how this works. Although we don't provide any detailed algorithms for quantum simulation, our high-level description at least helps illustrate the important limitations of these techniques.

How it works

The many approaches to quantum simulation follow a similar set of steps. Given a Hermitian matrix H we proceed as follows:

1. *Deconstruct.* We find a way to split H into a *sum* of some number (n) of other *simpler* Hermitian matrices, $H = H_1 + \ldots H_n$. These matrices $H_1, \ldots, H_n$ are simpler in the sense that they are easier to simulate efficiently in the manner mentioned in the previous section.

2. *Simulate components.* We then efficiently find quantum circuits (in terms of fundamental QPU operations) for these simpler component matrices.

3. *Reconstruction.* We reconstruct a circuit for implementing the full matrix H of interest from the smaller quantum circuits found for its deconstructed components.

For this plan of action to work the two steps that need most clarification are: finding a way to break down a Hermitian matrix into a summation of easy-to-simulate pieces (step 1) and showing how to piece together simulations of each of these smaller pieces into a full-blown simulation of H (step 3). Quantum simulation approaches differ in how they achieve this. Here we summarize one group of methods, known as *product formula methods.*

It's actually easiest to start at the end and first explain how product formula methods perform the final reconstruction of H (step 3, from the preceding list), so let's do that.

Reconstruction

Suppose that we do find some way to write $H = H_1 + \ldots + H_n$, with $H_1, \ldots, H_n$ being Hermitian matrices for which we can easily find QPU operations. If this is the case, we can reconstruct H itself thanks to a mathematical relationship known as the *Lie product formula.* This formula allows the unitary matrix $U = \exp(-iHt)$ to be approximated by performing each of the component QPU operations

$$U_1 = \exp\left(-iH_1\delta t\right), \ldots, U_n = \exp\left(-iH_n\delta t\right)$$

in sequence for very short times δt, and then repeating this whole procedure some number of times m, as illustrated in Figure 9-9.

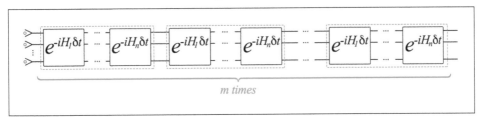

Figure 9-9. Quantum simulation reconstructs a hard-to-simulate Hermitian matrix by repeatedly simulating a sequence of easier-to-simulate Hermitian matrices

Crucially, the Lie product formula shows that *if* we can deconstruct H into matrices having efficient circuits, then we can also approximate $U = \exp(-iHt)$ with an efficient runtime.

Deconstructing H

That takes care of step 3, but how do we deconstruct our matrix as a sum of easy-to-simulate Hermitian matrices in the first place?

Different approaches from the product formula class of quantum simulation techniques perform this deconstruction in different ways. All approaches are quite mathematically involved, and place differing additional requirements on H. For example, one approach that is suitable if H is sparse (and we can efficiently access these sparse components) is to consider H to be an adjacency matrix for a graph. By solving a certain coloring problem on this graph, the different colors we identify group together elements of H that form the easy-to-simulate $H_1, ...H_n$ deconstructing it.

Here we use the term *graph* in the mathematical sense, meaning a structure containing a series of vertices connected by edges relating them. A *coloring problem* on a graph is the task of associating one of several available colors to each vertex subject to the constraint that if two vertices are directly connected by an edge, they cannot share the same color. How deconstructing Hermitian matrices relates to graph coloring is not obvious, and results from the problem's underlying mathematical structure.

The cost of quantum simulation

This summary of product formula approaches to quantum simulation hopefully gives you a feel for the lengths one must go to represent matrix data as QPU operations. As we previously mentioned, other quantum simulation approaches also exist, many of which exhibit better performance through either needing smaller circuits or reduced access to the matrix to be encoded. In Table 9-2 we compare the runtimes of some common quantum simulation techniques. Here "runtime" refers the size of the circuit a method produces for simulating a matrix (where circuit size is the required number of fundamental QPU operations). d is a measure of the matrix's sparsity (the maximum number of nonzero elements per row), and ϵ is a measure of the desired precision of the representation.[2]

Table 9-2. Runtimes of selected quantum simulation techniques

Technique	Circuit runtime
Product formula[a]	$O\left(d^4\right)$
Quantum walks	$O(d/\sqrt{\epsilon})$
Quantum signal processing	$O\left(d + \dfrac{\log\ (1/\epsilon)}{\log\ \log\ (1/\epsilon)}\right)$

[a] It is also possible to slightly improve the runtime of product formula quantum simulation techniques through the use of "higher order" approximations to the Lie product formula used within the approach.

---

2 Note that these runtimes are also dependent on some other important parameters, like the input matrix and quantum simulation technique we might use. We have excluded these for simplicity in this overview.

CHAPTER 10

Quantum Search

In Chapter 6 we saw how the amplitude amplification (AA) primitive changes differences in phases within a register into detectable variations in magnitude. Recall that when introducing AA, we assumed that applications would provide a subroutine to flip the phases of values in our QPU register. As a simplistic example, we used the flip circuit as a placeholder, which simply flipped the phase of a single known register value. In this chapter we will look in detail at several techniques for flipping phases in a quantum state based on the result of nontrivial logic.

Quantum Search (QS) is a particular technique for modifying the flip subroutine such that AA allows us to reliably READ solutions from a QPU register for a certain class of problems. In other words, QS is really just an application of AA, formed by providing an all-important subroutine[1] marking solutions to a certain class of problems in a register's phases.

The class of problems that QS allows us to solve is those that repeatedly evaluate a subroutine giving a yes/no answer. The yes/no answer of this subroutine is, generally, the output of a conventional boolean logic statement.[2] One obvious problem that can be cast in this form is searching through a database for a specific value. We simply imagine a boolean function that returns a 1 if and only if an input is the database element we're searching for. This was in fact the prototypical use of Quantum Search, and is known, after its discoverer, as *Grover's search algorithm*. By applying the Quantum Search technique, Grover's search algorithm can find an element in a database using only $O(\sqrt{N})$ database queries, whereas conventionally $O(N)$ would be required.

---

1 In the literature, a function that flips phases according to some logic function is referred to as an *oracle*, in a similar sense to how the term is used in conventional computer science. We opt for slightly less intimidating terminology here, but more thoroughly relate this to prevalent technical language in Chapter 14.

2 We provide a more detailed description of this class of problems at the end of this chapter and in Chapter 14.

However, this assumes an unstructured database—a rare occurrence in reality—and faces substantial practical implementation obstacles.

Although Grover's search algorithm is the best known example of a Quantum Search application, there are many other applications that can use QS as a subroutine to speed up performance. These range from applications in artificial intelligence to software verification.

The piece of the puzzle that we're missing is just how Quantum Search allows us to find subroutines encoding the output of any boolean statement in a QPU register's phases (whether we use this for Grover's database search or other QS applications). Once we know how to do this, AA takes us the rest of the way. To see how we can build such subroutines, we'll need a sophisticated set of tools for manipulating QPU register phases—a repertoire of techniques we term *phase logic*. In the rest of this chapter, we outline phase logic and show how QS can leverage it. At the end of the chapter, we summarize a general recipe for applying QS techniques to various conventional problems.

Phase Logic

In Chapter 5, we introduced a form of quantum logic—i.e., a way of performing logic functions that's compatible with quantum superpositions. However, these logic operations used register values with non-zero *magnitudes* as inputs (e.g. $|2\rangle$ or $|5\rangle$), and similarly would output results as register values (possibly in scratch qubits).

In contrast, the quantum phase logic we need for Quantum Search should output the results of logic operations in the *relative phases* of these registers.

More specifically, to perform phase logic we seek QPU circuits that can achieve *quantum phase logic*, which represents a given logic operation (such as an AND, OR, etc.) by flipping the phases of values in a register for which the operation would return a 1 value.

The utility of this definition requires a little explaining. The idea is that we feed the phase-logic circuit a state (which may be in superposition) and the circuit flips the relative phases of all inputs that would satisfy the logic operation it represents. If the state fed in is *not* in superposition, this phase flip will simply amount to an unusable global phase, but when a superposition is used, the circuit encodes information in relative phases, which we can then access using the amplitude amplification primitive.

 The expression *satisfy* is often used to describe inputs to a logic operation (or a collection of such operations forming a logical *statement*) that produce a 1 output. In this terminology, phase logic flips the phases of all QPU register values that *satisfy* the logic operation in question.

We've already seen one such phase-manipulating operation: the PHASE operation itself! The action of PHASE was shown in Figure 5-13. When acting on a single qubit, it simply writes the logical value of the qubit into its phase (only flipping the phase of the $|1\rangle$ value; i.e., when the output is 1). Although so far we've simply thought of PHASE as a tool for rotating the relative phases of qubits, it satisfies our quantum phase logic definition, and we can also interpret it as a phase-based logic operation.

The difference between binary logic and phase logic is important to understand and a potential point of confusion. Here's a summary:

Conventional binary logic
    Applies logic gates to an input, producing an output

Quantum magnitude logic
    Applies logic gates to a *superposition* of inputs, producing a *superposition* of outputs

Quantum phase logic
    Flips the phase of every input value that would produce a 1 as output; this works when the register is in superposition too

It's perhaps easier to grasp the action of phase logic by seeing some examples in circle notation. Figure 10-1 illustrates how phase-logic versions of OR, NOR, XOR, AND, and NAND operations affect a uniform superposition of a two-qubit register.

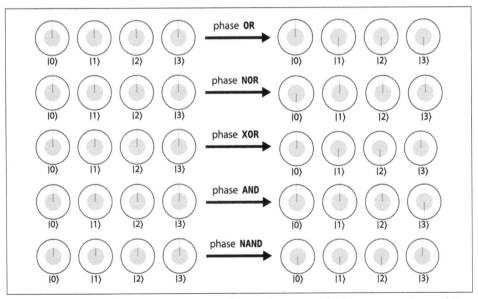

Figure 10-1. Phase-logic representations of some elementary logic gates on a two-qubit register

In Figure 10-1 we have chosen to portray the action of these phase-logic operations on superpositions of the register, but the gates will work regardless of whether the register contains a superposition or a single value. For example, a conventional binary logic XOR outputs a value 1 for inputs 10 and 01. You can check in Figure 10-1 that only the phases of $|1\rangle$ and $|2\rangle$ have been flipped.

Phase logic is fundamentally different from any kind of conventional logic—the results of the logic operations are now hidden in unREADable phases. But the advantage is that by flipping the phases in a superposition we have been able to mark *multiple* solutions in a *single* register! Moreover, although solutions held in a superposition are normally unobtainable, we already know that by using this phase logic as the flip subroutine in amplitude amplification, we *can* produce READable results.

Building Elementary Phase-Logic Operations

Now that we know what we want phase-logic circuits to achieve, how do we actually build phase-logic gates such as those alluded to in Figure 10-1 from fundamental QPU operations?

Figure 10-2 shows circuits implementing some elementary phase-logic operations. Note that (as was the case in Chapter 5) some of these operations make use of an extra scratch qubit. In the case of phase logic, any scratch qubits will always be initialized[3] in the state $|-\rangle$. It is important to note that this scratch qubit will *not* become entangled with our input register, and hence it is not necessary to uncompute the entire phase-logic gate. This is because the scratch qubits implement the phase-logic gates using the *phase-kickback* trick introduced in Chapter 3.

 It's crucial to keep in mind that *input* values to these phase-logic implementations are encoded in the states of QPU registers (e.g. $|2\rangle$ or $|5\rangle$), but *output* values are encoded in the *relative phases*. Don't let the name *phase logic* trick you into thinking that these implementations also take phase values as inputs!

---

3 For example, the phase-logic XOR in Figure 10-2 uses a scratch qubit, which is prepared in the $|-\rangle$ state using a NOT and a HAD operation.

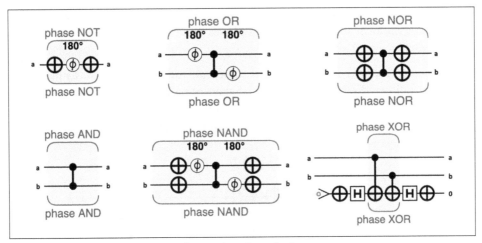

Figure 10-2. QPU operations implementing phase logic

Building Complex Phase-Logic Statements

The kind of logic we want to explore with QS will concatenate together many different elementary logic operations. How do we find QPU circuits for such full-blown, composite phase-logic statements? We've carefully cautioned that the implementations in Figure 10-2 output phases but require magnitude-value inputs. So we can't simply link together these elementary phase-logic operations to form more complex statements; their inputs and outputs aren't compatible.

Luckily, there's a sneaky trick: we take the full statement that we want to implement with phase logic and perform all but the *final* elementary logic operation from the statement using magnitude-based quantum logic, of the kind we saw in Chapter 5. This will output the values from the statement's penultimate operation encoded in QPU register magnitudes. We then feed this into a *phase-logic* implementation of the statement's final remaining logic operation (using one of the circuits from Figure 10-2). Voilà! We have the final output from the whole statement encoded in phases.

To see this trick in action, suppose that we want to evaluate the logical statement (a OR NOT b) AND c (involving the three boolean variables a, b, and c) in phase logic. The conventional logic gates for this statement are shown in Figure 10-3.

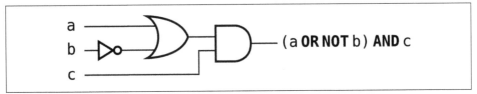

Figure 10-3. An example logic statement, expressed as conventional logic gates

For a phase-logic representation of this statement, we want to end up with a QPU register in a uniform superposition with phases flipped for all input values satisfying the statement.

Our plan is to use magnitude-based quantum logic for the (a OR NOT b) part of the statement (all but the last operation), and then use a phase-logic circuit to AND this result with c—yielding the statement's final output in register phases. The circuit in Figure 10-4 shows how this looks in terms of QPU operations.[4]

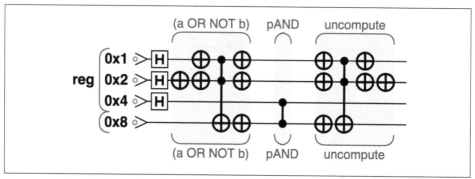

Figure 10-4. Example statement expressed in phase logic

Note that we also needed to include a scratch qubit for our binary-value logic operations. The result of (a OR NOT b) is written to the scratch qubit, and our phase-logic AND operation (which we denote pAND) is then performed between this and qubit c. We finish by uncomputing this scratch qubit to return it to its initial, unentangled |0⟩ state.

Sample Code

Run this sample online at *http://oreilly-qc.github.io?p=10-1*.

Example 10-1. Encoding example in phase logic

```
qc.reset(4);
var reg = qint.new(4, 'reg');

qc.write(0);
reg.hadamard();

// (a OR NOT b)
qc.not(2);
```

---

4 Note that there are some redundant operations in this circuit (e.g., canceling NOT operations). We have kept these for clarity.

```
bit_or(1,2,8);

// pAND
phase_and(4|8);

// uncompute
inv_bit_or(1,2,8);
qc.not(2);

// Logic Definitions

// binary logic OR using ancilla as output
function bit_or(q1,q2,out) {
    qc.not(q1|q2);
    qc.cnot(out,q1|q2);
    qc.not(q1|q2|out);
}

// reversed binary logic OR (to uncompute)
function inv_bit_or(q1,q2,out) {
    qc.not(q1|q2|out);
    qc.cnot(out,q1|q2);
    qc.not(q1|q2);
}

// Phase-logic AND (pAND)
function phase_and(qubits) {
    qc.cz(qubits);
}
```

Running the preceding sample code, you should find that the circuit flips the phases of values $|4\rangle$, $|5\rangle$, and $|7\rangle$, as shown in Figure 10-5.

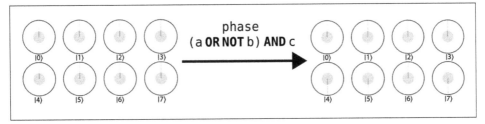

Figure 10-5. State transformation

These states encode the logical assignments (a=0, b=0, c=1), (a=1, b=0, c=1), and (a=1, b=1, c=1), respectively, which are the only logic inputs satisfying the original boolean statement illustrated in Figure 10-3.

Solving Logic Puzzles

With our newfound ability to mark the phases of values satisfying boolean statements, we can use AA to tackle the problem of *boolean satisfiability*. Boolean satisfiability is the problem of determining whether input values exist satisfying a given boolean statement—precisely what we've learned to achieve with phase logic!

Boolean satisfiability is an important problem in computer science[5] and has applications such as model checking, planning in artificial intelligence, and software verification. To understand this problem (and how to solve it), we'll take a look at how QPUs help us with a less financially rewarding but much more fun application of the boolean satisfiability problem: solving logic puzzles!

Of Kittens and Tigers

On an island far, far away, there once lived a princess who desperately wanted a kitten for her birthday. Her father the king, while not opposed to this idea, wanted to make sure that his daughter took the decision of having a pet seriously, and so gave her a riddle for her birthday instead (Figure 10-6).[6]

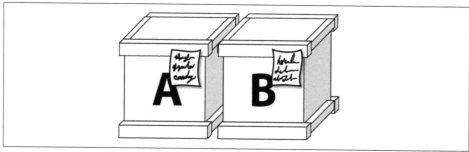

Figure 10-6. A birthday puzzle

On her big day, the princess received two boxes, and was allowed to open at most one. Each box might contain her coveted kitten, but might also contain a vicious tiger. Fortunately, the boxes came labeled as follows:

Label on box A
> *At least one of these boxes contains a kitten.*

---

5 Boolean satisfiability was the first problem proven to be NP-complete. *N*-SAT, the boolean satisfiability problem for boolean statements containing clauses of *N* literals, is NP-complete when $N > 2$. In Chapter 14 we give more information about basic computational complexity classes, as well as references to more in-depth material.

6 Adaptation of a logic puzzle from the book *The Lady or the Tiger?* by Raymond Smullyan.

Label on box B
    The other box contains a tiger.

"That's easy!" thought the princess, and quickly told her father the solution.

"There's a twist," added her father, having known that such a simple puzzle would be far too easy for her. "The notes on the boxes are either both true, or they're both false."

"Oh," said the princess. After a brief pause, she ran to her workshop and quickly wired up a circuit. A moment later she returned with a device to show her father. The circuit had two inputs, as shown in Figure 10-7.

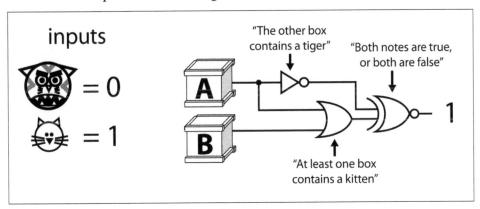

Figure 10-7. A digital solution to the problem

"I've set it up so that 0 means tiger and 1 means kitten," she proudly declared. "If you input a possibility for what's in each box, you'll get a 1 output only if the possibility satisfies all the conditions."

For each of the three conditions (the notes on the two boxes plus the extra rule her father had added), the princess had included a logic gate in her circuit:

- For the note on box A, she used an OR gate, indicating that this constraint would only be satisfied if box A *or* box B contained a kitten.

- For the note on box B, she used a NOT gate, indicating that this constraint would only be satisfied if box A did *not* contain a kitten.

- Finally, for her father's twist, she added an XNOR gate to the end, which would be satisfied (output true) *only* if the results of the other two gates were the same as each other, both true or both false.

"That'll do it. Now I just need to run this on each of the four possible configurations of kittens and tigers to find out which one satisfies all the constraints, and then I'll know which box to open."

"Ahem," said the king.

The princess rolled her eyes, "What now, dad?"

"And… you are only allowed to run your device once."

"Oh," said the princess. This presented a real problem. Running the device only once would require her to guess which input configuration to test, and would be unlikely to return a conclusive answer. She'd have a 25% chance of guessing the correct input to try, but if that failed and her circuit produced a 0, she would need to just choose a box randomly and hope for the best. With all of this guessing, and knowing her father, she'd probably get eaten by a tiger. No, conventional digital logic just would not do the job this time.

But fortunately (in a quite circular fashion), the princess had recently read an O'Reilly book on quantum computation. So, gurgling with delight, she once again dashed to her workshop. A few hours later she returned, having built a new, somewhat larger, device. She switched it on, logged in via a secure terminal, ran her program, and cheered in triumph. Running to the correct box, she threw it open and happily hugged her kitten.

The end.

Example 10-2 is the QPU program that the princess used, as illustrated in Figure 10-8. The figure also shows the conventional logic gate that each part of the QPU circuit ultimately implements in phase logic. Let's check that it works!

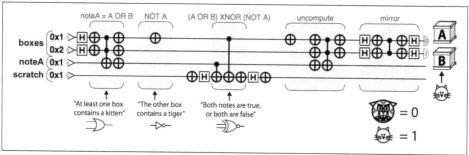

Figure 10-8. Logic puzzle: Kitten or tiger?

Sample Code

Run this sample online at *http://oreilly-qc.github.io?p=10-2*.

Example 10-2. Kittens and tigers

```
qc.reset(4);
var boxes = qint.new(2, 'boxes')
var noteA = qint.new(1, 'noteA')
```

```
var anc = qint.new(1,'anc')
qc.write(0);

// Put both boxes into a quantum kitten/tiger superposition
boxes.hadamard();

// Satisfy the note on box A using binary logic
// noteA = A OR B
qc.not(0x1|0x2);
qc.cnot(0x4,0x1|0x2)
qc.not(0x1|0x2|0x4);

// Satisfy the note on box B using binary logic
// NOT A
qc.not(0x1);

// Put the phase-logic scratch qubit into the |+> state
anc.not();
anc.hadamard();

// Satisfy the final condition using phase-logic
// (A OR B) XNOR (NOT A)
qc.cnot(0x8,0x4);
qc.cnot(0x8,0x1);
qc.not(0x8);

// Return the scratch to |0>
anc.hadamard();
anc.not();

// Uncompute all of the binary logic
qc.not(0x1);
qc.nop();
qc.not(0x1|0x2|0x4);
qc.cnot(0x4,0x1|0x2);
qc.not(0x1|0x2);

// Use mirror to convert the flipped phase
boxes.Grover();

// Read and interpret the result!
var result = boxes.read();
var catA = result & 1 ? 'kitten' : 'tiger';
var catB = result & 2 ? 'kitten' : 'tiger';
qc.print('Box A contains a ' + catA + '\n');
qc.print('Box B contains a ' + catB + '\n');
```

After just a single run of the QPU program in Example 10-2, we can solve the riddle!
Just as in Example 10-1, we use magnitude logic until the final operation, for which
we employ phase logic. The circuit output shows clearly (and with 100% probability)

that the birthday girl should open box B if she wants a kitten. Our phase-logic sub-routines take the place of flip in an AA iteration, so we follow them with the mirror subroutine originally defined in Example 6-1.

As discussed in Chapter 6, the number of times that we need to apply a full AA itera-tion will depend on the number of qubits involved. Luckily, this time we only needed one! We were also lucky that there *was* a solution to the riddle (i.e., that *some* set of inputs did satisfy the boolean statement). We'll see shortly what would happen if there wasn't a solution.

 Remember the subtlety that the mirror subroutine increases the magnitude of values that have their phases *flipped* with respect to other ones. This doesn't necessarily mean that the phase has to be negative for this particular state and positive for the rest, so long as it is flipped with respect to the others. In this case, one of the options will be correct (and have a *positive* phase) and the others will be incorrect (with a *negative* phase). But the algorithm works just as well!

General Recipe for Solving Boolean Satisfiability Problems

The princess's puzzle was, of course, a feline form of a boolean satisfiability problem. The approach that we used to solve the riddle generalizes nicely to other boolean sat-isfiability problems with a QPU:

1. Transform the boolean statement from the satisfiability problem in question into a form having a number of clauses that have to be satisfied simultaneously (i.e., so that the statement is the AND of a number of independent clauses).[7]

2. Represent each individual clause using magnitude logic. Doing so will require a number of scratch qubits. As a rule of thumb, since most qubits will be involved in more than one clause, it's useful to have one scratch qubit per logical clause.

3. Initialize the full QPU register (containing qubits representing all input variables to the statement) in a uniform superposition (using HADs), and initialize all scratch registers in the $|0\rangle$ state.

4. Use the magnitude-logic recipes given in Figure 5-25 to build the logic gates in each clause one by one, storing the output value of each logical clause in a scratch qubit.

---

7 This form is the most desirable, since the final pAND combining all the statements in phase logic can be imple-mented using a single CPHASE with no need for extra scratch qubits. However, other forms can be imple-mented with carefully prepared scratch qubits.

5. Once all the clauses have been implemented, perform a phase-logic AND between all the scratch qubits to combine the different clauses.

6. Uncompute all of the magnitude-logic operations, returning the scratch qubits to their initial states.

7. Run a mirror subroutine on the QPU register encoding our input variables.

8. Repeat the preceding steps as many times as is necessary according to the amplitude amplification formula given in Equation 6-2.

9. Read the final (amplitude-amplified) result by reading out the QPU register.

In the following sections we give two examples of applying this recipe, the second of which illustrates how the procedure works in cases where a statement we're trying to satisfy *cannot* actually be satisfied (i.e., no input combinations can yield a 1 output).

Hands-on: A Satisfiable 3-SAT Problem

Consider the following 3-SAT problem:

```
(a OR b) AND (NOT a OR c) AND (NOT b OR NOT c) AND (a OR c)
```

Our goal is to find whether any combination of boolean inputs a, b, c can produce a 1 output from this statement. Luckily, the statement is already the AND of a number of clauses (how convenient!). So let's follow our steps. We'll use a QPU register of seven qubits—three to represent our variables a, b, and c, and four scratch qubits to represent each of the logical clauses. We then proceed to implement each logical clause in magnitude logic, writing the output from each clause into the scratch qubits. Having done this, we implement a phase-logic AND statement between the scratch qubits, and then uncompute each of the magnitude-logic clauses. Finally, we apply a mirror subroutine to the seven-qubit QPU register, completing our first amplitude amplification iteration. We can implement this solution with the sample code in Example 10-3, as shown in Figure 10-9.

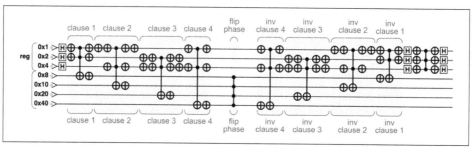

Figure 10-9. A satisfiable 3-SAT problem

Sample Code

Run this sample online at *http://oreilly-qc.github.io?p=10-3*.

Example 10-3. Satisfiable 3-SAT problem

```
var num_qubits = 3;
var num_ancilla = 4;

qc.reset(num_qubits+num_ancilla);
var reg = qint.new(num_qubits, 'reg');
qc.write(0);

reg.hadamard();

// clause 1
bit_or(0x1,0x2,0x8);

// clause 2
qc.not(0x1);
bit_or(0x1,0x4,0x10);
qc.not(0x1);

// clause 3
qc.not(0x2|0x4);
bit_or(0x2,0x4,0x20);
qc.not(0x2|0x4);

// clause 4
bit_or(0x1,0x4,0x40);

// flip phase
phase_and(0x8|0x10|0x20|0x40);

// inv clause 4
inv_bit_or(0x1,0x4,0x40);

// inv clause 3
qc.not(0x2|0x4);
```

```
inv_bit_or(0x2,0x4,0x20);
qc.not(0x2|0x4);

// inv clause 2
qc.not(0x1);
inv_bit_or(0x1,0x4,0x10);
qc.not(0x1);

// inv clause 1
inv_bit_or(0x1,0x2,0x8);

reg.Grover();

/////////// Definitions

// Define bit OR and inverse
function bit_or(q1, q2, out)
{
    qc.not(q1|q2);
    qc.cnot(out,q1|q2);
    qc.not(q1|q2|out);
}

function inv_bit_or(q1, q2, out)
{
    qc.not(q1|q2|out);
    qc.cnot(out,q1|q2);
    qc.not(q1|q2);
}

// Define phase AND
function phase_and(qubits)
{
    qc.cz(qubits);
}
```

Using circle notation to follow the progress of the three qubits representing a, b, and c, we see the results shown in Figure 10-10.

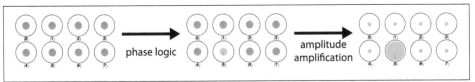

Figure 10-10. Circle notation for a satisfiable 3-SAT problem after one iteration

This tells us that the boolean statement can be satisfied by values a=1, b=0, and c=1.

In this example, we were able to find a set of input values that satisfied the boolean statement. What happens when no solution exists? Luckily for us, NP problems like boolean satisfiability are such that although finding an answer is computationally expensive, checking whether an answer is correct is computationally cheap. If a problem is unsatisfiable, no phase in the register will get flipped and no magnitude will change as a consequence of the mirror operation. Since we start with an equal superposition of all values, the final READ will give one value from the register at random. We simply need to check whether it satisfies the logical statement; if it *doesn't*, we can be sure that the statement is unsatisfiable. We'll consider this case next.

Hands-on: An Unsatisfiable 3-SAT Problem

Now let's look at an unsatisfiable 3-SAT problem:

```
(a OR b) AND (NOT a OR c) AND (NOT b OR NOT c) AND (a OR c) AND b
```

Knowing that this is unsatisfiable, we expect that no value assignment to variables a, b, and c will be able to produce an output of 1. Let's determine this by running the QPU routine in Example 10-4, as shown in Figure 10-11, following the same prescription as in the previous example.

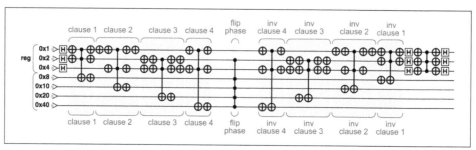

Figure 10-11. An unsatisfiable 3-SAT problem

```
// clause 1
bit_or(0x1,0x2,0x8);

// clause 2
qc.not(0x1);
bit_or(0x1,0x4,0x10);
qc.not(0x1);

// clause 3
qc.not(0x2|0x4);
bit_or(0x2,0x4,0x20);
qc.not(0x2|0x4);

// clause 4
bit_or(0x1,0x4,0x40);

// flip phase
phase_and(0x2|0x8|0x10|0x20|0x40);

// inv clause 4
inv_bit_or(0x1,0x4,0x40);

// inv clause 3
qc.not(0x2|0x4);
inv_bit_or(0x2,0x4,0x20);
qc.not(0x2|0x4);

// inv clause 2
qc.not(0x1);
inv_bit_or(0x1,0x4,0x10);
qc.not(0x1);

// inv clause 1
inv_bit_or(0x1,0x2,0x8);

reg.Grover();

/////////////// Definitions

// Define bit OR and inverse
function bit_or(q1, q2, out) {
    qc.not(q1|q2);
    qc.cnot(out,q1|q2);
    qc.not(q1|q2|out);
}

function inv_bit_or(q1, q2, out) {
    qc.not(q1|q2|out);
    qc.cnot(out,q1|q2);
    qc.not(q1|q2);
}
```

```
// Define phase AND
function phase_and(qubits) {
    qc.cz(qubits);
}
```

So far, so good! Figure 10-12 shows how the three qubits encoding the a, b, and c input values are transformed throughout the computation. Note that we only consider a single AA iteration, since (as we can see in the figure) its effect, or lack thereof, is clear after only one iteration.

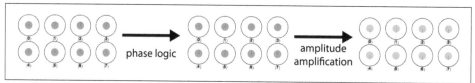

Figure 10-12. Circle notation for an unsatisfiable 3-SAT problem

Nothing has happened! Since none of the eight possible values of the register satisfy the logical statement, no phase has been flipped with respect to any others; hence, the mirror part of the amplitude amplification iteration has equally affected all values. No matter how many AA iterations we perform, when READing these three qubits we will obtain one of the eight values completely at random.

The fact that we could equally have obtained any value on READing might make it seem like we learned nothing, but whichever of these three values for a, b, and c we READ, we can try inputting them into our boolean statement. If we obtain a 0 outcome then we can conclude (with high probability) that the logical statement is *not* satisfiable (otherwise we would have expected to read out the satisfying values).

Speeding Up Conventional Algorithms

One of the most notable features of amplitude amplification is that, in certain cases, it can provide a quadratic speedup not only over brute-force conventional algorithms, but also over the best conventional implementations.

The algorithms that amplitude amplification can speed up are those with one-sided error. These are algorithms for decision problems containing a subroutine outputting a yes/no answer, such that if the answer to the problem is "no," the algorithm always outputs "no," while if the answer to the problem is "yes," the algorithm outputs the answer "yes" with probability $p > 0$. In the case of 3-SAT, which we have seen in the previous examples, the algorithms outputs the the "yes" answer (the formula is satisfiable) only if it finds a satisfiable assignment.

To find a solution with some desired probability, these conventional algorithms must repeat their probabilistic subroutine some number of times (k times if the algorithm has a runtime of $O(k^n poly(n))$). To obtain a QPU speedup, combine them with the quantum routine we simply need to substitute the repeated probabilistic subroutine with an amplitude amplification step.

Any conventional algorithm of this form can be combined with amplitude amplification to make it faster. For example, the naive approach to solving 3-SAT in the earlier examples runs in $O(1.414^n poly(n))$, while the best conventional algorithm runs faster, in $O(1.3(29^n poly(n))$. However, by combining this conventional result with amplitude amplification, we can achieve a runtime of $O(1.1(53^n poly(n)))$!

There are a number of other algorithms that can be sped up using this technique. For example:

Element distinctness
    Algorithms which, given a function f acting on a register, can determine whether there exist two distinct elements in the register i, j for which $f(i) = f(j)$. This problem has applications such as finding triangles in graphs or calculating matrix products.

Finding global minima
    Algorithms which, given an integer-valued function acting on a register with N entries, find the index i of the register such that $f(i)$ has the lowest value.

Chapter 14 provides a reference list where many of these algorithms can be found.

CHAPTER 11

Quantum Supersampling

From pixel-based adventure games to photorealistic movie effects, computer graphics has a history of being at the forefront of computing innovations. Quantum Image Processing (QIP) employs a QPU to enhance our image processing capabilities. Although very much in its infancy, QIP already offers exciting examples of how QPUs might impact the field of computer graphics.

What Can a QPU Do for Computer Graphics?

In this chapter we explore one particular QIP application called *Quantum Supersampling (QSS)*. QSS leverages a QPU to find intriguing improvements to the computer graphics task of *supersampling*, as is summarized in Figure 11-1. Supersampling is a conventional computer graphics technique whereby an image generated by a computer at high resolution is reduced to a lower-resolution image by selectively sampling pixels. Supersampling is an important step in the process of producing usable output graphics from computer-generated images.

QSS was originally developed as a way to *speed up* supersampling with a QPU, and by this metric it failed. However, numerical analysis of the results revealed something interesting. Although the final image quality of QSS (measured as error per pixel) is about the same as for existing conventional methods, the output image has a different kind of advantage.

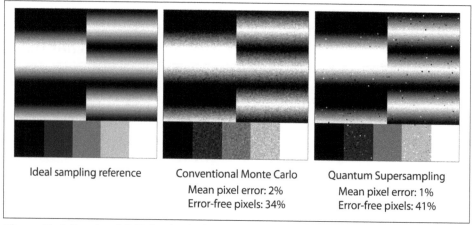

| Ideal sampling reference | Conventional Monte Carlo
Mean pixel error: 2%
Error-free pixels: 34% | Quantum Supersampling
Mean pixel error: 1%
Error-free pixels: 41% |

Figure 11-1. Results of QSS (with ideal and conventional cases for comparison); these reveal a change in the character of the noise in a sampled image

Figure 11-1 shows that the average pixel noise[1] in the conventional and QSS sampled images is about the same, but the *character* of the noise is very different. In the conventionally sampled image, each pixel is a little bit noisy. In the quantum image, some of the pixels are *very* noisy (black and white specks), while the rest are perfect.

Imagine you've been given an image, and you're allowed 15 minutes to manually remove the visible noise. For the image generated by QSS the task is fairly easy; for the conventionally sampled image, it's nearly impossible.

QSS combines a range of QPU primitives: quantum arithmetic from Chapter 5, amplitude amplification from Chapter 6, and the Quantum Fourier Transform from Chapter 7. To see how these primitives are utilized, we first need a little more background in the art of supersampling.

Conventional Supersampling

Ray tracing_ is a technique for producing computer-generated images, where increased computational resources allow us to produce results of increasing quality. Figure 11-2 shows a schematic representation of how ray tracing produces images from computer-generated scenes.

---

1 Here pixel noise is defined as the difference between the sampled and ideal results.

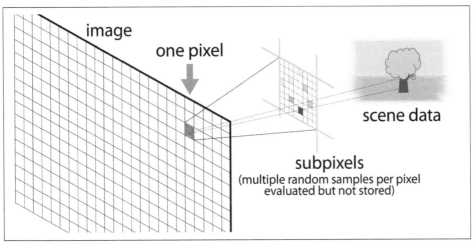

Figure 11-2. In ray tracing, many samples are taken for each pixel of the final image

For each pixel in the final image, a mathematical ray is projected in 3D space from the camera through the pixel and toward the computer-generated scene. The ray strikes an object in the scene, and in the simplest version (ignoring reflections and transparency) the object's color determines the color of the corresponding pixel in the image.

While casting just one ray per pixel would produce a correct image, for faraway details such as the tree in Figure 11-2 edges and fine details in the scene are lost. Additionally, as the camera or the object moves, troublesome noise patterns appear on objects such as tree leaves and picket fences.

To solve this without making the image size ridiculously large, ray-tracing software casts multiple rays per pixel (hundreds or thousands is typical) while varying the direction slightly for each one. Only the *average* color is kept, and the rest of the detail is discarded. This process is called *supersampling*, or *Monte Carlo sampling*. As more samples are taken, the noise level in the final image is reduced.

Supersampling is a task where we perform parallel processing (calculating the results of many rays interacting with a scene), but ultimately only need the *sum* of the results, not the individual results themselves. This sounds like something a QPU might help with! A full QPU-based ray-tracing engine would require far more qubits than are currently available. However, to demonstrate QSS we can use a QPU to draw higher-resolution images by less-sophisticated methods (ones not involving ray-tracing!), so that we can study how a QPU impacts the final resolution-reducing supersampling step.

Hands-on: Computing Phase-Encoded Images

To make use of a QPU for supersampling, we'll need a way of representing images in a QPU register (one that isn't as tricky as full-blown ray tracing!).

There are many different ways to represent pixel images in QPU registers and we summarize a number of approaches from the quantum image processing literature at the end of this chapter. However, we'll use a representation that we refer to as *phase encoding*, where the values of pixels are represented in the phases of a superposition. Importantly, this allows our image information to be compatible with the amplitude amplification technique we introduced in Chapter 6.

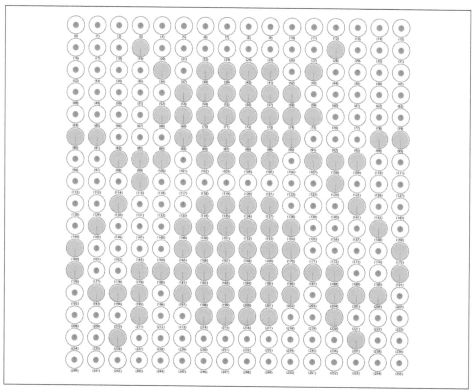

Figure 11-3. Ce n'est pas une mouche[2]

---

2 In *La trahison des images*, the painter René Magritte highlights the realization that an image of a pipe is not a pipe. Similarly, this phase-encoded *image* of a fly is not the complete quantum state of an actual fly.

Encoding images in the phases of a superposition isn't entirely new to us. At the end of Chapter 4 we used an eight-qubit register to phase-encode a whimsical image of a fly,[3] as shown in Figure 11-3.

In this chapter we'll learn how phase-encoded images like this can be created, and then use them to demonstrate Quantum Supersampling.

A QPU Pixel Shader

A *pixel shader* is a program (often run on a GPU) that takes an x and y position as input, and produces a color (black or white in our case) as output. To help us demonstrate QSS, we'll construct a *quantum* pixel shader.

To begin, Example 11-1 initializes two four-qubit registers, qx and qy. These will serve as the x and y input values for our shader. As we've seen in previous chapters, performing a HAD on all qubits produces a uniform superposition of all possible values, as in Figure 11-4. This is our blank canvas, ready for drawing.

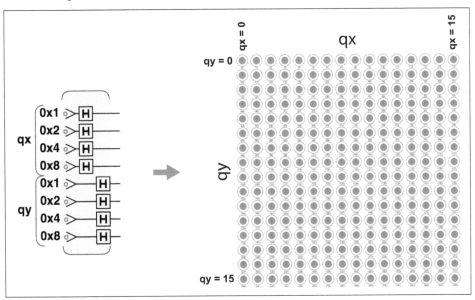

Figure 11-4. A blank quantum canvas

---

3 The complete code for the fly-in-the-teleporter experiment can be found at *http://oreilly-qc.github.io?p=4-2*. In addition to phase logic, the mirror subroutine from Chapter 6 was applied to make the fly easier to see.

Using PHASE to Draw

Now we're ready to draw. Finding concise ways to draw into register phases can get complicated and subtle, but we can start by filling the right half of the canvas simply by performing the operation "if qx >= 8 then invert phase." This is accomplished by applying a PHASE(180) to a single qubit, as demonstrated in Figure 11-5:

```
// Set up and clear the canvas
qc.reset(8);
var qx = qint.new(4, 'qx');
var qy = qint.new(4, 'qy');
qc.write(0);
qx.hadamard();
qy.hadamard();

// Invert if qx >= 8
qc.phase(180, qx.bits(0x8));
```

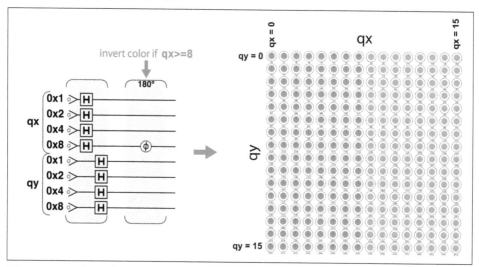

Figure 11-5. Phase-flipping half of the image

 In a sense, we've used *just one* QPU instruction to fill 128 pixels. On a GPU, this would have required the pixel shader to run 128 times. As we know only too well, the catch is that if we try to READ the result we get only a random value of qx and qy.

With a little more logic, we can fill a square with a 50% gray dither pattern.[4] For this, we want to flip any pixels where qx and qy are both greater than or equal to 8, *and* where the low qubit of qx is not equal to the low qubit of qy. We do this in Example 11-1, and the results can be seen in Figure 11-6.

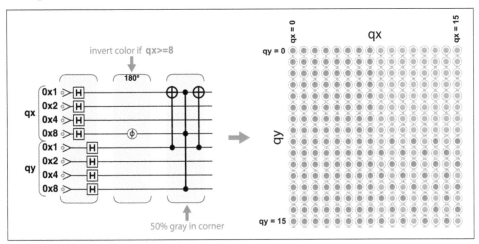

Figure 11-6. Adding a dither pattern

---

4 Dithering is the process of applying a regular pattern to an image, normally to approximate otherwise unobtainable colors by visually "blending" a limited color palette.

```
qc.cphase(180, qy.bits(0x8, qx.bits(0x8|0x1)));
qx.cnot(qy, 0x1);
```

With a little arithmetic from Chapter 5, we can create more interesting patterns, as shown in Figure 11-7:

```
// Clear the canvas
qc.reset(8);
var qx = qint.new(4, 'qx');
var qy = qint.new(4, 'qy');
qc.write(0);
qx.hadamard();
qy.hadamard();

// fun stripes
qx.subtractShifted(qy, 1);
qc.phase(180, qx.bits(0x8));
qx.addShifted(qy, 1);
```

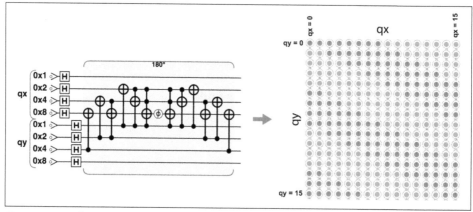

Figure 11-7. Playing with stripes

Drawing Curves

To draw more complex shapes, we need more complex math. Example 11-2 demonstrates the use of the addSquared() QPU function from Chapter 5 to draw a quarter-circle with a radius of 13 pixels. The result is shown in Figure 11-8. In this case, the math must be performed in a larger 10-qubit register, to prevent overflow when we square and add qx and qy. Here we've used the trick learned in Chapter 10 of storing the value of a logical (or mathematical) operation in the phase of a state, through a combination of magnitude and phase-logic operations.

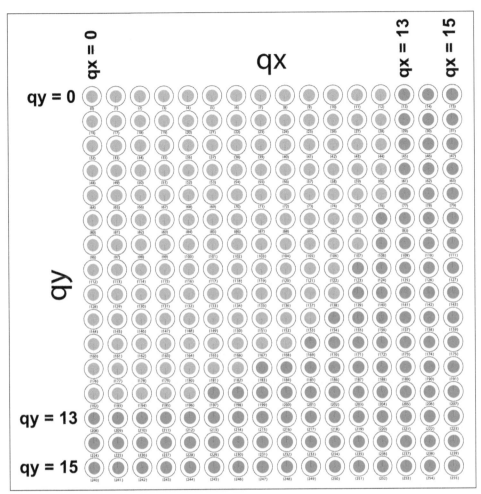

Figure 11-8. Drawing curves in Hilbert space

Sample Code

Run this sample online at *http://oreilly-qc.github.io?p=11-2*.

Example 11-2. Drawing curves in Hilbert space

```
var radius = 13;
var acc_bits = 10;

// Clear the canvas
qc.reset(18);
var qx = qint.new(4, 'qx');
var qy = qint.new(4, 'qy');
var qacc = qint.new(10, 'qacc');
```

```
qc.write(0);
qx.hadamard();
qy.hadamard();

// fill if x^2 + y^2 < r^2
qacc.addSquared(qx);
qacc.addSquared(qy);
qacc.subtract(radius * radius);
qacc.phase(180, 1 << (acc_bits - 1));
qacc.add(radius * radius);
qacc.subtractSquared(qy);
qacc.subtractSquared(qx);
```

If the qacc register is too small, the math performed in it will overflow, resulting in curved bands. This overflow effect will be used deliberately in Figure 11-11, later in the chapter.

Sampling Phase-Encoded Images

Now that we can represent images in the phases of quantum registers, let's return to the problem of supersampling. Recall that in supersampling we have many pieces of information calculated from a computer-generated scene (corresponding to different rays we have traced) that we want to combine to give a single pixel in our final output image. software verification To simulate this, we can consider our 16×16 array of quantum states to be made of 16 4×4 tiles as shown in Figure 11-9.

We imagine that the full 16×16 image is the higher-resolution data, which we then want reduce into 16 final pixels.

Since they're only 4×4 subpixels, the qx and qy registers needed to draw into these tiles can be reduced to two qubits each. We can use an overflow register (which we call qacc since such registers are often referred to as *accumulators*) to perform any required logical operations that won't fit in two qubits. Figure 11-10 (Example 11-3) shows the circuit for performing the drawing shown in Figure 11-9, tile by tile.

Note that in this program, the variables tx and ty are digital values indicating which tile of the image the shader is working on. We get the absolute x value of a subpixel that we want to draw by adding qx and (tx x 4), which we can easily compute since tx and ty are not quantum. Breaking our images into tiles this way makes it easier for us to subsequently perform supersampling.

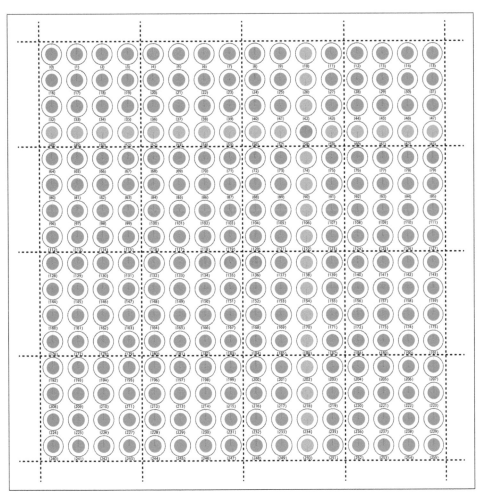

Figure 11-9. A simple image divided into subpixels

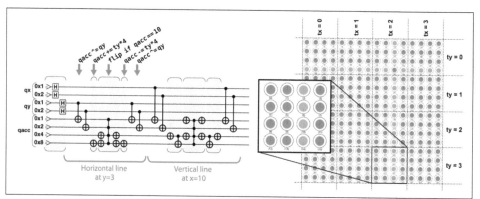

Figure 11-10. Drawing the subpixels of one tile in superposition

Sample Code

Run this sample online at *http://oreilly-qc.github.io?p=11-3*.

Example 11-3. Drawing lines using an accumulator

```
// Set up and clear the canvas
qc.reset(8);
var qx = qint.new(2, 'qx');
var qy = qint.new(2, 'qy');
var qacc = qint.new(4, 'qacc');
qc.write(0);
qx.hadamard();
qy.hadamard();

// Choose which tile to draw
var tx = 2;  // tile column
var ty = 1;  // tile row

// Hz line y=3
qacc.cnot(qy)
qacc.add(ty * 4);
qacc.not(~3);
qacc.cphase(180);
qacc.not(~3);
qacc.subtract(ty * 4);
qacc.cnot(qy);

// Vt line x=10
qacc.cnot(qx)
qacc.add(tx * 4);
qacc.not(~10);
qacc.cphase(180);
qacc.not(~10);
```

```
qacc.subtract(tx * 4);
qacc.cnot(qx);
```

A More Interesting Image

With a more sophisticated shader program, we can produce a more interesting test for the quantum supersampling algorithm. In order to test and compare supersampling methods, here we use circular bands to produce some very high-frequency detail. The full source code for the image in Figure 11-11, which also splits the phase-encoded image into tiles as we mentioned earlier, can be run at *http://oreilly-qc.github.io?p=11-A*.

Figure 11-11. A more involved image with some high-frequency detail conventionally rendered at 256×256 pixels (shown here).

 It may seem like we've had to use a range of shortcuts and special-case tricks to produce these images. But this is not so different from the hacks and workarounds that were necessary in the very early days of conventional computer graphics.

Now that we have a higher-resolution phase-encoded image broken up into tiles, we're ready to apply the QSS algorithm. In this case, the full image is drawn at 256×256 pixels. We'll use 4,096 tiles, each composed of 4×4 subpixels, and supersample all the subpixels in a single tile to generate one pixel of the final sampled image from its 16 subpixels.

Supersampling

For each tile, we want to estimate the number of subpixels that have been phase-flipped. With black and white subpixels (represented for us as flipped or unflipped phases), this allows us to obtain a value for each final pixel representative of the intensity of its original constituent subpixels. Handily, this problem is exactly the same as the Quantum Sum Estimation problem from "Multiple Flipped Entries" on page 114.

To make use of Quantum Sum Estimation, we simply consider the quantum program implementing our drawing instructions to be the `flip` subroutine we use in amplitude amplification from Chapter 6. Combining this with the Quantum Fourier Transform from Chapter 7 allows us to approximate the total number of flipped subpixels in each tile. This involves running our drawing program multiple times for each tile.

Note that, without a QPU, sampling a high-resolution image into a lower-resolution one would still require running a drawing subroutine multiple times for each tile, randomizing the values `qx` and `qy` for each sample. Each time we would simply receive a "black" or "white" sample, and by adding these up we would converge on an approximated image.

The sample code in Example 11-4 shows the results of both quantum and conventional supersampling (typically performed in the conventional case by a technique known as Monte Carlo sampling), and we see them compared in Figure 11-12. The *ideal reference* shows the result we would get from perfect sampling, and the QSS lookup table is a tool we discuss in detail in the coming pages.

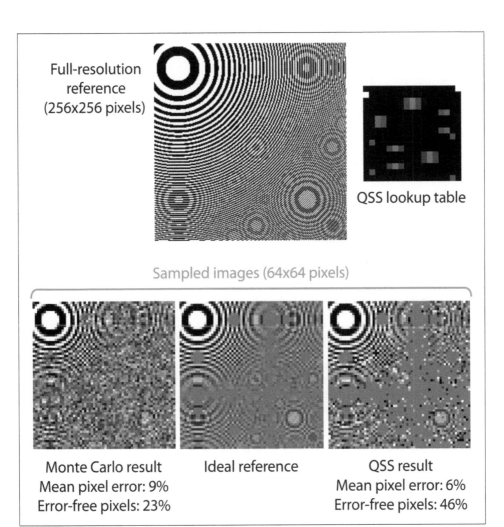

Figure 11-12. Comparison of quantum and conventional supersampling

Sample Code

Run this sample online at *http://oreilly-qc.github.io?p=11-4*.

Example 11-4. Supersampling

```javascript
function do_qss_image()
{
    var sp = {};
    var total_qubits = 2 * res_aa_bits + num_counter_bits
                       + accum_bits;

    // Set up the quantum registers
```

```
qc.reset(total_qubits);
sp.qx = qint.new(res_aa_bits, 'qx');
sp.qy = qint.new(res_aa_bits, 'qy');
sp.counter = qint.new(num_counter_bits, 'counter');
sp.qacc = qint.new(accum_bits, 'scratch');
sp.qacc.write(0);

// For each tile in the image, run the qss_tile() function
for (var sp.ty = 0; sp.ty < res_tiles; ++sp.ty) {
    for (var sp.tx = 0; sp.tx < res_tiles; ++sp.tx)
        qss_tile(sp);
    }
}

function qss_tile(sp)
{
    // Prepare the tile canvas
    sp.qx.write(0);
    sp.qy.write(0);
    sp.counter.write(0);
    sp.qx.hadamard();
    sp.qy.hadamard();
    sp.counter.hadamard();

    // Run the pixel shader multiple times
    for (var cbit = 0; cbit < num_counter_bits; ++cbit) {
        var iters = 1 << cbit;
        var qxy_bits = sp.qx.bits().or(sp.qy.bits());
        var condition = sp.counter.bits(iters);
        var mask_with_condition = qxy_bits.or(condition);
        for (var i = 0; i < iters; ++i) {
            shader_quantum(sp.qx, sp.qy, sp.tx, sp.ty, sp.qacc,
                           condition, sp.qcolor);
            grover_iteration(qxy_bits, mask_with_condition);
        }
    }
    invQFT(sp.counter);

    // Read and interpret the result
    sp.readVal = sp.counter.read();
    sp.hits = qss_count_to_hits[sp.readVal];
    sp.color = sp.hits / (res_aa * res_aa);
    return sp.color;
}
```

As mentioned at the beginning of this chapter, the interesting advantage we obtain with QSS is not to do with the number of drawing operations that we have to perform, but rather relates to a difference in the *character* of the noise we observe.

In this example, when comparing equivalent numbers of samples, QSS has about 33% lower mean pixel error than Monte Carlo. More interestingly, the number of zero-error pixels (pixels in which the result *exactly* matches the ideal) is almost double that of the Monte Carlo result.

QSS Versus Conventional Monte Carlo Sampling

In contrast to conventional Monte Carlo sampling, our QSS shader never actually outputs a single subpixel value. Instead, it uses the superposition of possible values to estimate the *sum* you would have gotten from calculating them all and adding them up. If you actually need to calculate every subpixel value along the way, then a conventional computing approach is a better tool for the job. If you need to know the sum, or some other characteristic of groups of subpixels, a QPU offers an interesting alternative approach.

The fundamental difference between QSS and conventional supersampling can be characterized as follows:

Conventional supersampling
    As the number of samples increases, the result converges toward the exact answer.

Quantum supersampling
    As the number of samples increases, the probability of getting the exact answer increases.

Now that we have an idea of what QSS can do for us, let's expand a little on how it works.

How QSS Works

The core idea behind QSS is to use the approach we first saw in "Multiple Flipped Entries" on page 114, where combining amplitude amplification iterations with the Quantum Fourier Transform (QFT) allows us to estimate the number of items flipped by whatever logic we use in the `flip` subroutine of each AA iteration.

In the case of QSS, `flip` is provided by our drawing program, which flips the phase of all of the "white" subpixels.

We can understand the way that AA and QFT and work together to help us count flipped items as follows. First, we perform a single AA iteration *conditional on the value of a register of "counter" qubits*. We call this register a "counter" precisely because its value determines how many AA iterations our circuit will perform. If we now use HAD operations to prepare our counter register in superposition we will be performing a *superposition* of different numbers of AA iterations. Recall from "Multiple Flipped

Entries" on page 114 that the READ probabilities for multiple flipped values in a register are dependent on the number of AA iterations that we perform. We noted in this earlier discussion that oscillations are introduced depending on the number of flipped values. Because of this, when we perform a superposition of different numbers of AA iterations, we introduce a periodic oscillation across the amplitudes of our QPU register having a frequency that depends on the number of flipped values.

When it comes to READing frequencies encoded in QPU registers, we know that the QFT is the way to go: using the QFT we can determine this frequency, and consequently the number of flipped values (i.e., number of shaded subpixels). Knowing the number of subpixels we've supersampled for a single pixel in our final lower-resolution image, we can then use this to determine the *brightness* we should use for that pixel.

Although this might be a little difficult to parse in text on a page, stepping through the code in Example 11-4 and inspecting the resulting circle notation visualizations will hopefully make the approach taken by QSS more apparent.

Note that the more counter qubits we use, the better the sampling of the image will be, but at the cost of having to run our drawing code more times. This trade-off is true for both quantum and conventional approaches, as can be seen in Figure 11-13.

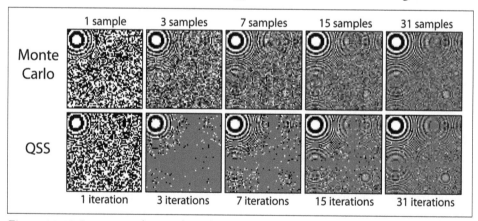

Figure 11-13. Increasing the number of iterations

The QSS lookup table

When we run the QSS algorithm and finish by READing out our QPU register, the number we get will be related but not directly equal to the number of white pixels within a given tile.

The QSS lookup table is the tool we need to look up how many subpixels a given READ value implies were within a tile. The lookup table needed for a particular image doesn't depend on the image detail (or more precisely, the details of the quantum pixel shader we used). We can generate and reuse a single QSS lookup table for any QSS applications having given tile and counter register sizes.

For example, Figure 11-14 shows a lookup table for QSS applications having a 4×4 tile size and a counter register consisting of four qubits.

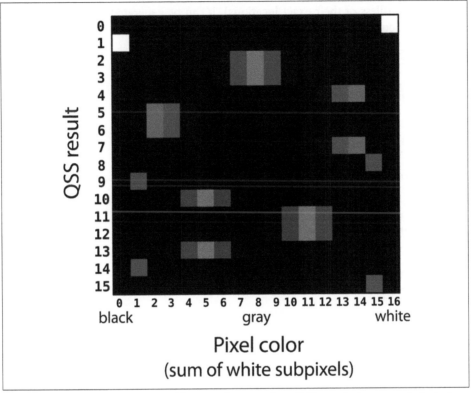

Figure 11-14. The QSS lookup table is used to translate QSS results into sampled pixel brightness

The rows (y-axis) of the lookup table enumerate the possible outcomes we might read in the output QPU register from an application of QSS. The columns (x-axis) enumerate the different possible numbers of subpixels within a tile that could lead to these READ values. The grayscale colors in the table graphically represent the probabilities associated with the different possible READ values (lighter colors here denoting higher probabilities). Here's an example of how we could use the lookup table. Suppose we read a QSS result of 10. Finding that row in the QSS lookup table, we see that this result most likely implies that we have supersampled five white subpixels. However, there's also a nonzero probability we supersampled four or six (or to a lesser extent three or seven) subpixels. Note that some error is introduced as we cannot always uniquely infer the number of sampled subpixels from a READ result.

Such a lookup table is used by the QSS algorithm to determine a final result. How do we get our hands on a QSS lookup table for a particular QSS problem? The code in Example 11-5 shows how we can calculate the QSS lookup table. Note that this code doesn't rely on a particular quantum pixel shader (i.e., particular image). Since the lookup table only associated the READ value with a given number of white subpixels per tile (regardless of their exact locations), it can be generated without any knowledge of the actual image to be supersampled.

Sample Code

Run this sample online at *http://oreilly-qc.github.io?p=11-5*.

Example 11-5. Building a QSS lookup table

```
function create_table_column(color, qxy, qcount)
{
    var true_count = color;

    // Put everything into superposition
    qc.write(0);
    qcount.hadamard();
    qxy.hadamard();

    for (var i = 0; i < num_counter_bits; ++i)
    {
        var reps = 1 << i;
        var condition = qcount.bits(reps);
        var mask_with_condition = qxy.bits().or(condition);
        for (var j = 0; j < reps; ++j)
        {
            flip_n_terms(qxy, true_count, condition);
            grover_iteration(qxy.bits(), mask_with_condition);
        }
    }
    invQFT(qcount);

    // Construct the lookup table
    for (var i = 0; i < (1 << num_counter_bits); ++i)
        qss_lookup_table[color][i] = qcount.peekProbability(i);
}
```

The QSS lookup table tells us a lot about how QSS performs for given counter register and tile sizes, acting as a sort of *fingerprint* for the algorithm. Figure 11-15 shows a few examples of how the lookup table changes as (for a fixed counter register size of four qubits) we increase the tile size (and therefore number of subpixels) used in our QSS algorithm.

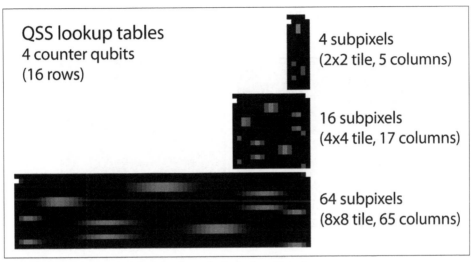

Figure 11-15. Increasing the number of subpixels adds columns

Similarly, Figure 11-16 shows how the lookup table changes as we increase the number of counter qubits used (for a given tile size).

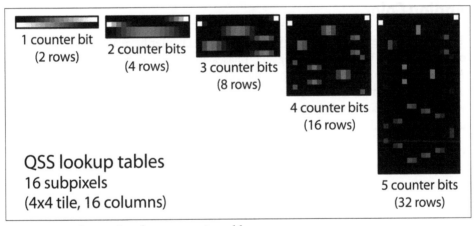

Figure 11-16. Increasing the counter size adds rows

Confidence maps

In addition to being a tool for interpreting READ values, we can also use a QSS lookup table to evaluate how confident we are in the final brightness of a pixel. By looking up a given pixel's QSS READ value in a row of the table, we can judge the probability that a pixel value we've inferred is correct. For example, in the case of the lookup table in Figure 11-14, we'd be very confident of values READ to be 0 or 1, but much less confident if we'd READ values of 2, 3, or 4. This kind of inference can be used to produce a "confidence map" indicating the likely locations of errors in images we produce with QSS, as illustrated in Figure 11-17.

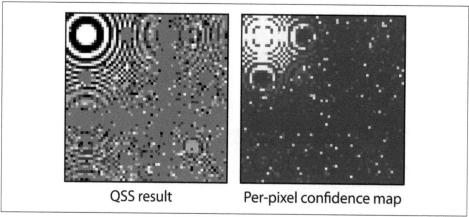

Figure 11-17. QSS result and associated confidence map generated from a QSS lookup table—in the confidence map brighter pixels denote areas where the result is more likely correct

Adding Color

The images we've been rendering with QSS in this chapter have all been one-bit monochrome, using flipped QPU register phases to represent black and white pixels. Although we're big fans of retro gaming, perhaps we can incorporate a few more colors? We *could* simply use the phases and amplitudes of our QPU register to encode a wider range of color values for our pixels, but then the Quantum Sum Estimation used by QSS would no longer work.

However, we can borrow a technique from early graphics cards known as *bitplanes*. In this approach we use our quantum pixel shader to render separate monochrome images, each representing one bit of our image. For example, suppose we want to associate three colors with each pixel in our image (red, green, and blue). Our pixel shader can then essentially generate three separate monochrome images, each of which represents the contribution of one of the three color channels. These three images can undergo supersampling separately, before being recombined into a final color image.

This only allows us eight colors (including black and white); however, supersampling allows us to blend *subpixels* together, effectively producing a 12-bit-per-pixel image (see Figure 11-18). The complete code for this can be found at *http://oreilly-qc.github.io?p=11-6*.

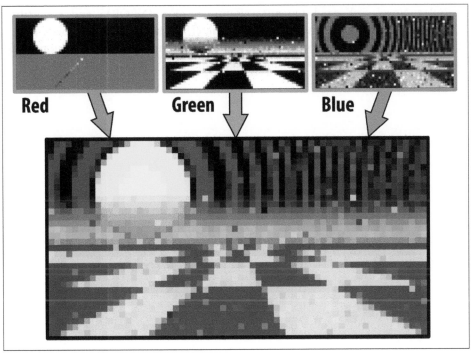

Figure 11-18. Combining supersampled color planes. Space Harrier eat your heart out!

Conclusion

This chapter demonstrated how exploring new combinations of QPU primitives with a little domain knowledge can potentially lead to new QPU applications. The ability to redistribute sampling noise also shows visually how sometimes we have to look beyond speedups to see the advantages of QPU applications.

It's also worth noting that the ability of Quantum Supersampling to produce novel noise redistributions potentially has relevance beyond computer graphics. Many other applications also make heavy use of Monte Carlo sampling, in fields such as artificial intelligence, computational fluid dynamics, and even finance.

To introduce Quantum Supersampling, we used a *phase encoding* representation of images in QPU registers. It is worth noting that Quantum Image Processing researchers have also proposed many other such representations. These include the so-called Qubit Lattice representation,[5] Flexible Representation of Quantum Images

---

5 Venegas-Andraca et al, 2003 (*http://bit.ly/2XMtx6t*).

(FRQI),[6] Novel Enhanced Quantum Representation (NEQR),[7] and Generalized Quantum Image Representation (GQIR).[8] These representations[9] have been used to explore other image processing applications including template matching,[10] edge detection,[11] image classification,[12] and image translation[13] to name but a few.[14]

6 Le et al, 2011 (*http://bit.ly/2JdoL8I*).

7 Zhang et al, 2013 (*http://bit.ly/2XePN4g*).

8 Jiang et al, 2015 (*http://bit.ly/2JcFo4h*).

9 For a more detailed review of these quantum image representations, see Yan et al, 2015 (*http://bit.ly/2ROGjMi*).

10 Curtis et al, 2004 (*http://bit.ly/2xvJqiV*).

11 Yuan et al, 2013 (*http://bit.ly/2RKPrkR*).

12 Ostaszewski et al, 2015 (*https://arxiv.org/abs/1504.00580*).

13 Wang et al, 2015 (*http://bit.ly/2XfEAW5*).

14 For more comprehensive reviews of QIP applications, see Cai et al, 2018 (*http://bit.ly/2XeR8bw*) and Yan et al, 2017 (*http://bit.ly/2ROeBPx*).

CHAPTER 12

Shor's Factoring Algorithm

If you'd heard about one application of quantum computing before you picked up this book, there's a good chance it was Shor's factoring algorithm.

Quantum computing was mostly considered to be of academic, rather than practical, interest until Peter Shor's 1994 discovery that a sufficiently powerful quantum computer can find the prime factors of a number exponentially faster than any conventional machine. In this chapter, we take a hands-on look at one specific implementation of Shor's QPU factoring algorithm.

Far from being a mere mathematical curiosity, the ability to quickly factorize large numbers can help break the Rivest–Shamir–Adleman (RSA) public-key cryptosystem. Anytime you spin up an `ssh` session you're making use of RSA. Public-key cryptosystems like RSA work by a process wherein a freely available public key can be used by anybody to *encrypt* information. But once encrypted, the information can only be *decrypted* using a secret, privately held key. Public-key cryptosystems are often compared to an electronic version of a mailbox. Imagine a locked box with a slit allowing anyone to post (but not retrieve) a message, and a door with a lock to which only the owner has the key. It turns out that the task of finding the prime factors of a large number N works really well as part of a public-key cryptosystem. The assurance that someone can only use the public key to encrypt and not to decrypt information rests on the assumption that finding the prime factors of N is a computationally infeasible task.

A full explanation of RSA is beyond the scope of this book, but the key point is that if Shor's algorithm provides a way to find the prime factors of a large number N, then it has implications for one of the modern internet's backbone components.

There are other very good reasons to get to grips with Shor's algorithm besides its cryptographic implications, as it's the best-known example of a class of algorithms solving instances of the so-called *hidden subgroup problem*. In this kind of problem, we want to determine the periodicity of a given periodic function, where the periodicity can be potentially quite complicated. A number of problems in discrete mathematics are instances of the hidden subgroup problem, such as period finding, order finding (which is the underlying difficult problem in factoring), finding discrete logarithms, and many others. A similar procedure to what we'll see in this chapter can also provide solutions to some of these other problems.[1]

Shor's algorithm is another prime example (pun intended) of how our QPU primitives are put to use. We've seen in Chapter 7 that the QFT is perfectly suited to investigating periodic signals, and Shor's algorithm makes heavy use of it.

An especially instructive aspect of Shor's algorithm is that it also ends by leveraging a conventional program to retrieve the desired prime factors from a periodicity learned with the QFT. The algorithm works so well because it accepts the QPU's role as a *coprocessor*, applying quantum ideas only in those parts of the problem to which they are well suited.

Let's take a closer look at the idea and code behind the algorithm.

Hands-on: Using Shor on a QPU

In keeping with the hands-on theme of this book, the sample code in Example 12-1 will allow you to see Shor's factoring algorithm in operation right away, using built-in functions from QCEngine.

Sample Code

Run this sample online at *http://oreilly-qc.github.io?p=12-1*.

Example 12-1. Complete factoring with Shor

```
function shor_sample() {
    var N = 35;                  // The number we're factoring
    var precision_bits = 4;      // See the text for a description
    var coprime = 2;             // Must be 2 in this QPU implementation

    var result = Shor(N, precision_bits, coprime);
}

function Shor(N, precision_bits, coprime) {
    // quantum part
```

---

1 Note that not all problems of this class are known to have solutions of this form. For example, graph isomorphism (which tests the equivalence of graphs under relabeling of vertices) also belongs to the hidden subgroup class, but it is unknown whether an efficient QPU algorithm exists for this problem.

```
      var repeat_period = ShorQPU(N, precision_bits, coprime);
      var factors = ShorLogic(N, repeat_period, coprime);
      // classical part
      return factors;
}

function ShorLogic(N, repeat_period, coprime) {
    // Given the repeat period, find the actual factors
    var ar2 = Math.pow(coprime, repeat_period / 2.0);
    var factor1 = gcd(N, ar2 - 1);
    var factor2 = gcd(N, ar2 + 1);
    return [factor1, factor2];
}
```

As mentioned earlier, the QPU is doing only part of the work here. The `Shor()` function makes calls to two other functions. The first, `ShorQPU()`, leverages our QPU (or a simulation thereof) to help find the *repeat period* of a function, while the rest of the work in `ShorLogic()` is performed with conventional software running on a CPU. We'll dive into each of these functions in more detail in the next section.

The `ShorLogic()` implementation we use in our example is for illustrative purposes only. Although simpler to explain, it will struggle with very large numbers. Full-scale Shor algorithms are the focus of ongoing research.

The remainder of the chapter walks through Shor's algorithm, presented in a standard and approachable way. Take note, however, that the implementation we present is *not* the most efficient realization of Shor's original idea, and actual implementations "in the wild" are likely to vary across QPU hardware.

What Shor's Algorithm Does

Let's start with the `ShorQPU()` function. We're going to assert without proof a useful fact from number theory.[2] Namely, it's possible to solve the problem of finding prime factors p and q of a number $N = pq$ if we are able to solve the seemingly unrelated problem of finding the repeat period of the function $a^x \bmod(N)$, as the integer variable x is varied. Here N is still the number we want to factor; a is called the *coprime*. The value of the coprime can be chosen to be any prime number that we like.

If the idea of finding the repeat period of $a^x \bmod(N)$ sounds obscure, fear not. All it means is that as you change the value of x, eventually the sequence of numbers

---

2 See Chapter 14 for more in-depth references.

returned by $a^x \bmod(N)$ repeats itself. The repeat period is just the number of x values between repeats, as you can see in Figure 12-1.

 To keep things simple, we'll choose 2 as our coprime. Besides being the smallest prime number, this choice has the advantage that our QPU implementation of a^x can be implemented by simply shifting bits. It's a good choice for the cases we cover in this chapter, but will not be appropriate in other cases.

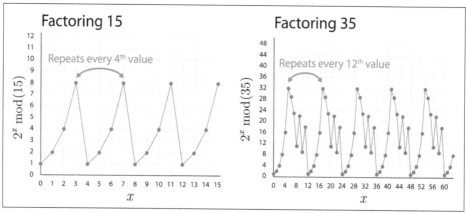

Figure 12-1. The repeat periods for two different values of N

Once we know the repeat period p, then one of N's prime factors *might* be given by $gcd\left(N, a^{p/2} + 1\right)$ and the other might be given by $gcd\left(N, a^{p/2} - 1\right)$. Again, these are statements that we give here without proof, but which follow from number theory arguments. Here, *gcd* is a function that returns the greatest common divisor of its two arguments. The well-known *Euclidean algorithm* can quickly work out *gcd* for us on a conventional CPU (see the online sample code at *http://oreilly-qc.github.io?p=12-1* for an implementation of *gcd*).

 While we *might* be able to find the prime factors from these two *gcd* expressions, this is not guaranteed. Success depends on the chosen value of the coprime a. As previously mentioned, we have chosen 2 as our coprime for illustrative purposes, and as a result there are some numbers that this implementation will fail to factor, such as 171 or 297.

Do We Need a QPU at All?

We've reduced the problem of prime factoring to finding the periodicity p of a^x $\bmod(N)$. It's actually possible to try to find p with a conventional CPU program. All we need do is repeatedly evaluate $a^x \bmod(N)$ for increasing values of x, counting how many values we have tried and keeping track of the return values we get. As soon as a return value repeats, we can stop and declare the period to be the number of values we tried.

 This brute-force method for finding the period of $a^x \bmod(N)$ assumes that if we get the same value back from the function, then we must have gone through one full repeat period p. Although not immediately obvious, a mathematical property of $a^x \bmod(N)$ is that it can only assume any given value once within one period. Hence the moment we get the same result twice, we know we have completed a full period.

Example 12-2 implements this nonquantum, brute-force approach to finding p.

Sample Code

Run this sample online at *http://oreilly-qc.github.io?p=12-2*.

Example 12-2. Factoring without a QPU

```
function ShorNoQPU(N, precision_bits, coprime) {
    // Classical replacement for the quantum part of Shor
    varwork = 1;
    var max_loops = Math.pow(2, precision_bits);
    for (var iter = 0; iter < max_loops; ++iter) {
        work = (work * coprime) % N;
        if (work == 1) // found the repeat
            return iter + 1;
    }
    return 0;
}
```

The code shown in Example 12-2 runs quickly on a whole range of numbers. The period-finding loop only needs to run until it finds the first repetition, and then it's done. So why do we need a QPU at all?

Although ShorNoQPU() in Example 12-2 might not *look* too costly to evaluate, the number of loops required to find the repeat pattern (which is given by the repeat period of the pattern itself) grows exponentially with the number of bits in N, as shown in Figure 12-2.

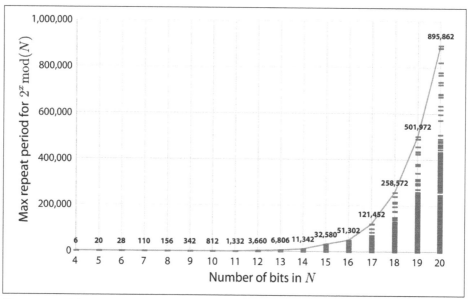

Figure 12-2. The maximum number of loops required to find the repeat period of an integer represented by a bitstring of length N. Each bar also displays a histogram showing the distribution of repeat periods for integers represented by a bitstring of length N.

 There are more efficient approaches to finding prime factors on a conventional CPU (such as the *General Number Field Sieve*), but they all run into similar scaling problems as the size of *N* increases. The runtime of the most efficient algorithm for factoring on a conventional CPU scales exponentially with the input size, whereas the runtime of Shor's algorithm scales polynomially with the input size.

So then, let's crack open the QPU.

The Quantum Approach

Although we'll give a step-by-step walkthrough of how ShorQPU() works in the next section, we'll first spend a little time highlighting the creative way it makes use of the QFT.

As we'll see shortly, thanks to some initial HAD operations, ShorQPU() leaves us with a^x mod(N) represented in the magnitudes and relative phases of our QPU register. Recall from Chapter 7 that the QFT implements the Discrete Fourier Transform, and leaves our output QPU register in a superposition of the different frequencies contained in the input.

Figure 12-3 shows what a DFT of a^x mod(N) looks like.

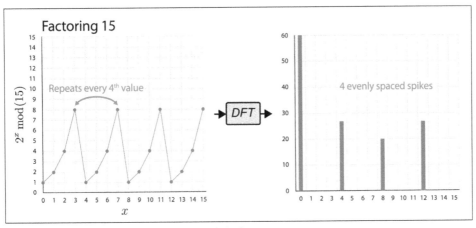

Figure 12-3. Computation performed while factoring 15

This DFT includes a spike at the correct signal frequency of 4, from which we could easily calculate p. That's all well and good for this conventional DFT, but recall from Chapter 7 that if we perform a QFT on the signal, these output peaks occur in super-position within our QPU output register. The value we obtain from the QFT after a READ is unlikely to yield the desired frequency.

It may look like our idea for using the QFT has fallen short. But if we play around with different values of N, we find something interesting about the DFT results for this particular kind of signal. Figure 12-4 shows the DFT of $a^x \bmod(N)$ with $N = 35$.

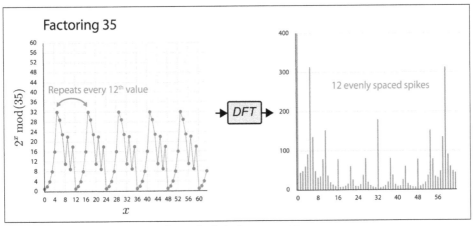

Figure 12-4. Computation performed while factoring 35

In this case, the repeat period of $a^x \bmod(N)$ is 12, and there are also 12 evenly spaced highest-weighted spikes in the DFT (these are the values we're most likely to observe in a readout after the QFT). Experimenting with different N values, we start to notice a trend: for a pattern with repeat period *p*, the magnitude of the Fourier Transform will have exactly *p* evenly spaced spikes, as shown in the figure.

Since the spikes are evenly spaced and we know the size of our register, we can estimate how many spikes there were in the QFT—even though we can't hope to observe more than one of them. (We give an explicit algorithm for doing this shortly.) From our experimenting, we know that this number of peaks is the same as the repeat period, *p*, of our input signal—precisely what we're after!

This is a more indirect use of the QFT than we covered in Chapter 7, but it demonstrates a crucial point—we shouldn't be afraid to use all the tools at our disposal to experiment with what's in our QPU register. It's reassuring to see that the hallowed programmer's mantra "Change the code and see what happens" remains fruitful even with a QPU.

Step by Step: Factoring the Number 15

Let's take a step-by-step look at using a QPU to factor the number 15. (Spoiler alert: the answer is 3 × 5.) Our Shor program grows in complexity as we try larger numbers, but 15 is a good place to start. The walkthrough we give will use the settings in Example 12-3 to demonstrate the algorithm's operation.

Sample Code

Run this sample online at *http://oreilly-qc.github.io?p=12-3*.

Example 12-3. Factoring the number 15

```
var N = 15;             // The number we're factoring
var precision_bits = 4; // See the text for a description of this
var coprime = 2;        // For this QPU implementation, this must be 2

var result = Shor(N, precision_bits, coprime);
```

The first argument, N, in this example is set to 15, the number we want to factor. The second argument, precision_bits, is 4. A larger number of precision bits will generally be more likely to return the correct answer, but conversely requires more qubits and many more instructions to execute. The third argument, coprime, will be left at 2, which is the only value that our simplified QPU implementation of Shor's algorithm supports.

We already know that our main Shor() function executes two smaller functions. A QPU program determines the repeat period, and then passes the result to a second function that determines the prime factors using conventional digital logic on a CPU. The steps taken by the constituent parts of Shor() are as follows:

- Steps 1–4 create a superposition of evaluations of $a^x \bmod(N)$.
- Steps 5–6 implement the QFT trick outlined previously for learning the period p of this signal.
- Steps 7–8 use p in a conventional CPU algorithm to find our prime factors.

We'll walk through these steps for the case of an eight-qubit register. Four of these qubits will be used to represent (superpositions of) the different values of x that we pass to $a^x \bmod(N)$, while the other four qubits will process and keep track of the values that this function returns.

This means that in total we will need to keep track of $2^8 = 256$ values—256 circles in our circle notation. By arranging all these circles into a 16×16 square, we can visualize the 16 states from each of our 4-qubit registers separately (see Chapter 3 for a recap on reading circle notation in this way). For convenience, we also add tags to these grids of 16×16 circles, showing the probabilities for each value from each of the two registers. Okay, enough talk; let's factor some numbers with a QPU!

Step 1: Initialize QPU Registers

To start the quantum part of the Shor program, we initialize the registers with the digital values 1 and 0 as shown in Figure 12-5. We'll see shortly that starting the work register with value 1 is necessary for the way we'll calculate $a^x \bmod(N)$.

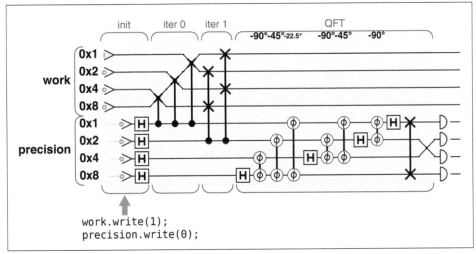

Figure 12-5. QPU instructions for step 1

Figure 12-6 shows the state of our two registers in circle notation after initialization.

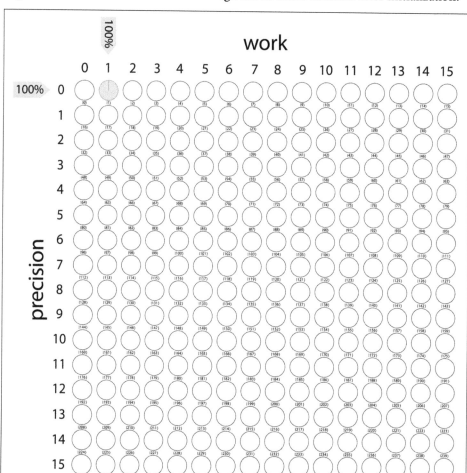

Figure 12-6. Step 1: Work and precision registers are initialized to values of 1 and 0, respectively

Step 2: Expand into Quantum Superposition

The precision register is used to represent the x values that we'll pass to the function $a^x \bmod(N)$. We'll use quantum superposition to evaluate this function for multiple values of x in parallel, so we apply HAD operations as shown in Figure 12-7 to place the precision register into a superposition of all possible values.

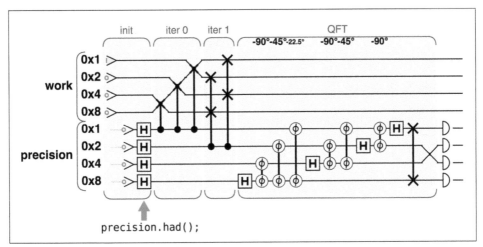

Figure 12-7. QPU instructions for step 2

This way, each row in the circle grid shown in Figure 12-8 is ready to be treated as a separate input to a parallel computation.

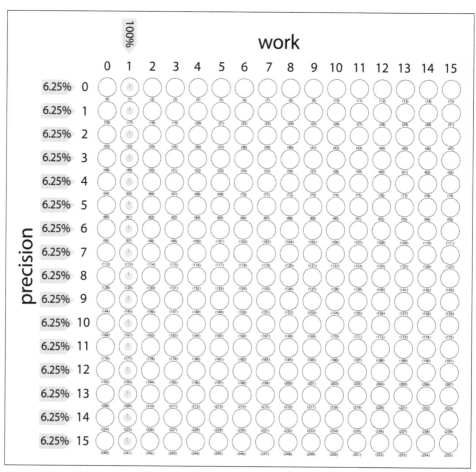

Figure 12-8. Step 2: A superposition of the precision register prepares us to evaluate a^x mod(N) in superposition

Step 3: Conditional Multiply-by-2

We now want to perform our function a^x mod(N) on the superposition of inputs we have within the precision register, and we'll use the work register to hold the results. The question is, how do we perform a^x mod(N) on our qubit register?

Recall that we have chosen $a = 2$ for our coprime value, and consequently the a^x part of the function becomes 2^x. In other words, to enact this part of the function we need to multiply the work register by 2. The number of times we need to perform this multiplication is equal to x, where x is the value represented in binary within our precision register.

Multiplication by 2 (or indeed any power of 2) can be achieved on any binary register with a simple bit shift. In our case, each qubit is exchanged with the next highest-weighted position (using the QCEngine `rollLeft()` method). To multiply by 2 a total of *x* times, we simply condition our multiplication on the qubit values contained in the `precision` register. Note that *we will only use the two lowest-weight qubits of the* `precision` *register to represent values of x* (meaning that *x* can take the values 0, 1, 2, 3). Consequently, we only need to condition on these two qubits.

Why is `precision` *a four-qubit register if we only need two qubits for x?* Although we will never directly use the additional `0x4` and `0x8` qubits that are present in the `precision` register, including them in all consequent calculations effectively *stretches out* the circle-notation patterns that we'll observe within our QPU registers. Shor's algorithm would run just fine without them, but pedagogically, it would be a little harder for us to point out the patterns explaining how the algorithm works.

If the lowest-weight qubit in `precision` has a value 1, then we will need to include one ×2 multiplication to the `work` register, and so we perform a single `rollLeft()` on `work` conditioned on this qubit's value, as shown in Figure 12-9.

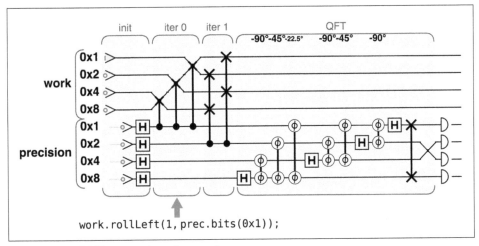

Figure 12-9. *QPU instructions for step 3*

The result is shown in Figure 12-10.

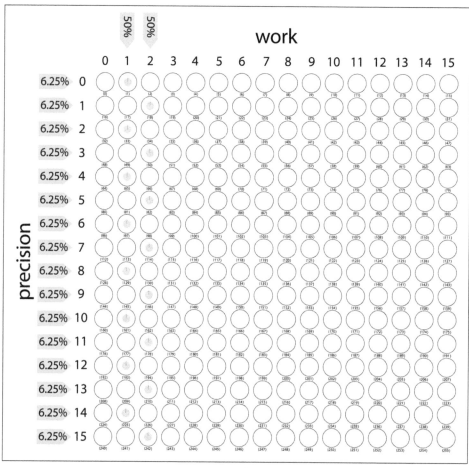

Figure 12-10. Step 3: To begin implementing a^x we multiply by 2 all qubits in the work register, conditioned on the lowest-weight qubit of precision being 1

In QPU programming, using conditional gates as the equivalent of if/then operations is extremely useful, as the "condition" is effectively evaluated for all possible values at once.

Step 4: Conditional Multipy-by-4

If the next-highest-weight qubit of the precision register is 1, then that implies a binary value of x also requiring another *two* multiplications by 2 on the work register. Therefore, as shown in Figure 12-11, we perform a shift by two qubits—i.e., two rollLeft() operations—conditional on the value of the 0x2 qubit from the precision register.

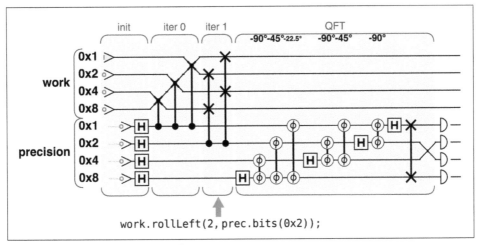

Figure 12-11. QPU instructions for step 4

We now have a value of a^x in the work register, for whatever value of x is encoded in the (first two) qubits of the precision register. In our case, precision is in a uniform superposition of possible x values, so we will obtain a corresponding superposition of associated a^x values in work.

Although we've performed all the necessary multiplications by 2, it may seem like we've fallen short of implementing the function $a^x \bmod(N)$ by taking no action to take care of the *mod* part of the function. In fact, for the particular example we've considered, our circuit manages to take care of the modulus automatically. We'll explain how in the next section.

Figure 12-12 shows how we've now managed to compute $a^x \bmod(N)$ on every value of x from the precision register in superposition.

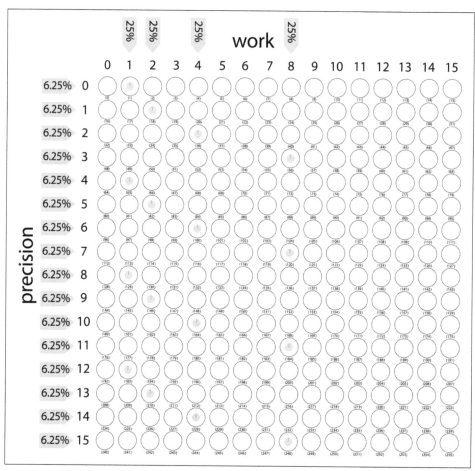

Figure 12-12. Step 4: The work register now holds a superposition of 2^x mod(15) for every possible value of x in the precision register

The preceding circle notation shows a familiar pattern. Having performed the function a^x mod(N) on our QPU register, the superposition amplitudes exactly match the plot of a^x mod(N) that we first produced at the beginning of the chapter in Figure 12-1 (albeit with the axes rotated 90°). We highlight this in Figure 12-13.

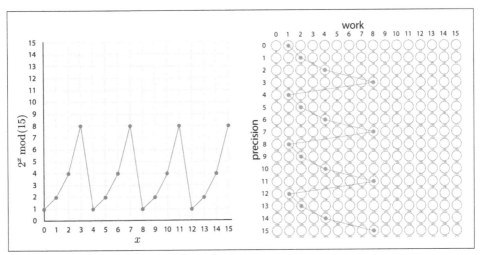

Figure 12-13. Hey, this looks familiar!

We now have the repeating signal for a^x mod(N) encoded into our QPU registers. Trying to read either register now will, of course, simply return a random value for the precision register, along with the corresponding work result. Luckily, we have the DFT-spike-counting trick up our sleeves for finding this signal's repeat period. It's time to use the QFT.

Step 5: Quantum Fourier Transform

By performing a QFT on the precision register as shown in Figure 12-14, we effectively perform a DFT on each column of data, transforming the precision register states (shown as the rows of our circle-notation grid) into a superposition of the periodic signal's component frequencies.

Looking at the periodic pattern shown in the circle notation of Figure 12-12, you might wonder why we don't need to QFT both registers (after all, it was the work register that we applied a^x mod(N) to!). Pick a work value with nonzero amplitude from the circle-notation grid and look up and down the circles of that column. You should clearly see that as the precision register value is varied, we get a periodic variation of amplitude (with a period of 4 in this case). This is the register for which we therefore want to find the QFT.

Reading from top to bottom, Figure 12-15 now resembles the DFT plot we originally saw toward the beginning of the chapter in Figure 12-3, as we highlight in

Figure 12-16. Note in Figure 12-15 that the QFT has also affected the relative phases of the register amplitudes.

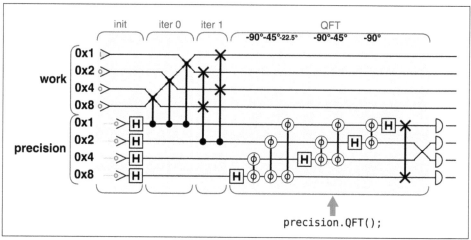

Figure 12-14. QPU instructions for step 5

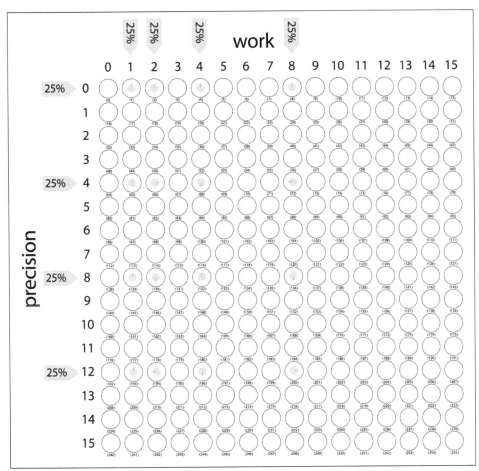

Figure 12-15. Step 5: Frequency spikes along the precision register following application of the QFT

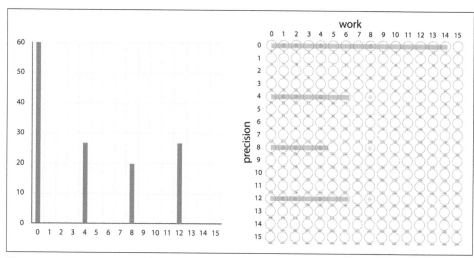

Figure 12-16. Once again, this resembles something we've seen

Each column in Figure 12-16 now contains the correct number of frequency spikes (four in this case). Recall from our earlier discussion that if we can count these spikes, that's all we need to find the factor we seek via some conventional digital logic. Let's READ out the precision register to get the information we need.

Step 6: Read the Quantum Result

The READ operation used in Figure 12-17 returns a random digital value, weighted by the probabilities in the circle diagram. Additionally, the READ destroys all values from the superposition that are in disagreement with the observed digital result.

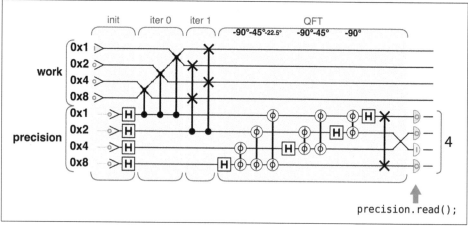

Figure 12-17. QPU instructions for step 6

In the example readout shown in Figure 12-18, the number 4 has been randomly obtained from the four most probable options. The QPU-powered part of Shor's algorithm is now finished, and we hand this READ result to the conventional logic function `ShorLogic()` used in the next step.

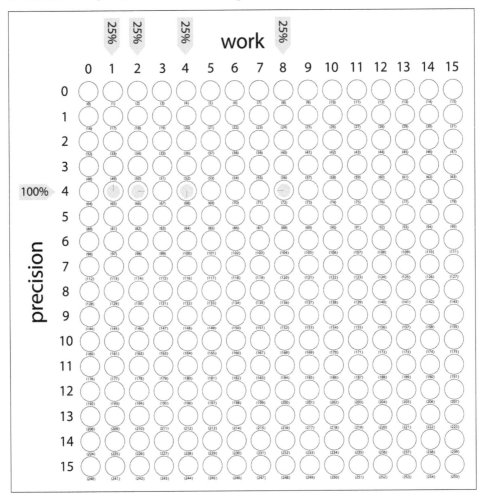

Figure 12-18. Step 6: After a READ on the precision register

Step 7: Digital Logic

Our work up until this point has produced the number 4, although looking back at Figure 12-15, we could equally have randomly received the results 0, 4, 8, or 12.

As noted earlier, given our knowledge that the QFT spikes are evenly distributed across the register, we can determine what periods are consistent with our READ value using conventional digital logic. The `estimate_num_spikes()` function in

Example 12-4 explicitly shows the logic for doing this. In some cases, this function may return more than one candidate number of spikes for the DFT plot. For example, if we pass it our READ value of 4, then it returns the two values 4 and 8, either of which is a number of spikes in the DFT consistent with our READ value.

Sample Code

Run this sample online at *http://oreilly-qc.github.io?p=12-4.*

Example 12-4. A function to estimate the number of spikes based on the QPU result

```
function estimate_num_spikes(spike, range)
{
    if (spike < range / 2)
        spike = range - spike;
    var best_error = 1.0;
    var e0 = 0, e1 = 0, e2 = 0;
    var actual = spike / range;
    var candidates = []
    for (var denom = 1.0; denom < spike; ++denom)
    {
        var numerator = Math.round(denom * actual);
        var estimated = numerator / denom;
        var error = Math.abs(estimated - actual);
        e0 = e1;
        e1 = e2;
        e2 = error;
        // Look for a local minimum which beats our
        // current best error
        if (e1 <= best_error && e1 < e0 && e1 < e2)
        {
            var repeat_period = denom - 1;
            candidates.push(denom - 1);
            best_error = e1;
        }
    }
    return candidates;
}
```

Since (in this example) we've ended up with two candidate results (4 and 8), we'll need to check both to see whether they give us prime factors of 15. We introduced the method ShorLogic(), implementing the *gcd* equations that determine prime factors from a given number of DFT spikes back at the start of the chapter, in Example 12-1. We first try the value 4 in this expression, and it returns the values 3 and 5.

Not all of the available values will lead to a correct answer. What happens if we receive the value 0? This is 25% likely, and in this case the estimate_num_spikes() function returns no candidate values at all, so the program fails. This is a common situation with quantum algorithms, and not a problem when we can check the validity of our answer quickly. In this case, we make such a check and then, if necessary, run the program again, from the beginning.

Step 8: Check the Result

The factors of a number can be difficult to find, but once found the answer is simple to verify. We can easily verify that 3 and 5 are both prime and factors of 15 (so there's no need to even try checking the second value of 8 in ShorLogic()).

Success!

The Fine Print

This chapter presented a simplified version of what is typically a very complicated algorithm. In our version of Shor's algorithm, a few aspects were simplified for ease of illustration, although at the cost of generality. Without digging too deeply, we here mention some of the necessary simplifications. More information can also be found in the online sample code.

Computing the Modulus

We already mentioned that in our QPU calculation of $a^x \bmod(N)$ the modulus part of the function was somehow automatically taken care of for us. This was a happy coincidence specific to the particular number we wanted to factor, and sadly won't happen in general. Recall that we multiplied the work register by powers of two through the rolling of bits. If we simply start with the value 1 and then shift it 4 times, we should get $2^4 = 16$; however, since we only used a 4-bit number and allowed the shifted bits to wrap around, instead of 16 we get 1, which is precisely what we should get if we're doing the multiplications followed by mod(15).

You can verify that this trick also works if we're trying to factor 21; however, it fails on a larger (but still relatively tiny) number such as 35. What can we do in these more general cases?

When a conventional computer calculates the modulus of a number, such as 1024 % 35, it performs integer division and then returns the remainder. The number of conventional logic gates required to perform integer division is very (*very*) large, and a QPU implementation is well beyond the scope of this book.

Nevertheless, there is a way we can solve the problem, by using an approach to calculating the modulus that, although less sophisticated, is well suited to QPU operations. Suppose we wanted to find $y \bmod(N)$ for some value y. The following code will do the trick:

```
y -= N;
if (y < 0) {
    y += N;
}
```

We simply subtract N from our value, and use the sign of the result to determine whether we should allow the value to wrap around or return it to its original value. On a conventional computer this might be considered bad practice. In this case, it gives us exactly what we need: the correct answer, using decrements, increments, and comparisons—all logic we know can be implemented with QPU operations from our discussions in Chapter 5.

A circuit for performing the modulus by this method (on some value `val`) is shown in Figure 12-19.

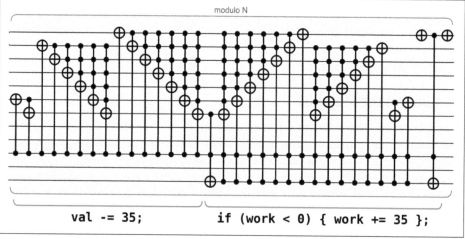

Figure 12-19. Quantum operations to perform a multiply by 2 modulo 35

While this example does use a large number of complicated operations to perform a simple calculation, it is able to perform the modulus in superposition.

 The modulus implementation in Figure 12-19 actually uses one additional scratch qubit to stash away the sign bit of the `work` register, for use in the conditional addition.

Time Versus Space

The modulus operation described in the preceding section slows things down considerably for the general factoring case, primarily because it requires the multiply-by-2 operations to be performed one at a time. This increase in the number of operations needed (and therefore overall operation time) destroys our QPU's advantage. This can be solved by increasing the number of qubits used, and then applying the modulus operation a logarithmic number of times. For an example of this, see *http://oreilly-qc.github.io?p=12-A*. Much of the challenge of QPU programming involves finding ways to balance program *depth* (the number of operations) against required number of qubits.

Coprimes Other Than 2

The implementation covered here will factor many numbers, but for some it returns undesired results. For example, using it to factor 407 returns [407, 1]. While this is technically correct, we would much prefer the *nontrivial* factors of 407, which are [37, 11].

A solution to this problem is to replace our coprime=2 with some other prime number, although the quantum operations required to perform non-power-of-2 exponentiation are outside the scope of this book. The choice of coprime=2 is a useful illustrative simplification.

CHAPTER 13

Quantum Machine Learning

At the time of writing, quantum machine learning (QML) is just about the greatest combination of buzzwords you could hope to synthesize. A lot is written about QML, and the topic is often (confusingly) both overhyped and undersold at the same time. In this section we'll try to give a flavor for how QPUs might transform machine learning, while also being careful to point out the caveats inherent in manipulating quantum data.

Useful QML applications require very large numbers of qubits. For this reason, our overview of QML applications is necessarily very high-level. Such a summary is also fitting given the rapidly changing nature of this nascent field. Although our discussion will be more schematic than pragmatic, it will heavily leverage our hands-on experience of primitives from earlier chapters.

We summarize three different QML applications: *solving systems of linear equations, Quantum Principal Component Analysis,* and *Quantum Support Vector Machines.* These have been selected due to both their relevance to machine learning and their simplicity to discuss. These are also applications whose conventional counterparts are hopefully familiar to anyone who has dabbled in machine learning. We only give a brief description of the conventional progenitors of each QML application as it's introduced.

In discussing QML, we'll frequently make use of the following pieces of machine-learning terminology:

Features
> Term used to describe measurable properties of data points available to a machine-learning model for making predictions. We often imagine the possible values of these features to define a *feature space.*

Supervised

Refers to machine-learning models that must be *trained* on a collection of points in feature space for which correct classes or responses are already known. Only then can the adequately trained model be used to classify (or predict) responses for new points in the feature space.

Unsupervised

Refers to machine-learning models that are able to learn patterns and structure in training data that does not include known responses.

Classification

Used to describe supervised predictive models that assign a given point in feature space to one of several discrete classes.

Regression

Used to describe supervised models predicting some continuously varying *response variable*.

Dimensionality reduction

One form of unsupervised data preprocessing that can benefit machine-learning models of all types. Dimensionality reduction aims to reduce the number of features needed to describe a problem.

In addition to this terminology, we'll also make use of mathematical descriptions of machine-learning problems. As such, this chapter is slightly more mathematically involved than our previous discourse.

Our first QML application teaches us how a QPU can help solve systems of linear equations.

Solving Systems of Linear Equations

Although systems of linear equations are certainly fundamental to much of machine learning, they also underlie vast areas across all of applied mathematics. The *HHL algorithm* [1] (often referred to simply as HHL) we present for leveraging a QPU to efficiently solve these systems is consequently a fundamental and powerful tool, and we'll see that it's a key building block in *other* QML applications too. HHL has also been considered for applications ranging from modeling electrical effects to streamlining computer graphics calculations.

We begin our summary of the HHL algorithm by recapping the mathematics needed to describe conventional systems of linear equations. We then summarize the distinctly quantum operation of HHL, outlining its performance improvements and—

---

[1] Harrow et al., 2009 (*https://arxiv.org/abs/0811.3171*).

just as importantly—its constraints. Finally, we give a more detailed description of how HHL works "inside the box."

Describing and Solving Systems of Linear Equations

The most concise way of representing a system of linear equations is in terms of matrix multiplication. In fact, for the seasoned equation solver the terms *matrices* and *linear equations* are synonymous. For example, suppose we have a system of two linear equations, $3x_1 + 4x_2 = 3$ and $2x_1 + x_2 = 3$. We can equivalently, and much more concisely, represent these as the single matrix equation shown in Equation 13-1.

Equation 13-1. Using matrices to describe systems of linear equations

$$\begin{bmatrix} 3 & 4 \\ 2 & 1 \end{bmatrix} \begin{bmatrix} x_1 \\ x_2 \end{bmatrix} = \begin{bmatrix} 3 \\ 3 \end{bmatrix}$$

We can recover our two linear equations through the rules of matrix multiplication. More generally, a system of n linear equations for n variables can be written as a matrix equation containing an $n \times n$ matrix, $\mathbf{A}$, and an n-dimensional vector $\vec{b}$:

$$\mathbf{A}\vec{x} = \vec{b}$$

Here we have also introduced a vector $\vec{x} = [x_1, ..., x_n]$ of the n variables we want to solve for.

In this matrix formulation, the task of solving the system of equations boils down to being able to invert the matrix $\mathbf{A}$. If we can obtain the inverse $\mathbf{A}^{-1}$, then we can easily determine the n unknown variables via Equation 13-2.

Equation 13-2. Solving systems of linear equations by inverting matrices

$$\vec{x} = \mathbf{A}^{-1}\vec{b}$$

Many conventional algorithms exist for finding the inverse of a matrix, and the most efficient rely on the matrix in question possessing certain helpful properties.

The following matrix parameters can affect the performance of both conventional and quantum algorithms:

n

The *size of the system of linear equations*. Equivalently, this is the dimensionality of **A**—if we want to solve a system of n linear equations to find n variables, then **A** will be an $n \times n$ matrix.

κ

The *condition number* of the matrix **A** representing the system of linear equations. Given the system of equations $\mathbf{A}\vec{x} = \vec{b}$, the condition number tells us how much an error in our specification of $\vec{b}$ affects the error we can expect to find in our solution for $\vec{x} = \mathbf{A}^{-1}\vec{b}$. κ is calculated as the maximum ratio between the relative error in the input $\vec{b}$ and the output $\vec{x} = \mathbf{A}^{-1}\vec{b}$. It turns out that κ can equivalently be found as[2] the ratio $|\lambda_{max}|/|\lambda_{min}|$ of the absolute values of the maximum and minimum eigenvalues of **A**.

s

The *sparsity* of the matrix **A**. This is the number of nonzero entries in **A**.

ε

The *precision* we require in our solution. In the case of HHL, we'll shortly see that a state $|\vec{x}\rangle$ is output that amplitude-encodes the solution vector $\vec{x}$. Increasing ϵ means increasing the precision with which the values in $\vec{x}$ are represented within these amplitudes.

Our assessment of how efficiently HHL can invert a matrix will be with respect to these parameters. By *efficiency* we mean the *runtime* of the algorithm (a measure of how many fundamental operations it must employ). For comparison, at the time of writing, the leading conventional algorithm for solving systems of linear equations is probably the *conjugate gradient descent* method. This has a runtime of $O(ns\kappa \log(1/\epsilon))$.

Solving Linear Equations with a QPU

HHL (named after its 2009 discoverers Harrow, Hassidim, and Lloyd) employs the primitives we've learned thus far to find (in a particular sense) the inverse of a matrix faster than is possible with conjugate gradient descent. We say *in a particular sense* because HHL solves a distinctly *quantum* version of the problem. HHL provides the solutions to a system of linear equations amplitude-encoded in a QPU register, and as such, they are inaccessibly quantum. Although HHL cannot solve systems of linear

---

2 The expression for condition number in terms of eigenvalues only holds if **A** is a *normal* matrix. All matrices used in HHL are necessarily normal because of its reliance on quantum simulation and Hermitian matrices.

equations in a conventional sense, amplitude-encoded solutions can still be very useful, and are in fact critical building blocks in other QML applications.

What HHL does

Before decomposing HHL into primitives, we'll give an executive summary of its inputs, outputs, and performance.

The inputs and outputs of HHL are as shown in Figure 13-1.

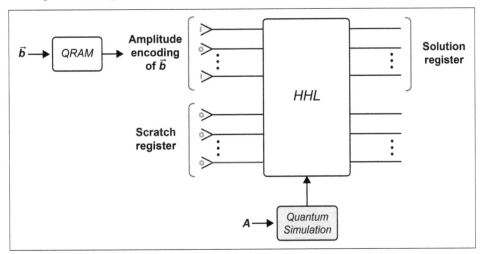

Figure 13-1. A high-level view of the inputs and outputs utilized by the HHL algorithm to solve systems of linear equations.

Inputs. This schematic shows that HHL accepts two sets of input registers, and a matrix (via a quantum simulation):

Scratch register
    This contains a number of scratch qubits used by various primitives within HHL, all prepared in the $|0\rangle$ state. Because HHL deals with fixed-point (or floating-point) data and involves nontrivial arithmetic operations (such as taking the square root), we require a *lot* of scratch qubits. This makes HHL difficult to simulate for even the simplest cases.

Amplitude encoding of $\vec{b}$
    We also need to provide HHL with the vector $\vec{b}$ from Equation 13-2, amplitude-encoded in a QPU register (in the sense we discussed in Chapter 9). We will denote the state of a register amplitude encoding $\vec{b}$ as $|\vec{b}\rangle$. Note that to prepare

an amplitude encoding of $\vec{b}$ we will need to use QRAM. Thus, HHL fundamentally relies on the existence of QRAM.

*QPU operation representing **A***

Naturally, HHL also needs access to the matrix encapsulating the system of linear equations we wish to solve. The bottom of Figure 13-1 illustrates how HHL requires us to represent **A** as a QPU operation, which we can achieve via the process of quantum simulation outlined in Chapter 9. This means that the matrix **A** must meet the requirements we noted for performing quantum simulation.

Outputs.   Figure 13-1 also shows that two registers are output from HHL.

Solution register

The solution vector $\vec{x}$ is amplitude-encoded within a single output QPU register (we denote this state as $|\vec{x}\rangle$). As we've already stressed, this implies that *we cannot access the individual solutions*, since they're *hidden* in the amplitudes of a quantum superposition that we cannot hope to efficiently extract with READ operations.

Scratch register

The scratch qubits are returned to their starting state of $|0\rangle$, allowing us to continue using them elsewhere in our QPU.

Here are some examples of ways in which the quantum output from HHL can still be incredibly useful despite its inaccessible nature:

1. Rather than a specification of solutions for all n variables in $\vec{x}$, we may only wish to know some derived property, such as their sum, mean value, or perhaps even whether or not they contain a certain frequency component. In such cases we may be able to apply an appropriate quantum circuit to $|\vec{x}\rangle$, allowing us to READ the derived value.

2. If we are satisfied with checking only whether or not the solution vector $\vec{x}$ is equal to one particular suspected vector, then we can employ the *swap test* introduced in Chapter 3 between $|\vec{x}\rangle$ and another register encoding the suspected vector.

3. If, for example, we plan to use the HHL algorithm as a component in a larger algorithm, $|\vec{x}\rangle$ may be sufficient for our needs as is.

Since systems of linear equations are fundamental in many areas of machine learning, HHL is the starting point for many other QML applications, such as regression[3] and data fitting.[4]

Speed and fine print. The HHL algorithm has a runtime[5] of $O\left(\kappa^2 s^2 \epsilon^{-1} \log n\right)$.

In comparison with the conventional method of conjugate gradient descent and its runtime of $O(ns\kappa \log (1/\epsilon))$, HHL clearly offers an exponential improvement in the dependence on the size of the problem (n).

One could argue that this is an unfair comparison, since conventional conjugate gradient descent reveals the full set of solutions to us, unlike the quantum answer generated by HHL. We could instead compare HHL to the best conventional algorithms for determining derived statistics from solutions to systems of linear equations (sum, mean, etc.), which have n and κ dependencies of $O(n\sqrt{\kappa})$, but HHL still affords an exponential improvement in the dependence on n.

Although it's tempting to focus solely on how algorithms scale with the problem size n, other parameters are equally important. Though offering an impressive exponential speedup in terms of n, HHL's performance is worse than conventional competitors once we consider poorly conditioned or less sparse problems (where κ or s becomes important).[6] HHL also suffers if we demand more precision and place importance on the parameter ϵ.

For these reasons, we have the following fine print:

> The HHL algorithm is suited to solving systems of linear equations represented by sparse, well-conditioned matrices.

Additionally, since HHL leverages a quantum simulation primitive, we need to take note of any requirements particular to whichever quantum simulation technique we employ.

Having done our best to give a realistic impression of HHL's usage, let's break down how it works.

---

3 Kerenidis and Prakash, 2017 (*https://arxiv.org/abs/1704.04992*).

4 Wiebe et al., 2012 (*http://bit.ly/2RQ03iA*).

5 Several improvements and extensions have been made to the original HHL algorithm, resulting in runtimes with different trade-offs between the various parameters. Here we focus on the conceptually simpler original algorithm.

6 A more recent result by Childs, et al., 2015 (*https://arxiv.org/pdf/1511.02306.pdf*), actually manages to improve the dependence of HHL on ϵ to *poly*(log $(1/\epsilon)$).

Inside the box

The intuition behind HHL relies on one particular method for finding the inverse of a matrix via its eigendecomposition. Any matrix has an associated set of eigenvectors and eigenvalues. Since our focus in this chapter is machine learning, we'll assume some familiarity with this concept. If the idea is new to you, eigenvectors and eigenvalues are essentially the matrix equivalents of the eigenstates and eigenphases of QPU operations that we introduced while discussing phase estimation in Chapter 8.

In "Phase Estimation in Practice" on page 163 we also noted that any QPU register state can be considered to be some superposition of the eigenstates of any QPU operation. Through its dependence on quantum simulation, HHL is restricted to solving systems of linear equations that are represented by *Hermitian* matrices.[7] For such matrices a similar fact regarding its eigendecomposition is true. Any vector we might want to act a Hermitian matrix A on can be expressed in the basis of (i.e., written as a linear combination of) A's eigenvectors.

For example, consider the Hermitian matrix A and vector $\vec{z}$ shown in Equation 13-3.

Equation 13-3. Example matrix and vector for introducing eigendecomposition

$$A = \begin{bmatrix} 2 & 2 \\ 2 & 3 \end{bmatrix}, \quad \vec{z} = \begin{bmatrix} 1 \\ 0 \end{bmatrix}$$

The two eigenvectors of this particular matrix A are $\vec{v}_1 = [-0.7882, 0.615]$ and $\vec{v}_2 = [-0.615, -0.788]$, with associated eigenvalues $\lambda_1 = 0.438$ and $\lambda_2 = 4.56$, as you can check by confirming that $A\vec{v}_1 = \lambda_1 \vec{v}_1$ and $A\vec{v}_2 = \lambda_2 \vec{v}_2$. Since the example A considered here is Hermitian, $\vec{z}$ can be written in the basis of its eigenvectors, and in fact $\vec{z} = -0.788\vec{v}_1 - 0.615\vec{v}_2$. We could simply write this as $\vec{z} = [-0.788, -0.615]$ with the understanding that the components are expressed in the basis of A's eigenvectors.

---

7 However, as discussed in Chapter 9, we can always extend an $n \times n$ non-Hermitian matrix to a $2n \times 2n$ Hermitian one.

We can also write **A** in its own *eigenbasis*.[8] It turns out that when written this way a matrix is always diagonal, with its main diagonal consisting of its eigenvalues. For our preceding example, **A** is therefore written in its eigenbasis as shown in Equation 13-4.

Equation 13-4. Writing a matrix in its eigenbasis

$$\mathbf{A} = \begin{bmatrix} 0.438 & 0 \\ 0 & 4.56 \end{bmatrix}$$

Expressing **A** in its eigenbasis is very helpful for finding its inverse, because inverting a diagonal matrix is trivial. To do so you simply numerically invert the nonzero values along its diagonal. For example, we can find $\mathbf{A}^{-1}$ as shown in Equation 13-5.

Equation 13-5. Inverting a matrix written in its eigenbasis

$$\mathbf{A}^{-1} = \begin{bmatrix} \dfrac{1}{0.438} & 0 \\ 0 & \dfrac{1}{4.56} \end{bmatrix} = \begin{bmatrix} 2.281 & 0 \\ 0 & 0.219 \end{bmatrix}$$

We should note, of course, that this gives us $\mathbf{A}^{-1}$ *expressed in the eigenbasis* of **A**. We can either leave the inverse like this (if we wish to act it on vectors that are also expressed in **A**'s eigenbasis), or rewrite it in the original basis.

So in summary, if we can find the eigenvalues of some general matrix **A**, then we can determine $\vec{x} = \mathbf{A}^{-1}\vec{b}$ as shown in Equation 13-6.

Equation 13-6. General approach for determining the inverse of a matrix via its eigendecomposition

$$\vec{x} = \begin{bmatrix} \dfrac{1}{\lambda_1} & \cdots & 0 \\ \vdots & \ddots & \vdots \\ 0 & \cdots & \dfrac{1}{\lambda_n} \end{bmatrix} \begin{bmatrix} \tilde{b}_1 \\ \vdots \\ \tilde{b}_n \end{bmatrix} = \begin{bmatrix} \dfrac{1}{\lambda_1}\tilde{b}_1 \\ \vdots \\ \dfrac{1}{\lambda_n}\tilde{b}_n \end{bmatrix}$$

Where $\lambda_1, ..., \lambda_n$ are the eigenvalues of **A** and we use $\tilde{b}_1, ..., \tilde{b}_n$ to denote the components of $\vec{b}$ expressed in **A**'s eigenbasis.

---

8 By this we mean finding the elements **A** must have in order to correctly relate vectors expressed in its eigenbasis.

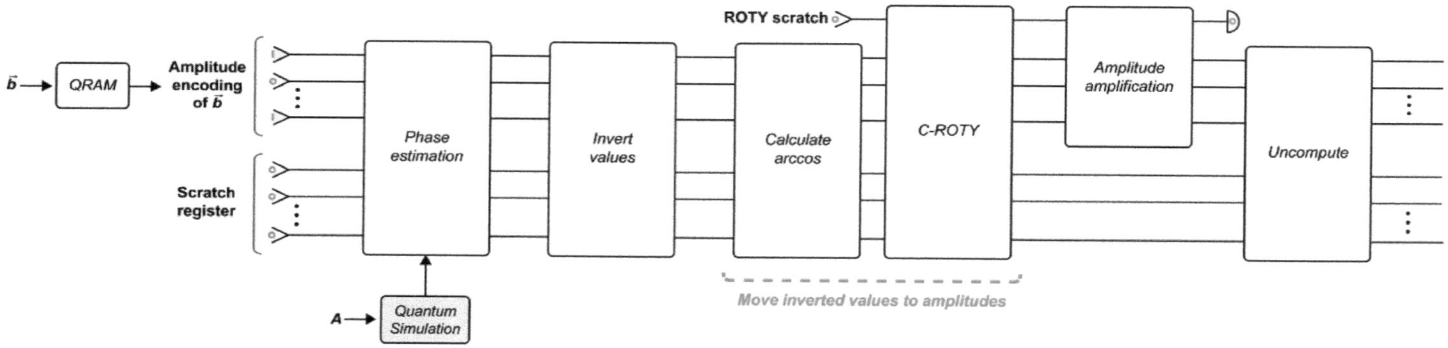

Figure 13-2. Schematic outline of the primitives contained in the HHL algorithm

HHL manages to employ this matrix inversion method using the quantum parallelism of a QPU. The output register from HHL contains an amplitude encoding of precisely the vector shown in Equation 13-6; i.e., one where the amplitude of state $|i\rangle$ is $\tilde{b}_i/\lambda_i$. The schematic in Figure 13-2 shows what's inside the HHL box from Figure 13-1, outlining how HHL uses our familiar QPU primitives to produce the output state in Equation 13-6.

Although we don't explicitly show them in Figure 13-2, HHL will also require other input registers specifying certain configuration parameters needed for the quantum simulation of **A**.

Let's step through each of the primitive components used in Figure 13-2.

1. Quantum simulation, QRAM, and phase estimation. We already know that the phase estimation primitive can efficiently find the eigenstates and eigenphases of a QPU operation. You might suspect that this could help us in using the eigendecomposition approach to inverting a matrix—and you'd be right!

Figure 13-2 shows that we begin by using QRAM to produce a register with an amplitude encoding of $\vec{b}$ and quantum simulation to produce a QPU operation representing **A**. We then feed both of these resources into the phase estimation primitive as shown in Figure 13-3.

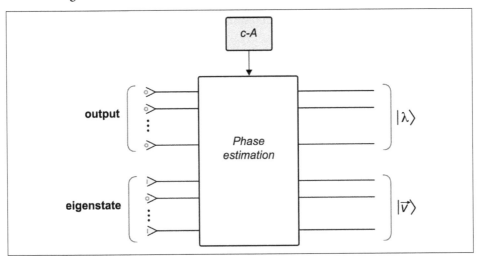

Figure 13-3. Recap of phase estimation primitive, where we have identified the eigenphase obtained in the output register as the eigenvalue of A

Figure 13-3 helps us recall that two input registers are passed to the phase estimation primitive. The lower `eigenstate` register takes an input specifying an eigenstate of the QPU operation for which we would like the associated eigenphase. The upper `output` register (initialized in state $|0\rangle$) produces a representation of the eigenphase, which in our case is an eigenvalue of **A**.

So phase estimation provides *an* eigenvalue of *A*. But how do we get all *n* eigenvalues?

Running phase estimation *n* separate times would reduce HHL's runtime to O(*n*)—no better than its conventional counterparts. We *could* input a uniform superposition in the `eigenstate` register and calculate the eigenvalues in parallel, producing a uniform superposition of them in the `output` register. But suppose we take a slightly different approach and instead send the amplitude encoding of $\vec{b}$ in the `eigenstate` register? This results in the `output` register being a superposition of A's eigenvalues, but one that is entangled with the amplitude encoding of $\vec{b}$ produced in the `output` register.

This will be far more useful to us than just a uniform superposition of the eigenvalues, since now each $|\lambda_i\rangle$ within the entangled state of `eigenstate` and `output` registers has an amplitude of $\tilde{b}_i$ (thanks to the `eigenstate` register). This isn't quite what we want to produce the solution as shown in Equation 13-6, however. The `output` register's *state* represents the eigenvalues of **A**. What we really want is to invert these eigenvalues and—instead of them being held in another (entangled) register—move them into values multiplying the *amplitudes* of the `eigenstate` register. The next steps in HHL achieve this inversion and transfer.

2. Invert values. The second primitive in Figure 13-2 inverts each λ_i value stored in the (entangled) superposition of the `output` and `eigenstate` registers.

At the end of this step the `output` register encodes a superposition of $|1/\lambda_i\rangle$ states, still entangled with the `eigenstate` register. To invert numerical values encoded in a quantum state we actually utilize a number of the arithmetic primitives introduced in Chapter 5. There are many different ways we could build a QPU numerical inversion algorithm from these primitives. One possibility is to use the Newton method for approximating the inverse. Whatever approach we take, as we noted in Chapter 12, division is hard. This seemingly simple operation requires a *significant* overhead in qubit numbers. Not only will the constituent operations require scratch qubits, but dealing with inverses means that we have to encode the involved numerical values in either fixed- or floating-point representations (as well as dealing with overflow, etc.). In fact, the overheads required by this step are a contributing factor to why a full code sample of even the simplest HHL implementation currently falls outside the scope (and capabilities!) of what we can reasonably present here.[9]

Regardless, at the end of this step, the `eigenstate` register will contain a superposition of $1/\lambda_i$ values.

3. Move inverted values into amplitudes.

We now need to move the state-encoded inverted eigenvalues of **A** into the *amplitudes* of this state. Don't forget that the amplitude-encoded state of $\vec{b}$ is still entangled with all this, so getting those inverted eigenvalues into the state amplitudes would yield the final line in Equation 13-6, and therefore an amplitude encoding of the solution vector $|\vec{x}\rangle$.

The key to achieving this is applying a `C-ROTY` (i.e., a conditional ROTY operation; see Chapter 2). Specifically, we set the target of this conditional operation to a new single scratch qubit (labeled `ROTY scratch` in Figure 13-2), initially in state $|0\rangle$. It's possible to show (although not without resorting to much more mathematics) that if we condition this ROTY on the *inverse cosine* of the $1/\lambda_i$ values stored in the `output` register, then the *amplitudes* of all parts of the entangled `output` and `eigenstate` registers where `ROTY scratch` is in the $|1\rangle$ state acquire precisely the $1/\lambda_i$ factors that we're after.

Consequently, this transfer step of the algorithm consists of two parts:

1. Calculate arccos $\left(1/\lambda_i\right)$ in superposition on each state in the `output` register. This can be achieved in terms of our basic arithmetic primitives,[10] although again with a significant overhead in the number of additional qubits required.

2. Perform a `C-ROTY` between the first register and the `ROTY scratch` (prepared in $|0\rangle$).

At the end of this we will have the state we want *if* `ROTY scratch` is in state $|1\rangle$. We can ensure this if we READ the `ROTY scratch` and get a 1 outcome. Unfortunately, this only occurs with a certain probability. To increase the likelihood that we get the needed 1 outcome we can employ another of our QPU primitives, performing amplitude amplification on the `ROTY scratch`.

---

9 There's something poetic and possibly profound about the fact that attempting to perform *conventional* notions of arithmetic on a QPU can cause such crippling overheads.

10 We actually need to include a constant value in this calculation, and calculate arccos $\left(C/\lambda_i\right)$ rather than just arccos $\left(1/\lambda_i\right)$. Since we're not implementing the HHL algorithm fully here we omit this for simplicity.

4. Amplitude amplification. Amplitude amplification allows us to increase the probability of getting an outcome of 1 when we READ the single-qubit ROTY register. This then increases the chance that we end up with the eigenstate register having the desired $\tilde{b}_i/\lambda_i$ amplitudes.

If despite the amplitude amplification a READ of ROTY scratch still produces the undesired 0 outcome, we have to discard the states of the registers and rerun the whole HHL algorithm from the beginning.

5. Uncompute. Assuming success in our previous READ, the eigenstate register now contains an amplitude encoding of the solutions $\vec{x}$. But we're not quite done. The eigenstate register is still entangled not only with the output register, but also with the many other scratch qubits we've introduced along the way. As mentioned in Chapter 5, having our desired state entangled with other registers is troublesome for a number of reasons. We therefore apply the uncomputation procedure (also outlined in Chapter 5) to disentangle the eigenstate register.

Bingo! The eigenstate register now contains a disentangled amplitude encoding of $\vec{x}$ ready to be used in any of the ways suggested at the start of this section.

HHL is a complex and involved QPU application. Don't feel intimidated if it takes more than one parse to get to grips with; it's well worth the effort to see how a more substantial algorithm masters our QPU primitives.

Quantum Principle Component Analysis

Quantum Principal Component Analysis (QPCA) is a QPU implementation of the eponymous data-processing routine. QPCA not only offers a potentially more efficient approach to this widely used machine-learning task, but can also act as a building block in other QML applications. Like HHL, QPCA relies on QRAM hardware. Before outlining how a QPU allows us to soup up conventional Principal Component Analysis (PCA), we first review PCA itself.

Conventional Principal Component Analysis

PCA is an invaluable tool in data science, machine learning, and beyond. Often used as a preprocessing step, PCA can transform an input set of features into a new, uncorrelated set. The uncorrelated features produced by PCA can be ordered in terms of the amount of the data's variance that they encode. By retaining only some of these new features, PCA is often employed as a *dimensionality reduction* technique. Keeping only the first few principal components allows us to reduce the number of features we need to deal with while retaining as much as possible of the interesting variation within the data.

The process of Principal Component Analysis also goes by many other names in different disciplines, such as the Karhunen-Loève transform or Hotelling transform. It is also equivalent to a *Singular Value Decomposition*.

A common geometrical way to understand the action of PCA is to envision m data points, each described by n features, as being a set of a m points in an n-dimensional *feature space*. In this setting PCA produces a list of n directions in feature space, ordered such that the first is the direction along which there is the most variance in the data, while the second contains the second most variance, and so on. These directions are the so-called *principal components* of our data. This is often illustrated in a simple two-dimensional feature space (i.e., $n = 2$), as shown in Figure 13-4.

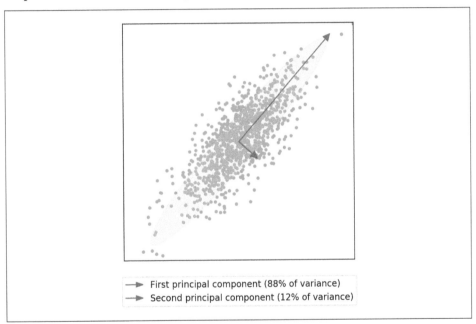

Figure 13-4. The two principal components of 1,000 data points in a two-dimensional feature space. The directions of the arrows show the principal component vectors, while their lengths represent the variance of the data in that direction.

One disadvantage in using the principal components generated by PCA as a new set of features is that they may not have any physical interpretation. However, if we're ultimately interested in building models having the greatest predictive power, this may not be our greatest concern.

Although a geometric description of PCA is useful for building intuition, to actually *compute* principal components we need a mathematical prescription for finding them. First we calculate the covariance matrix of the dataset in question. If we arrange our data into an $m \times n$ matrix $\mathbf{X}$ (where each row corresponds to one of the m original data points and each column contains values for one of the n different features), then the covariance matrix σ is given by:

$$\sigma = \frac{1}{n-1} \mathbf{X}^T \mathbf{X}$$

Conveniently, the principal components are given by finding the eigendecomposition of this covariance matrix. The eigenvectors correspond to the principal component directions, while each associated eigenvalue is proportional to the variance of the data along that principal component. If we want to use PCA for dimensionality reduction, we can then rearrange the eigenvectors in order of decreasing eigenvalue and pick only the top p as our new, reduced set of features.

 When performing PCA in practice it is important to *normalize* data before calculating its covariance matrix, as the PCA process is sensitive to the scale of the data. One common normalization technique is finding the deviation of each feature from its mean value and scaling the result by the standard deviation of the data.

The most computationally expensive step in PCA is performing the eigendecomposition of the covariance matrix σ. As with HHL, the need to determine eigenvalues immediately brings to mind the phase estimation primitive from Chapter 8. When carefully applied, phase estimation can help us run PCA on a QPU.

PCA with a QPU

We might suspect that something like the following steps could help us find the eigendecomposition that we need for PCA:

1. Represent the covariance matrix of the data as a QPU operation.
2. Perform phase estimation on this QPU operation to determine its eigenvalues.

However, there are a few problems with this proposed approach:

Problem 1: Quantum simulation with σ

In the first step we might assume that quantum simulation techniques would help us represent the covariance matrix as a QPU operation, as they did for the matrices involved with HHL. Sadly, covariance matrices rarely satisfy the sparsity requirements of quantum simulation techniques, so we'll need a different way to find a QPU operation representation of σ.

Problem 2: Input for phase estimation

In the second proposed step, how do we learn both the eigenvalues *and* eigenvectors that we need? Recall from Figure 13-3 that phase estimation has two input registers, one of which we must use to specify the eigenstate for which we want the associated eigenphase (and hence eigenvalue). But knowing any of the eigenvectors of σ is precisely part of the problem we want to solve with QPCA! We got around this seemingly circular problem when using phase estimation in HHL because we were able to use $|\vec{b}\rangle$ in the `eigenstate` input register. Even though we didn't know precisely what eigenstates $|\vec{b}\rangle$ superposed, phase estimation acted on them all in parallel—without us ever needing to learn them. Is there also some kind of clever `eigenstate` input we can use for QPCA?

Remarkably, by introducing one critical trick we can solve both of the problems just described. The trick in question is a way to represent the covariance matrix σ in a QPU *register* (not a QPU operation!). How this trick fixes the preceding problems is quite circuitous (and mathematically involved), but we give a brief outline next.

Representing a covariance matrix in a QPU register

The idea of representing a *matrix* in a register is new to us—so far we've gone to some length to represent matrices as QPU *operations*.

We've exclusively used circle notation to describe QPU registers, but have occasionally hinted that a full-blown mathematical description involves using (complex-valued) vectors. However, though we've carefully avoided introducing the notion, there's an *even more general* mathematical description of a QPU register that uses a matrix known as a density operator.[11] The details of density operators are far beyond the scope of this book (though Chapter 14 contains tips and references for starting to learn about them), but the important point for QPCA is that if we have QRAM access to our data, then a trick exists for initializing a QPU register so that its density operator description is precisely the covariance matrix of our data. While encoding matrices in a QPU register's density operator description like this is not normally very useful, for QPCA it affords us the following fixes to the two problems we highlighted earlier.

---

11 Density operators provide a more general description of a QPU register's state than using a complex vector (or circle notation) because they allow for cases where the register might not only be in superposition, but subject to some statistical uncertainty as to precisely what that superposition is. These quantum states that contain statistical uncertainty are usually called *mixed states*.

The trick QPCA uses to represent a covariance matrix as a density operator works because covariance matrices are always in *Gram form*, meaning that they can be written in the form $\mathbf{V}^T\mathbf{V}$ for some other matrix $\mathbf{V}$. For other matrices it's not such a useful trick.

Fixing problem 1

Having our covariance matrix in a QPU register's density operator allows us to perform a trick where by leveraging the SWAP operation (see Chapter 3) we repeatedly perform a kind of partial "mini-SWAP" (partial in a *quantum superposition* sense) between the register encoding σ and a second register. Although we won't go into any detail about how to modify SWAP to perform this mini-SWAP subroutine, it turns out that using it effectively results in a quantum simulation of σ being implemented on the second register.[12] This is precisely the result we would normally achieve using more standard quantum simulation techniques,[13] only this mini-SWAP approach to generating a QPU operation representing σ works efficiently even if σ isn't sparse, so long as it is of low rank. Despite this trick requiring us to repeatedly apply SWAP operations (and consequently repeatedly reencode σ as a QPU register's density operator), it still proves to be efficient.

The rank of a matrix is the number of its columns that are linearly independent. Since the columns of σ are the features of our data, saying that a covariance matrix is of "low rank" means that our data is actually well described by some smaller subspace of the full feature space. The number of features we would need to describe this subspace is the rank of σ.

Fixing problem 2

It transpires that a density operator representation of σ is also precisely the right state for us to use in the phase estimation eigenstate input register. If we do this, then the eigenstate register output by the phase estimation primitive will encode an eigenvector of σ (i.e., one of the principal components) and the output register will encode the associated eigenvalue (i.e., the amount of variance along that principal component). Precisely which principal component, eigenvalue/eigenvector pair we get is randomly determined, but the probability of getting a given principal component is, conveniently, determined by its variance.

---

12 For more technical detail on how this operation is built and how it enables such a quantum simulation, see Lloyd et al., 2013 (*https://arxiv.org/abs/1307.0401*).

13 Note that this mini-SWAP approach to representing a matrix as a QPU operation won't always be better than quantum simulation approaches. It only works well here because covariance matrices happen to be simple to encode in a QPU register's density operator thanks to them being in Gram form.

With these proposed fixes, a full schematic for QPCA is as shown in Figure 13-5.

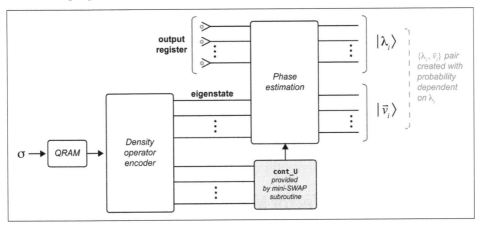

Figure 13-5. Schematic for QPCA

Figure 13-5 illustrates how the mini-SWAP subroutine's ability to perform quantum simulation with a density operator allows us to use it as the cont_U input to phase estimation. Note that the density operator encoder must be run multiple times and its output passed to the mini-SWAP subroutine, which provides the (conditional) QPU operation required by the phase estimation primitive (see Chapter 8). Also note that one run of the density operator encoder is input into the eigenstate register of the phase estimation primitive.

We've used the term *density operator encoder* to denote the process that allows us to represent our covariance matrix as a register's density operator. We won't go into detail about how the encoder works here, but Figure 13-5 summarizes how access to such an ability allows us to turn the phase estimation primitive to the task of PCA.

The output

After all this, we have an algorithm returning all the information we need about one (randomly chosen) principal component of our data—most likely to be the component having highest variance (exactly the ones we often care about when using PCA). But both the principal components and their variances are stored in QPU registers, and we must assert our usual important caveat that *our solutions are output in a quantum form*. Nevertheless, as was the case with HHL, it may still be possible to READ useful derived properties. Furthermore, we could pass the QPU register states onward to other QPU applications, where their quantum nature is likely advantageous.

Performance

Conventional algorithms for PCA have runtimes of $O(d)$, where d is the number of features we wish to perform PCA on.

In contrast, QPCA has a runtime of $O(R \log d)$, with R being the lowest-rank acceptable approximation to the covariance matrix σ (i.e., the smallest number of features that allow us to still represent our data to an acceptable approximation). In cases where $R < d$ (the data is well described by the low-rank approximation of our principal components), QPCA gives an exponential improvement in runtime over its conventional counterpart.

The runtime of QPCA qualifies our earlier assertion that it only offers an improvement for *low-rank* covariance matrices. This requirement is not as restrictive as it may seem. We are (presumably) normally using PCA on data that we expect is amenable to such a low-rank approximation—otherwise we'd be remiss to consider representing it with a subset of its principal components.

Quantum Support Vector Machines

Quantum support vector machines (QSVMs) demonstrate how QPUs can implement *supervised* machine-learning applications. Like a conventional supervised model, the QSVM we describe here must be trained on points in feature space having known classifications. However, QSVM comes with a number of unconventional constraints. First, a QSVM requires that training data be accessible in superposition using QRAM. Furthermore, the parameters that describe our learned model (used for future classification) are produced amplitude-encoded in a QPU register. As always, this means that we must take special care in how we plan to utilize a QSVM.

Conventional Support Vector Machines

Support vector machines (SVMs) are a popular type of supervised classifier finding wide application. As with other *linear classifiers*, the idea of SVMs is to use training data to find hyperplanes in feature space that separate different output classes of the problem. Once an SVM has learned such hyperplanes, a new data point in feature space can be classified by checking on which sides of these hyperplanes it lies. For a simple example, suppose we only have two features (and therefore a two-dimensional feature space), and furthermore that there are only two possible output classes the data can assume. In that case the hyperplane we seek is a line, as shown in Figure 13-6, where the x- and y-axes represent values of the two features, and we use blue and red markers to represent training data from the two output classes.

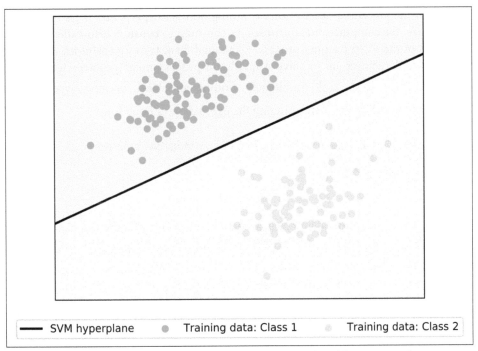

| — SVM hyperplane | ● Training data: Class 1 | ● Training data: Class 2 |

Figure 13-6. Example of the classification hyperplane produced by an SVM for a two-class classification problem with two features

How does an SVM learn a suitable hyperplane from training data? Geometrically we can think of the SVM training process as considering *two* parallel hyperplanes separating the training data classes, and trying to maximize the distance between this pair of hyperplanes. If we then choose a third hyperplane halfway between these as our classifier, we will have the classification hyperplane with the maximum *margin* between the training classes. The optimized hyperplane learned by the SVM is mathematically described[14] by a normal vector $\vec{w}$ and offset b. Having learned this description of the hyperplane, we predict the class of a new data point $\vec{x}$ according to the following rule:

$$\text{class} = \text{sign}\left(\vec{w} \cdot \vec{x} - b\right)$$

This mathematically determines on which side of the hyperplane the new point lies.

---

14 These parameters describe the hyperplane through the equation $\vec{w} \cdot \vec{x} - b = 0$, where $\vec{x}$ is a vector of feature values.

Although the preceding description of finding optimal hyperplanes is perhaps easier to visualize, for computational purposes it's common to consider a so-called *dual formulation* of the SVM training process.[15] The dual form is more useful for describing QSVMs, and requires us to solve a quadratic programming problem for a set of parameters $\vec{\alpha} = [\alpha_1, ..., \alpha_m]$. Specifically, finding an SVM's optimal hyperplane is equivalent to finding the $\vec{\alpha}$ maximizing the expression in Equation 13-7.

Equation 13-7. Dual description of the SVM optimization problem

$$\sum_i \alpha_i y_i - \frac{1}{2} \sum_i \sum_j \alpha_i \vec{x}_i \cdot \vec{x}_j \alpha_j$$

Here $\vec{x}_i$ is the ith training data point in feature space and y_i is the associated known class. The set of inner products $\vec{x}_i \cdot \vec{x}_j = K_{ij}$ between the training data points take on a special role if we generalize SVMs (as we'll discuss briefly in the next section) and are often collected into a matrix known as the *kernel matrix*.

Finding an $\vec{\alpha}$ satisfying this expression subject to the constraints that $\sum_i \alpha_i = 0$ and $y_i \alpha_i \geq 0 \forall i$ gives us the information needed to recover the optimal hyperplane parameters $\vec{w}$ and b. In fact, we can classify new data points directly in terms of $\vec{\alpha}$ according to Equation 13-8, where the intercept b can also be calculated from the training data.[16]

Equation 13-8. Classification rule for an SVM in the dual representation

$$\mathrm{sign}\left(\sum_i \alpha_i \vec{x}_i \cdot \vec{x} - b \right)$$

The key thing to note here for our forthcoming discussion of a *quantum* SVM is that classifying a new data point $\vec{x}$ requires us to calculate its inner product with every training data point, $\vec{x} \cdot \vec{x}_i$.

We won't delve any further into the detailed derivation or usage of these equations; instead we'll see how the calculations they require can be performed much more efficiently if we have access to a QPU.

---

15 Optimization problems often have such a dual form that can be easier to deal with. It's worth noting that sometimes these dual forms can contain subtle differences from the original (*primal*) optimization problem.

16 In fact, b can be determined from a single piece of training data lying on one of the two parallel hyperplanes defining the margin. The points lying on these defining hyperplanes are known as the *support vectors*.

SVM generalizations

First, though, it's worth noting that the kind of SVMs we have described so far are restricted to certain classification problems. To begin with, our discussion has assumed that the data to be modeled is *linearly separable*; i.e., that there definitely exists a hyperplane that could completely and unambiguously separate data from the two classes. Often, of course, this might not be the case, and while linearly separating the data could still provide a good fit, data from different classes may somewhat overlap in the feature space, as exemplified in Figure 13-7.

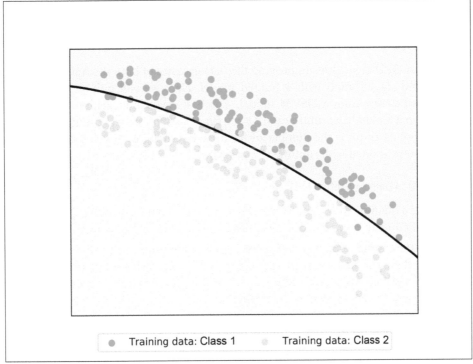

Figure 13-7. Data that cannot be fit by a linear SVM model—the training data from different classes overlap in feature space, and furthermore the correct decision boundary is clearly nonlinear.

SVMs deal with this possibility through the introduction of so-called *soft margins* in the training process. Although we won't expand on them here, it's worth noting that the QPU speedups we outline shortly persist for soft-margin SVMs.

Even soft-margin SVMs are still restricted to a linear separation of the data, though. In some cases a simple hyperplane may not do a good job of separating classes. When this is the case, we can try embedding our feature space in an even higher-dimensional space. If we perform this embedding carefully, we may be able to find a hyperplane in the higher-dimensional space that *does* effectively segregate the data from different classes. In other words, we use the projection of an $n + m$-dimensional hyperplane into an n-dimensional feature space, since a linear $n + m$-dimensional hyperplane can have a nonlinear n-dimensional projection. Such a nonlinear SVM is shown in Figure 13-7. Though this may sound like a complex modification to our SVM training process, it turns out we can very easily implement this kind of nonlinear generalization. By replacing the kernel matrix of inner products appearing in Equation 13-7 with a carefully chosen alternative kernel matrix, we're able to encapsulate higher-dimensional, nonlinear margins. This extension is often referred to as training an SVM with a *nonlinear kernel*.

SVM with a QPU

There exist QPU algorithms improving the performance of both the training of SVM models and classification with a trained model. Here we will only outline using a QPU to efficiently train a QSVM model. The best classical algorithms for training conventional SVMs have runtimes of $O(poly(m,n))$, where m is the number of training data points and n is the number of features describing each point. In contrast, a QSVM can be trained with runtime $O(log(mn))$.

Using a QPU to train a quantum SVM

Obtaining a quantum advantage for training SVMs is contingent on us being content with a fully quantum model. What we mean by this is that a trained QSVM is a set of QPU registers containing *amplitude encodings* of the hyperplane parameters $\vec{w}$ and b. Although these parameters are locked in superpositions, we'll see that they can still be used to classify new points in feature space, so long as the data for these new points can be accessed in superposition via a QRAM.

Training an SVM on a set of m training data points, $\left\{ \vec{x}_i, y_i \right\}_{i=1}^{m}$, requires us to find optimal values of the $\vec{\alpha}$ solving the quadratic programming problem stated in Equation 13-7. This seems like a tricky problem to speed up with a QPU. However, there is a reformulation of the SVM training problem known as a *Least Squares Support Vector Machine* (LS-SVM) that casts the building of an SVM classifier into a least-squares optimization problem.[17] As a consequence, to find the $\vec{\alpha}$ required by the SVM dual formulation, we are now presented with a linear system of equations, the solution of

---

[17] There are some subtle differences between SVM and LS-SVM models, although the two have been shown to be equivalent under certain reasonable conditions. See, for example, Ye and Xiong, 2007 (*http://bit.ly/ 31Wo8Jb*).

which is given by the matrix equation shown in Equation 13-9 (where $\vec{y}$ is a vector containing the training data classes).

Equation 13-9. LS-SVM equation

$$\begin{bmatrix} b \\ \vec{\alpha} \end{bmatrix} = \mathbf{F}^{-1} \begin{bmatrix} 0 \\ \vec{y} \end{bmatrix}$$

This looks more like something amenable to a QPU speedup, via the HHL algorithm from "Solving Systems of Linear Equations" on page 262. The matrix $\mathbf{F}$ is constructed from the kernel matrix K of training data inner products as outlined in Equation 13-10.

Equation 13-10. How the F matrix is built from the kernel matrix

$$\mathbf{F} = \begin{bmatrix} 0 & 1^T \\ 1 & K + \dfrac{1}{\gamma}\mathbb{1} \end{bmatrix}$$

Here, γ is a real number hyperparameter of the model (that in practice would be determined by cross-validation), $\mathbb{1}$ is the identity matrix, and we use 1 to denote a vector of m ones. Once we've used $\mathbf{F}$ to obtain values of $\vec{\alpha}$ and b, we can classify new data points using the LS-SVM just as we did with the standard SVM model, by using the criterion in Equation 13-8.

Using the HHL algorithm to efficiently solve Equation 13-9 and return registers' amplitude encoding $|b\rangle$ and $|\vec{\alpha}\rangle$ requires us to address a few key concerns:

Concern 1: Is $\mathbf{F}$ suitable for HHL?
    In other words, is the matrix $\mathbf{F}$ of the type we can invert with HHL (i.e., Hermitian, sufficiently sparse, etc.)?

Concern 2: How can we act $\mathbf{F}^{-1}$ on $\left[0, \vec{y}\right]$?
    If we *can* calculate $\mathbf{F}^{-1}$ using HHL, then how do we ensure it correctly acts on the vector $\left[0, \vec{y}\right]$ as Equation 13-9 requires?

Concern 3: How do we classify data?
    Even if we address concerns 1 and 2, we still need a way to make use of the obtained quantum representations of b and $\vec{\alpha}$ to train data presented to us in the future.

Let's address each of these concerns in turn to help convince ourselves that the training of a QSVM can indeed leverage the HHL algorithm.

Concern 1: Is F suitable for HHL?.   It's not too tricky to see that the matrix **F** is Hermitian, and so we can potentially represent it as a QPU operation using the quantum simulation techniques from Chapter 9. As we previously noted, being Hermitian, although necessary, is not sufficient for a matrix to be efficiently used in quantum simulation. However, it's also possible to see that a matrix of the form **F** can be decomposed into a sum of matrices, each of which satisfies all the requirements of quantum simulation techniques. So it turns out that we *can* use quantum simulation to find a QPU operation representing **F**. Note, however, that the nontrivial elements of **F** consist of inner products between the training data points. To efficiently use quantum simulation for representing **F** as a QPU operation we will need to be able to access the training data points using QRAM.

Concern 2: How can we act F^{-1} on $\left[0, \vec{y}\right]$?.   If we're using HHL to find $\mathbf{F}^{-1}$ then we can take care of this concern during the phase estimation stage of the algorithm. We input an amplitude encoding of the vector of training data classes, $|\vec{y'}\rangle$, into the phase estimation's eigenstate register. Here we use $|\vec{y'}\rangle$ to denote a QPU register state amplitude-encoding the vector $\left[0, \vec{y}\right]$. This, again, assumes that we have QRAM access to the training data classes. By the same logic we described when originally explaining HHL in "Solving Systems of Linear Equations" on page 262, $|\vec{y'}\rangle$ can be thought of as a superposition of the eigenstates of F. As a consequence, when we follow through the HHL algorithm we will find that $|F^{-1}\vec{y}\rangle$ is contained in the final output register, which is equal to precisely the solutions that we desire: $|b, \vec{\alpha}\rangle$. So we don't have to do anything fancy—HHL can output $\mathbf{F}^{-1}$ acted on the required vector, just as it did when we originally used it for solving systems of linear equations more generally.

Concern 3: How do we classify data?.   Suppose we are given a new data point $\vec{x}$, which we want to classify with our trained QSVM. Recall that a "trained QSVM" is really just access to the state $|b, \vec{\alpha}\rangle$. We can perform this classification efficiently so long as we have QRAM access to the new data point $\vec{x}$. Classifying the new point requires computing the sign given by Equation 13-8. This, in turn, involves determining the inner products of $\vec{x}$ with all the training data points $\vec{x}_i$, weighted by the LS-SVM dual hyperplane parameters α_i. We can calculate the requisite inner products in superposition and assess Equation 13-8 as follows. First we use our trained LS-SVM state $|b, \vec{\alpha}\rangle$ in the address register of a query to the QRAM holding the training data. This gives us a superposition of the training data with amplitudes containing the α_i. In another register we perform a query to the QRAM containing the new data point $\vec{x}$.

Having both of these states, we can perform a special *swap-test subroutine*. Although we won't go into full detail, this subroutine combines the states resulting from our two QRAM queries into an entangled superposition and then performs a carefully constructed swap test (see Chapter 3). Recall that as well as telling us whether the states of two QPU registers are equal or not, the exact success probability p of the READ involved in the swap test is dependent on the *fidelity* of the two states—a quantitative measure of precisely how close they are. The swap test we use here is carefully constructed so that the probability p of READing a 1 reflects the sign we need in Equation 13-8. Specifically, $p < 1/2$ if the sign is +1 and $p >= 1/2$ if the sign is –1. By repeating the swap test and counting 0 and 1 outcomes, we can estimate the value of the probability p to a desired accuracy, and classify the data point $\vec{x}$ accordingly.

Thus, we are able to train and use a quantum LS-SVM model according to the schematic shown in Figure 13-8.

Without delving into mathematical details, like those of the swap-test subroutine, Figure 13-8 gives only a very general overview of how LS-SVM training proceeds. Note that many details of the swap-test subroutine are not shown, although the key input states are highlighted. This gives some idea of the key roles the QPU primitives we've introduced throughout the book play.

Our QSVM summary also provides an important take-home message. A key step was recasting the SVM problem in a format that is amenable to techniques a QPU is well suited for (in particular, matrix inversion). This exemplifies a central ethos of this book—through awareness of *what* a QPU can do well, domain expertise may allow the discovery of new QPU applications simply by casting existing problems in QPU-compatible forms.

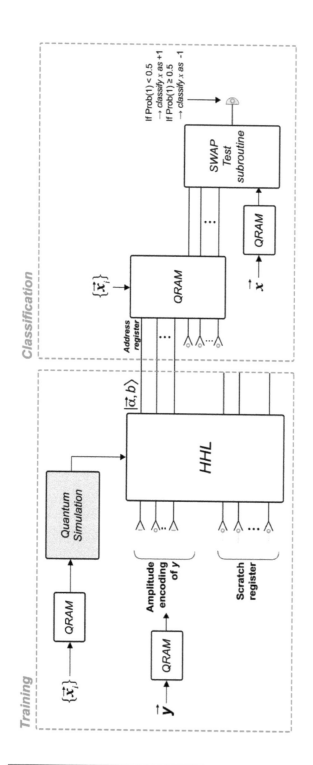

Figure 13-8. Schematic showing the stages in training and classifying with a QSVM

Other Machine Learning Applications

Quantum machine learning is still an extremely dynamic area of research. In this chapter we presented three canonical examples, but new developments in QML are constantly being made. At the same time, *conventional* approaches to machine learning are being inspired by QPU algorithms—in fact, within the time period of us writing this book, all three of the QML applications presented in this chapter have inspired the development of conventional algorithms with similar runtime improvements.[18] This should not shake your confidence in QML's potential; these results were unlikely to have been discovered without the inspiration of their QPU counterparts, showing that QML applications have far-reaching and unexpected consequences.[19] There are also many other QML applications that we simply didn't have space to properly mention. These include efficient QPU applications for linear regression,[20] unsupervised learning,[21], Boltzmann machines,[22] semidefinite programming,[23] and quantum recommender systems[24] (quantum recommender systems have also inspired improvements in conventional algorithms[25]).

18 HHL: Chia et al., 2018 (*https://arxiv.org/abs/1811.04852*); QPCA and QSVM: Tang, 2018 (*https://arxiv.org/abs/1811.00414*).

19 In fact, it's not obvious how practical these quantum-inspired algorithms will be in actual usage. See for example Arrazola et al., 2019 (*https://arxiv.org/abs/1905.10415*).

20 Chakraborty et al., 2018 (*https://arxiv.org/abs/1804.01973*).

21 Lloyd et al., 2013 (*https://arxiv.org/abs/1307.0411*).

22 Wiebe et al., 2014 (*https://arxiv.org/abs/1412.3489*).

23 Brandão et al., 2017 (*https://arxiv.org/abs/1710.02581*).

24 Kerenidis and Prakash, 2016 (*https://arxiv.org/abs/1603.08675*).

25 Tang, 2018 (*https://arxiv.org/abs/1807.04271*).

PART IV

Outlook

CHAPTER 14

Staying on Top: A Guide to the Literature

We hope you've enjoyed tinkering with the computational problems we presented in this book! Before closing, we'll briefly introduce a few subjects we didn't have space to go into previously, and provide pointers on where to go to learn more about these and other topics in quantum computing. We won't go into too much depth here; the aim here is rather to link what you've learned so far to material reaching beyond the scope of this book. Let the intuition you've built here be only the first step in your exploration of quantum programming!

From Circle Notation to Complex Vectors

The $|x\rangle$ notation that we use throughout the book to refer to states in a quantum register is called *bra-ket notation* or, sometimes *Dirac notation*, in honor of the 20th-century physicist of the same name. Throughout the quantum computing literature, this—rather than circle notation—is the notation used to represent quantum states. In Chapter 2 we hinted at the equivalence between these two notations, but it's worth saying a little more to set you on your way. A general superposition within a single-qubit register can be expressed in Dirac notation as $\alpha|0\rangle + \beta|1\rangle$, where α and β are the states' *amplitudes*, represented as complex numbers satisfying the equation $|\alpha|^2 + |\beta|^2 = 1$. The magnitude and relative phase of each value in the circle notation we've been using are given by the *modulus* and *argument* of the complex numbers α and β, respectively. The probability of a READ outcome for a given binary output value from a QPU register is given by the *squared modulus* of the complex number describing the amplitude of that value. For example, in the preceding single-qubit case, $|\alpha|^2$ would give the probability of READing a 0 and $|\beta|^2$ would give the probability of READing a 1.

The complex vectors describing QPU register states satisfy some very specific mathematical properties, meaning that they can be said to exist in a structure known as a *Hilbert space*. You likely don't need to know that much about Hilbert space, but will hear the term used a lot—mostly simply to refer to the collection of possible complex vectors representing a given QPU register.

In the case of single qubits, a common way to parameterize α and β is as $\cos\theta|0\rangle + e^{i\phi}\sin\theta|1\rangle$. In this case, the two variables θ and ϕ can be interpreted as angles on a sphere, which many references will refer to as the *Bloch* sphere. As mentioned in Chapter 2, the Bloch sphere provides a visual representation of single-qubit states. Unlike circle notation, though, it's unfortunately difficult to use the Bloch sphere to visualize registers with more than one qubit.

Another complication regarding qubit states that we didn't cover in the book is the so-called *mixed states*, which are represented mathematically by so-called *density operators* (although we did mention density operators briefly in Chapter 13). These are a statistical mixture of the kind of *pure states* that we've been working with in our quantum registers throughout the book (i.e., how you should describe a qubit if you're not sure precisely *what* superposition it's in). To some extent it is possible to represent mixed states in circle notation, but if we have a QPU with error correction (more on that later), pure states are enough to get started with QPU programming.

As visualizations of many-qubit registers are not common in most textbooks and academic references, quantum registers are most often represented solely by complex vectors,[1] with the length of the vector needed for representing n qubits being 2^n (just as the number of circles needed in circle-notation to represent n qubits was 2^n. When writing down the amplitudes of an n-qubit register's state in a column vector, the amplitude of the state $|00\ldots0\rangle$ is conventionally placed at the top with the remaining possible states following below in ascending binary order.

QPU operations are described by unitary matrices acting on these complex vectors. The order in which the matrices are written is right to left (exactly opposite of how we would write a quantum circuit diagram—left to right), so that the first matrix that acts on our complex vector corresponds to the first (leftmost) gate in an associated circuit diagram. Equation 14-1 shows a simple example, where a NOT gate (often also referred to as X in the literature) is applied to an input qubit in the state $\alpha|0\rangle + \beta|1\rangle$. We can see how it flips the values of α and β, as expected.

---

1 Recall from Chapter 13, though, that mixed states are represented by matrices, called *density operators*, instead of vectors.

Equation 14-1. NOT gate acting on qubit in standard complex-vector notation

$$\begin{bmatrix} 0 & 1 \\ 1 & 0 \end{bmatrix} \begin{bmatrix} \alpha \\ \beta \end{bmatrix} = \begin{bmatrix} \beta \\ \alpha \end{bmatrix}$$

Single-qubit gates are represented as 2×2 matrices since they transform vectors with two entries, corresponding to the single-qubit register values of $|0\rangle$ and $|1\rangle$. Two-qubit gates are represented by 4×4 matrices and, in general, n-qubit gates are represented by $2^n \times 2^n$ matrices. In Figure 14-1 we show the matrix representations of some of the most commonly used single- and two-qubit gates. If you have an understanding of matrix multiplication and really want to test your understanding, you might try to predict the action of these operations on different input states and see whether your predictions match what you see in QCEngine's circle notation.

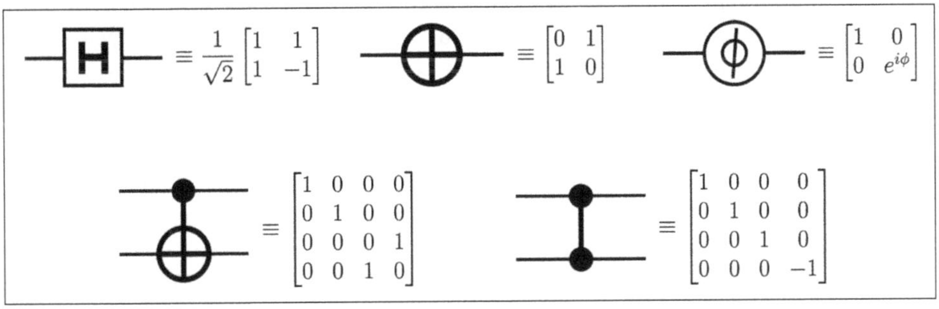

Figure 14-1. Matrix representations of the most basic single- and two-qubit gates

Some Subtleties and Notes on Terminology

There are a few subtleties we wanted to mention with regard to to the terminology used in this book.

- Throughout the book we've referred to pre-quantum computing as "conventional." You may also hear people use the term *classical* to refer to traditional binary computing that doesn't operate with quantum registers.

- We have often used so-called *scratch qubits* to help perform some aspects of the quantum computation. These are instead referred to as *ancilla qubits* in many quantum computing resources.

- In Chapter 2 we introduced the PHASE gate, which takes an angle as an input parameter. In this book we have used *degrees* to represent angles, ranging from 0° to 360°. It is common in the quantum computing literature to specify angles in *radians*. Radians are an angular unit corresponding to an angle at the center of the circle such that its arc has the same length as its radius. The following table shows commonly used angles in both units:

Degrees	0°	45°	90°	135°	180°	225°	270°	315°
Radians	0	$\frac{\pi}{4}$	$\frac{\pi}{2}$	$\frac{3\pi}{4}$	π	$\frac{5\pi}{4}$	$\frac{3\pi}{2}$	$\frac{7\pi}{4}$

- There are three cases in which the PHASE gate receives a special name:

Angle (radians)	$\frac{\pi}{4}$	$\frac{\pi}{2}$	π
Name	T	S	Z

- In Chapter 6, we introduced the AA primitive. This primitive (more specifically, the mirror operation) allows us to *amplify the amplitude* of marked states in our register, thereby increasing the probability of READing out that register. Although this terminology may seem straightforward enough, it's worth noting that in the scholarly literature, these iterations are usually denoted as *Grover iterations*, while the expression *amplitude amplification* is reserved for a general class of algorithms that can use Grover iterations in order to improve their success probabilities.

- The particular configuration of a QPU register (eg: what superposition or entangled arrangement it might exist in) is commonly referred to as the *state* of the register. This terminology arises from the fact that a register's configuration is really described by a quantum state in the mathematical sense introduced briefly above (even if we we choose to visualize the register more conveniently using circle notation).

- When describing an N qubit QPU register in some superposition of its 2^N possible integer values, we have often referred to each of these possibilities (and their asociated amplitudes) as *values* within the superposition. An equivalent, more commonplace, expression is *term*. So one might talk (for example) about the amplitude of *"the |4⟩ term"* in a QPU register's superposition. If we're thinking of QPU register's in terms of their proper Dirac notation representation, then this terminology makes sense, as $|4\rangle$ (and it's amplitude) really is a *term* in a mathematical expression. We avoided using the expression *term* throughout most of the book, simply because of the unavoidable mathematical connotations.

- QPU operations are sometimes referred to as *quantum gates*, with reverance to the logic gates of conventional computation. You can consider the terms "QPU operation" and "quantum gate" to be snynonymous. Collections of quantum gates form a quantum circuit.

Measurement Basis

There's a widespread concept in quantum computing that we've carefully managed to avoid mentioning throughout the book—that of *measurement basis*. Understanding measurement more thoroughly in quantum computing really involves getting to grips with the full mathematical machinery of quantum theory, and we can't hope to begin to do so in this short space. The goal of this book is to give you an intuitive "in" to the concepts needed to program a QPU, and for more in-depth discussion we refer the interested reader to the recommended resources at the end of this chapter. That said, we'll try to briefly give an insight into how the core idea of measurement basis relates to the concepts and terminology we've used.

Wherever we used the READ operation, we always assumed it would give us an answer of 0 or 1. We saw that these two answers correspond to the states $|0\rangle$ and $|1\rangle$, in the sense that these are the states which will always give a 0 or 1 outcome, respectively. These states are, more technically, the eigenstates[2] of the PHASE(180) operation (also sometimes called a Z gate). Whenever we "READ in the Z basis," as we have implicitly done throughout the book, the complex vector describing our QPU register will, after the READ, end up in one of these two states. We say that we've *projected* our QPU register onto one of these states.[3] Although we've so far only thought about measurements in the Z basis, this is not the only option.

Different measurement bases are like different *questions* we are asking our QPU state. The possible questions we can ask with quantum READ operations are which of the eigenstates from certain QPU operations our system is in. This may sound incredibly abstract, but in quantum physics these operations and their eigenstates do have physical meanings, and understanding their precise nature requires a more in-depth understanding of the underlying physics. Since so far we've only been measuring in the basis of PHASE(180), we've actually always been asking the question, "is the QPU register in the eigenstate of PHASE(180) corresponding to the eigenvalue +1, or is it in the state corresponding to the eigenvalue -1?" Even if the QPU register is in a superposition of these possibilities, after the READ it will assume one of them.

Performing a READ in another basis means asking which eigenstate of some *other* QPU operation, *U*, our QPU register is in. After the READ our QPU register will end up in (i.e., be projected onto) one of the eigenstates of U.

---

2 For a refresher on eigenstates, see Chapter 8.

3 The term *project* here has a mathematical meaning. Projection operators in mathematics "select out" certain vectors from a linear combination. In quantum mechanics, the action of a READ in the Z basis is to "project" the complex vector representing our QPU register onto one of the complex vectors representing $|0\rangle$ or $|1\rangle$.

Since a QPU register's state can be thought of as a superposition of the eigenstates of any QPU operation (as we described in Chapter 13), writing out the complex vector representation of a QPU register state in the eigenbasis of some operation U allows us to work out the various READ probabilities in the U measurement basis. Another interesting aspect of this whole measurement basis business is that states that *always* have the same measurement outcome (with 100% probability) when measured in one basis may not be so definite in a different basis, possibly only *probabilistically* yielding each outcome. For example, we've seen multiple times that when reading out the state $|+\rangle = \frac{1}{\sqrt{2}}|0\rangle + \frac{1}{\sqrt{2}}|1\rangle$, we have a 50% chance of getting 0 and 50% chance of getting 1 when measuring in the Z basis. However, if we're measuring in the X (NOT) basis, we will always get 0; this is because $|+\rangle$ happens to be an eigenstate of X and therefore, when considered in the measurement basis of X, our state isn't in a superposition at all.

Gate Decompositions and Compilation

Controlled operations have played an important role throughout the book, and on occasion, you may have been left wondering how we would implement these operations. Cases that might particularly require elucidation are:

1. Controlled operations where the operation acting on the target qubit is something other than NOT or PHASE

2. Gates with controls on several qubits at once

For compactness of notation we've often drawn these kinds of operations as single diagrammatic units in our circuit diagrams. However, in general, they will not correspond to native instructions on QPU hardware and they'll need to be implemented in terms of more fundamental QPU operations.

Fortunately, more complex conditional operations can be written as series of single-qubit and two-qubit operations. In Figure 14-2 we show a general decomposition of a controlled QPU operation (corresponding to a general unitary matrix in the mathematics of quantum computing). The constituent operations in this decomposition need to be chosen such that A, B, and C satisfy $U = e^{i\alpha}AXBXC$ (where X is the NOT gate) and acting all three operations directly one after the other, $A \cdot B \cdot C$, has no overall effect on our QPU register state.

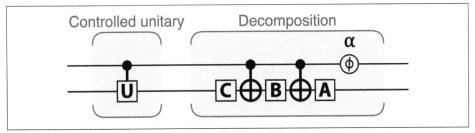

Figure 14-2. General decomposition of a controlled unitary

If we can find operations *A*, *B*, *C*, and *α* satisfying these requirements, then we can conditionally perform our desired operation *U*. Sometimes there may be more than one possible way to decompose a conditional operation according to this prescription.

What about conditional operations that are conditioned on *more than one qubit at once*? As an example, Figure 14-3 shows three different decompositions for implementing the CCNOT (Toffoli) gate, which is conditioned on two qubits.

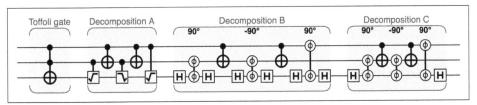

Figure 14-3. The familiar CCNOT gate can be decomposed into more basic operations

You may notice that all three of these decompositions follow the same pattern. This is not only the case for the CCNOT, any controlled-controlled operation (i.e., an operation conditioned on two other qubits) will have a similar decomposition. Figure 14-4 shows the general way we can implement a QPU operation controlled on two qubits, if we can find a QPU operation *V* satisfying $V^2 = U$ (i.e., where applying *V* twice to a register is the same as if we had applied *U*).

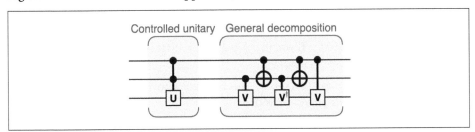

Figure 14-4. A general controlled-controlled unitary decomposition

Note that if we need help constructing the controlled-*V* operations in Figure 14-4, we can always refer back to Figure 14-3.

Finding the optimal decompositions of QPU algorithms in terms of simple QPU primitives and operations is not easy. The field of *quantum compiling* focuses on finding fast implementations of quantum algorithms. We'll mention a few more details about quantum compiling later in the chapter, and you can find some examples of quantum compiling optimizations online at *http://oreilly-qc.github.io?p=14-GD*.

Gate Teleportation

In Chapter 4, we used the quantum teleportation protocol to introduce ideas and notation that we used later throughout the book. While the teleportation of *information* does not feature heavily in most QPU applications, the ability to teleport *QPU operations* often does. This allows two parties to perform an operation on a quantum register, even if no one of the two parties has access to the state and operation in the same place. Like the teleportation protocol we saw in Chapter 4, this trick requires the use of a pair of entangled qubits.

A simple example of a gate teleportation protocol can be found online at *http://oreilly-qc.github.io?p=14-GT*.

QPU Hall of Fame

For most of the book, we have abstained from referring the reader to academic references. Here we've compiled a small list of the references that first introduced many of the ideas and algorithms that we've discussed in detail:

- Feynman (1982), "Simulating Physics with Computers" (*http://bit.ly/322FC6r*)
- Deutsch (1985), "Quantum theory, the Church-Turing principle and the universal quantum computer" (*http://bit.ly/2XmWKWc*)
- Deutsch (1989), "Quantum Computational Networks" (*http://bit.ly/2KNzJF6*)
- Shor (1994), "Algorithms for Quantum Computation: Discrete Log and Factoring" (*http://bit.ly/32119fP*)
- Barenco et al. (1995), "Elementary gates for quantum computation" (*https://arxiv.org/abs/quant-ph/9503016*)
- Grover (1996), "A fast quantum mechanical algorithm for database search" (*https://arxiv.org/abs/quant-ph/9605043*)
- Brassard et al. (1998), "Quantum Counting" (*https://arxiv.org/pdf/quant-ph/9805082.pdf*)

- Brassard et al. (1998), "Quantum Amplitude Amplification and Estimation" (*https://arxiv.org/abs/quant-ph/0005055*)
- Lloyd et al. (2009), "Quantum Algorithm for Solving Linear Systems of Equations" (*https://arxiv.org/abs/0811.3171*)

Further references and resources can also be found in the lists of selected books and lecture notes at the end of the chapter.

The Race: Quantum Versus Conventional Computers

When discussing various QPU applications we've often been interested in comparing the performance of our newly learned QPU algorithms with their conventional counterparts. Although we've made comparisons on a case-by-case basis, interesting general comparisons can be made between the capabilities of quantum and conventional computers in terms of computational complexity. The computational complexity of a problem in computer science is given (roughly speaking) by the resources required to run the most efficient algorithm solving the problem. Computational complexity theory studies the classification of difficult problems according to their computational complexity.[4] For example, some problems are classified as *P*, which means that the resources required to find a solution to the problem scale polynomially with the size of the problem (e.g., matrix diagonalization). *NP* refers to the class of problems that have a *correct* solution that can be *checked* in polynomial time, but where these solutions cannot necessarily be *found* in polynomial time. This class has a twin, *co-NP*, which corresponds to the problems for which an *incorrect* answer to the problem can be verified in polynomial time. For example, the problem of factoring that we discussed in Chapter 12 is in both the NP and co-NP classes—it's easy to *check* whether a pair of numbers are (or aren't) prime factors, but not so easy to find them in the first place. Whether P=NP is a notorious open problem, well known thanks to multiple references in popular culture and the small matter of a $1M prize awaiting anyone who can address the question! It is widely suspected, with good reason, that the two classes are not equal. The NP-complete class that we mentioned in Chapter 10 corresponds, in some sense, to the most difficult problems in the NP class. Any other problem in NP can be reduced to one of these NP-complete problems, and if a polynomial-time solution is found for any NP-complete problem, all the problems in NP will also become solvable in polynomial time and change class to P.

The excitement surrounding quantum computing is mainly due to the fact that it appears able to reduce the computational complexity of certain problems. Note that this is not a blanket speedup of any conventional computing problem; only very specific classes of algorithms are currently known to enjoy quantum speedups. This

---

4 A full description of its 500+ classes can be found in the Complexity Zoo (*http://bit.ly/2RIlge2*).

reduction can be polynomial (e.g., from higher-order polynomial to lower-order), as is the case for the 3-SAT problem we looked at in Chapter 10, or superpolynomial (e.g., from exponential to polynomial), as is the case for factoring. Where can quantum computers provide a superpolynomial speedup? It turns out that problems that are *both* in NP and co-NP are prime suspects (pun intended) to have exponentially faster QPU algorithms, and in fact, most of the algorithms for which such a speedup has been achieved belong to the intersection of these two classes.

Another important development that we initially mentioned in Chapter 13 is worth reiterating here. There have been a number of instances where completely conventional but quantum-inspired algorithms have emerged after quantum algorithms had been developed for those same problems. Therefore, research and understanding of quantum algorithms can lead to advances in conventional computing as well!

A Note on Oracle-Based Algorithms

Three of the earliest quantum algorithms shown to have a speedup on quantum versus conventional computers required calls to an *oracle*. An oracle provides information about a variable or a function, without revealing the variable or functions itself. The task in these early algorithms was to determine the variable or function used by the oracle in as few calls as possible. The required number of oracle calls in such a problem (and how this number scales with problem size) is usually referred to as the *query complexity*.

While these algorithms did not provide a useful computational advantage, they were crucial in the development of quantum computing, as they built understanding of the capabilities of quantum computers and eventually inspired researchers such as Peter Shor to develop more useful algorithms. Due to their pedagogical and historical importance, we briefly mention these early algorithms here, each of which is now known by the name of its inventor.

QCEngine code samples are also provided online at *http://oreilly-qc.github.io* to help you explore these pioneering quantum algorithms.

Deutsch-Jozsa

Oracle

Takes a binary string of n bits and outputs a single bit that is the result of applying a function f to the binary string. We are promised that the function f is either constant, in which case the output bit will always be the same, or balanced, in which case there will be the same number of 0 and 1 outputs.

Problem

Decide with absolute certainty whether f is constant or balanced in as few queries to the oracle as possible.

Query complexity

Conventionally, we will need to make $2^{n-1} + 1$ queries to the oracle to be absolutely sure about the nature of the function. With a QPU, we can solve the problem with zero probability of error *in a single quantum query!*

This algorithm can be run online at *http://oreilly-qc.github.io?p=14-DJ.*

Bernstein-Vazirani

Oracle

Takes a binary string, *x*, of *n* bits and outputs a single binary number. The output is obtained by $\Sigma_i x_i \cdot s_i$, where *s* is a secret string used by the oracle.

Problem

Find the secret string *s*.

Query complexity

Conventionally, we require *n* oracle queries, one to learn each of the input bits. However, using a QPU we can solve the problem with a single query.

This algorithm can be run online at *http://oreilly-qc.github.io?p=14-BV.*

Simon

Oracle

Takes an *n*-bit binary string, *x*, and outputs a single integer. All the possible input strings are paired through a secret string *s*, such that two strings (x,y) will result in the same output if and only if $y = x \oplus s$ (where $\oplus$ denotes bitwise addition modulo 2).

Problem

Find the secret string *s*.

Query complexity

A conventional deterministic algorithm will require at least $2^{n-1} + 1$ oracle queries. By using Simon's quantum algorithm, we can find the solution in a number of calls that scales linearly in *n*, rather than exponentially.

This algorithm can be run online at *http://oreilly-qc.github.io?p=14-S.*

Quantum Programming Languages

A topic we have not touched upon is that of *quantum programming languages*—i.e., programming languages specifically developed with the quirks of quantum computing in mind. The applications and algorithms we've covered have been described using basic QPU operations (analogous to conventional binary logic gates), which we have orchestrated and controlled from a conventional programming language. This approach was followed for two reasons. Firstly, our goal has been to allow you to get hands-on and experiment with the abilities of a QPU. At the time of writing, quantum programming is arguably too nascent a field, with no existing universal standards. Secondly, the majority of quantum computing resources available to take you beyond this book (other books, lecture notes, and online simulators) are all written in terms of the same basic QPU operations we have centered our discussion around.

On the topic of developing a quantum programming stack, one area that has seen a lot of recent interest and development is *quantum compiling*. Due to the characteristics of quantum error-correction codes, some QPU operations (such as HAD) are much easier to implement in a fault-tolerant manner than others (such as PHASE(45), also referred to as a T gate). Finding ways to compile quantum programs that account for such implementation constraints but don't adversely impact the speedup offered by a QPU is the task of quantum compiling. Literature surrounding quantum compiling often mentions the *T count* of a program, referring to the total number of difficult-to-perform T gates required. A common topic is also the preparation and distillation of so-called *magic states*,[5] particular quantum states that (when perfectly prepared) allow us to implement the elusive T gate.

At the time of writing, the study of quantum programming languages and quantum software toolchains would benefit greatly from input from experts in conventional computing—especially in the areas of debugging and verification. Some good starting points on the topic are listed here:

- Huang and Martonosi (2018), "QDB: From Quantum Algorithms Towards Correct Quantum Programs" (*https://arxiv.org/pdf/1811.05447.pdf*)
- Green et al. (2013), "Quipper: A Scalable Quantum Programming Language" (*https://arxiv.org/pdf/1304.3390.pdf*)
- Altenkirch and Grattage (2005), "A Functional Quantum Programming Language" (*https://arxiv.org/pdf/quant-ph/0409065.pdf*)
- Svore (2018), "Q#: Enabling Scalable Quantum Computing and Development with a High-Level Domain-Specific Language" (*https://arxiv.org/pdf/1803.00652.pdf*)
- Hietala et al. (2019), "Verified Optimization in a Quantum Intermediate Representation" (*https://arxiv.org/pdf/1904.06319.pdf*)
- Qiskit: An open-source software development kit (SDK) for working with OpenQASM and the IBM Q quantum processors (*http://qiskit.org*)

---

5 *Magic* is a technical term in quantum computing. As well as a magical one.

- Aleksandrowicz et al. (2019), "Qiskit: An Open-source Framework for Quantum Computing" (*http://www.doi.org/10.5281/zenodo.2562111*)

The Promise of Quantum Simulation

At the time of writing (circa 2019), quantum simulation is being proposed as the *killer app* of quantum computing. In fact, there are already some quantum algorithmic proposals to address quantum chemistry problems that are intractable with classical computers. Some of the problems that could be solved using quantum simulation routines are:

Nitrogen fixation
Find a catalyst to convert nitrogen to ammonia at room temperature. This process can be used to lower the cost of fertilizer, addressing hunger in third-world countries.

Room temperature superconductor
Find a material that superconducts at room temperature. This material would allow for power transmission with virtually no losses.

Catalyst for carbon sequestration
Find a catalyst to absorb carbon from the atmosphere, reducing the amount of CO_2 and slowing global warming.

It is clear that the potential for social and economic change that quantum computers can bring is unparalleled compared to most other technologies, which is one of the reasons there is such an interest in bringing about this technology.

Error Correction and NISQ Devices

The discussions of QPU operations, primitives, and applications in this book have all assumed (or simulated) the availability of *error-corrected* (also called logical) qubits. As with conventional computation, errors in registers and operations can quickly ruin quantum computation. A large body of research exists into quantum error-correction codes designed to counteract this effect. A remarkable result in the study of quantum error correction is the *threshold theorem*, which shows that if the rate of errors in a QPU falls below a certain threshold, then quantum error-correction codes will allow us to suppress the errors at the cost of only a small overhead to our computation. QPU applications only maintain their advantage over conventional algorithms under such low-noise conditions, and therefore likely require error-corrected qubits.

That said, at the time of writing there is a trend to search for QPU algorithms that might provide speedups over conventional computers even when run on Noisy Intermediate-Scale Quantum (NISQ) devices. These devices are understood to be composed of noisy qubits that do not undergo error correction. The hope is that algorithms might exist that are themselves intrinsically tolerant to QPU noise. However, circa 2019, no such algorithms capable of solving useful problems are known to exist.

Where Next?

In this book, we hope to have provided you with the conceptual tools and QPU intuition to further explore the fascinating topic of quantum computing. With the foundation you now have, the references we list in this section are good places to take your understanding of QPUs to the next stage. Be warned (but not dissuaded!) that these references often freely use the more advanced levels of linear algebra and other mathematics that we've aimed to avoid in this text.

Books

- Nielsen and Chuang (2011), *Quantum Computation and Quantum Information* (*http://bit.ly/2RGIFMU*)

- Mermin (2007), *Quantum Computer Science: An Introduction* (*https://amzn.to/2XfRwql*)

- Aaronson (2013), *Quantum Computing Since Democritus* (*http://bit.ly/2xmTkD8*)

- Kitaev et al. (2002), *Classical and Quantum Computation* (*https://amzn.to/2JduUBO*)

- Watrous (2018), *The Theory of Quantum Information* (*http://bit.ly/31ZTnmx*)

- Kaye et al. (2007), *An Introduction to Quantum Computing* (*https://g.co/kgs/2wradM*)

- Wilde (2013), *Quantum Information Theory* (*https://doi.org/10.1017/CBO9781139525343*)

Lecture Notes

- Aaronson, Quantum Information Science lecture notes (*http://bit.ly/2XdYSPM*)
- Preskill, lecture notes on Quantum Computation (*http://bit.ly/2xjlOxH*)
- Childs, lecture notes on quantum algorithms (*http://bit.ly/2FIibWR*)
- Watrous, Quantum Computation, lecture notes (*http://bit.ly/2XBUDgp*)

Online Resources

- Vazirani, Quantum Mechanics and Quantum Computation (*http://bit.ly/2YmvKST*)
- Shor, Quantum Computation (*http://bit.ly/2RHSuu8*)
- Quantum Algorithm Zoo (*http://quantumalgorithmzoo.org*)

Index

Gram form, 278
graph, 190
 color, 190
 isomorphism, 236
graphics, in relation to QSS, 211
greatest common divisor (gcd), 238, 256
Grover iteration, 110, 296
 (see also mirror operation)
Grover's search algorithm, 191

H

hacks, graphics, 223
HAD (Hadamard) operation, 22, 76, 86, 157, 161
Hamiltonian, 188
hardware limitations with QPU, 9
Hermitian matrix, 186
 constructing from non-Hermitian matrices, 187
 importance in HHL, 268
 relationship to Unitary matrices, 187
HHL algorithm, 262, 264, 265
HHL, fine print, 267
hidden subgroup problem, 236
Hilbert space, 294
Hotelling transform (see Principle Component Analysis (PCA))
hyperparameter (machine learning), 285
hyperplane, 280

I

IBM QX, 78
IBM simulator, 67
increment operators, 88-91
inner products, 283
integers, quantum, 87
intuition
 of amplitude amplification, 121-123
 of phase estimation, 165-167
 of QFT, 148
inverse QFT (invQFT), 143
invert values for solving systems of linear equations, 272
invQFT, 143
 (see also inverse QFT)
iterations in amplitude amplification, 111-114

J

JavaScript, 2

K

Karhunen-Loève transform (see Principle Component Analysis (PCA))
kernel matrix, 282
 nonlinear kernel, 284

L

Least Squares Support Vector Machine (LS-SVM), 284
Lie product formula, 189
linear classifier (machine learning), 280
linear equations, systems of, 263
linking payload to entangled pair in teleportation, 75
logic (see quantum arithmetic and logic)
logic puzzles, 198-202
 kittens and tigers, 198-202
 QS and, 198-202
logical qubits, 305
lookup table, for QSS, 224, 228

M

magic states, 304
magnitude
 converting between phase logic and, 107-110
 defined, 16, 17, 21
 of DFT, 133
magnitude logic
 defined, 193
 for building quantum arithmetic, 85
 usage in quantum search, 201
mapping between Boolean logic and QPU operations, 103-105
margin (of SVM), 281
marked value (in amplitude amplification), 108
matrix
 as a representation of a system of linear equations, 263
 eigenbasis of, 269
 inverting, 263, 269
 multiplication, 263
matrix encodings, 185, 185
 (see also quantum simulation)
 definition of a good representation, 186

ability to deal with generalizations of SVMs, 283

classifying with, 286-287

training, 284

usage of QPU, 284-287

quantum walks (as an approach to quantum simulation), 190

qubits

ancilla (see scratch qubits)

error-corrected, 305

logical, 305

naming with hexadecimal, 41

QPU measured in, 8

reading in multi-qubit registers, 43

single (see single qubit)

qubytes, 87

query complexity

Bernstein-Vazirani algorithm, 303

defined, 302

Deutsch-Jozsa algorithm, 303

Simon algorithm, 303

R

radians, 295

Random Access Memory, 175

shortcomings of, 177-177

usage in initializing QPU registers, 176

rank (of matrix), 278, 280

ray tracing, 212-214

READ, 23, 43, 79, 176, 297

reading qubits, 19

recommender systems, quantum, 289

regression

and HHL, 267

as a QML application, 289

regression (machine learning), defined, 262

relative phase, defined, 17, 17, 21

relative rotation of circles in circle notation, 19

remote-controlled randomness, 61-64

reversibility, 87, 89, 98-100

Rivest-Shamir-Adleman (RSA) public-key cryptosystem, 235

RNOT (ROOT-of-NOT), 30-32

rollLeft(), 247

room temperature superconductor, 305

ROOT-of-NOT (RNOT), 30-32

rotating circles phase by multiple value, 149

ROTX(θ), 29

ROTY(θ), 29

runtime, 190, 264

of approaches to quantum simulation, 190

of conventional algorithms employing amplitude amplification, 209

of HHL, 264

of QFT, 140

of QPCA, 279

of QSVMs, 284

S

sampling phase-encoded images, 220

satisfiable 3-SAT problem, 203-206

satisfy (in Boolean logic), 192

scenes, computer-generatedm id=scenes_computer_generatedm range=startofrange, 212

scratch qubits, 98-100, 295

scratch register, 265, 266

searching, database, 110, 191-192, 301

semidefinite programming, 289

Shor(), 242

Shor, Peter (see Peter Shor)

ShorLogic(), 237

ShorNoQPU(), 239

ShorQPU(), 237, 240

Shor's factoring algorithm, 235-259

computing modulus, 257

coprimes other than 2, 259

factoring number 15 (see factoring number 15)

overview of, 237-242

QFT and, 240-242

time vs. space, 259

signal processing with QFT, 141

Simon's algorithm, 303

simulation, molecular, 188

simulation, quantum (see quantum simulation)

simulator limitations with QPU, 8

single qubit, 13-36

about, 13-15

basic operations of (see single-qubit operations)

Bloch sphere and, 294

circle notation (see circle notation)

circle size in circle notation for, 18

generating random bit from, 24-27

quantum spy hunter, 32-35

relative rotation of circles in circle notation for, 19

superposition of, 15-18

single-qubit operations, 21-32
    combining, 30-32
    HAD, 22
    in multi-qubit registers, 41-44
    NOT, 21
    PHASE(θ), 28, 43
    READ and WRITE, 23
    ROOT-of-NOT, 30-32
    ROTX(θ) and ROTY(θ), 29
Singular Value Decomposition (see Quantum
    Principle Component Analysis (QPCA))
soft margins, 283, 283
software verification, 198
solution register, 266
solving systems of linear equations, 262-274
    amplitude amplification and, 274
    describing systems of linear equations, 263
    detailed explanation of, 268-271
    HHL and, 265
    inputs, 265
    inverting values for, 272
    moving inverted values into amplitudes for,
        273
    outputs, 266
    speed and fine print, 267
    uncomputing for, 274
    usage of quantum simulation, QRAM, and
        phase estimation, 271-272
Space Harrier, 233
space vs. time in Shor's factoring algorithm, 259
sparsity (of matrix), 190
    in QPCA, 276
    in quantum simulation, 190
    in solving systems of linear equations, 264
speed, 140, 208, 267
square waves, 136
state encoding for vectors (see vector encod-
    ings)
state, quantum, 296
stored data in QPU registers, 173
sum estimation, QFT as, 120
superconductor, room temperature, 305
superposition
    defined for single qubit, 15-18
    preparing, with inverse QFT, 143
    putting payload into, for teleportation, 76
    QPU operations and, 89
    writing, into QRAM, 179
supersampling, 212, 227

supervised (machine learning), defined, 262
Support Vector Machines (SVM), 280
    dual formulation of, 282
    generalizations of, 283
    Least Squares Support Vector Machine (LS-
        SVM), 284
    support vectors of, 282
    using soft margins, 283
support vectors, 282
SWAP, 54-58
swap test, 55, 287
    usage with output from HHL, 266

T

T count, 304
teleportation, 67
    creating entangled pair for, 74
    example of, 67-73
    famous accidents involving, 81
    interpreting results of, 79
    linking payload to entangled pair for, 75
    of quantum gates, 300
    preparing payload for, 74
    program walkthrough for, 73-79
    putting payload into superposition for, 76
    READing sent qubits, 76
    uses of, 80
    verifying the results of, 78
term, 296
threshold theorem, 305
time vs. space in Shor's factoring algorithm, 259
Toffoli (CCNOT), 53, 299

U

uncomputing, 100, 274
unitary matrix, 158, 187
    relationship to Hermitian matrices, 187
unsatisfiable 3-SAT problem, 206-208
unstructured database, 192
unsupervised (machine learning), defined, 262

V

value, marked, 108
vector encodings, 179-185
vertex (of graph), 190

W

WRITE, 23, 173, 176

About the Authors

Eric R. Johnston ("EJ") is the creator of the QCEngine simulator, and also an acrobat and competitive gymnast. As an engineer, EJ values surprise and whimsy above all other things. He studied Electrical Engineering and Computer Science at U. C. Berkeley, and worked as a researcher in Quantum Engineering at the University of Bristol Centre for Quantum Photonics. EJ spent two decades at Lucasfilm as a software engineer for video games and movie effects, along with occasional motion-capture stunt performance. Currently, he works as a senior quantum engineer in Palo Alto, California.

Nicholas Harrigan is a physicist, programmer, and easily excitable science communicator. He received his doctorate from Imperial College London for research into quantum computing and the foundations of quantum mechanics. His work on quantum mechanics has moderately convinced him that the moon is still there when he doesn't look at it. Nicholas has since worked at the University of Bristol, and spent time as a data scientist and teacher. He now works as a quantum architect in a quantum computing startup. Nicholas is also a keen climber who finds constant motivation from the Unix command yes.

Mercedes Gimeno-Segovia is a quantum physicist whose main scientific goal is to develop the next generation of quantum technologies. Mercedes has always been fascinated by the inner workings of conventional computers and decided to merge that interest with her passion for quantum physics; she received her PhD from Imperial College London for her work on the first photonic quantum architecture compatible with the silicon industry. As Director of Quantum Architecture at PsiQuantum, she is working on the design of a general-purpose quantum computer. When not thinking about physics, Mercedes can be found playing the violin, running (preferably on trails) and reading.

Colophon

The animal on the cover of *Programming Quantum Computers* is the musky octopus (*Eledone moschata*), a sea creature found at depths of up to ¼ mile in the Mediterranean Sea and the coastal waters of western Europe.

Its smooth skin and musky odor make the musky octopus easy to identify. As seen on the cover, the skin is beige to gray-brown, and marked with dark brown spots. At night, these tentacles appear fringed with an iridescent blue border. Its eight tentacles are relatively short and carry only one row of suckers.

Unlike other octopuses, which mainly take shelter in rock crevices or vegetation, the musky octopus burrows into the sediment of the continental platform.

The musky octopus has a carnivorous diet, aided by its parrot-like beak, and mostly dines on crustaceans, mollusks, and small fish. Its siphon, or funnel, allows it to propel itself after prey or away from predators, emitting a cloud of black ink as defense against the latter.

While the musky octopus's current conservation status is designated as of Least Concern, many of the animals on O'Reilly covers are endangered; all of them are important to the world.

The cover illustration is by Karen Montgomery, based on a black and white engraving from Dover's *Animals*. The cover fonts are Gilroy Semibold and Guardian Sans. The text font is Adobe Minion Pro; the heading font is Adobe Myriad Condensed; and the code font is Dalton Maag's Ubuntu Mono.

O'REILLY®

There's much more where this came from.

Experience books, videos, live online training courses, and more from O'Reilly and our 200+ partners—all in one place.

Learn more at oreilly.com/online-learning